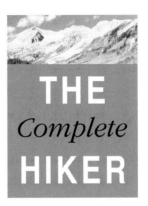

THE
Complete
HIKER

FROM THE LIBRARY OF

JB0-00019 Copyright © Antioch Publishing Company

THE *Complete* HIKER

Everything you'll need
for a day or a month
on the trail

JOHN LONG AND MICHAEL HODGSON

RAGGED MOUNTAIN PRESS/McGraw-Hill

CAMDEN, MAINE • NEW YORK • SAN FRANCISCO • WASHINGTON, D.C. • AUCKLAND • BOGOTÁ
CARACAS • LISBON • LONDON • MADRID • MEXICO CITY • MILAN • MONTRÉAL • NEW DELHI
SAN JUAN • SINGAPORE • SYDNEY • TOKYO • TORONTO

Ragged Mountain Press

A Division of The McGraw-Hill Companies

10   9   8   7   6   5   4   3   2   1

Copyright © 1996, 2000 John Long and Michael Hodgson

An earlier edition of this work was published as *The Dayhiker's Handbook*

Library of Congress Card Number: 00-102999

Questions regarding the content of this book should be addressed to
    Ragged Mountain Press
    P.O. Box 220
    Camden, ME 04843
    207-236-4837

Questions regarding the ordering of this book should be addressed to
    The McGraw-Hill Companies
    Customer Service Department
    P.O. Box 547
    Blacklick, OH 43004
    Retail customers: 1-800-262-4729
    Bookstores: 1-800-722-4726

Illustrations by Mike Clelland

Photograph on page ii by Chip Kamber

This book was typeset in Adobe Sabon and Adobe Helvetica Narrow

Printed by Quebecor Printing, Fairfield, PA
Design and Production by Dan Kirchoff
Edited by Jonathan Eaton, Sydne Silverstein Matus, Pamela Benner, and Don Graydon

The authors have made every attempt to reproduce trademarks accurately

To my wife, Mariana Rondon-Mendez.

—John Long

To my Mum and Dad, who inspired my love for walking and writing; my daughter, Nicole, who inspires me to see things in fresh new ways; and Wendy, who inspires me to love all that I do.

—Michael Hodgson

In that country they saw a diamond clear creek that was shadowed all day by narrowing mountains but for a little while at noon, when straight fingers of sunlight reached down through forest. On slopes open to the sun in summer, groves of quaking aspens showed here and there, creating little gardens of their own within immense wild parks. In winter the only green was that of evergreens, solemn and frowning amidst the silver and brown lichens—the colors of age—set off by heavy banks of snow. Far above, at timberline, like fixed images of the winds on the inhuman peaks, the last trees clutched the naked rock with gestures of agonized survival. Emerging from two flat-cliffed mountains of flesh-colored stone came a rush of diamond clear water that the prospectors named Willow Creek.

—The Green River, Paul Horgan

CONTENTS

INTRODUCTION . . . . . .

1   First Steps . . . . .

2   Clothing and Pack . . . .

3   Staying Safe and Found . . . .

4   Desert Travel . . . .

5   Mountain Walking . . .

6   Woodlands/Forest . . .

7   Stepping Out on Snow and Ice . . . .

8   Coastal Wandering . . . .

9   Canyons and Waterways . . . .

10   Jungle . . . .

11   Weekend Warrior . . . . .

12   Long-distance Hiking . . . .

AFTERWORD . . . .
     The "Secret" Dilemma of an Outdoor Writer

APPENDIX 1   The Hiking Adventurer's . . . . . .
              Checklist

APPENDIX 2   Gear Manufacturers . .

APPENDIX 3   Cyberhiking . . . .

INDEX . . . .

. . . . *1*

. . . . *4*

. . . . *44*

. . . . *72*

. . . . *106*

. . . . *120*

. . . . *136*

. . . . *150*

. . . . *168*

. . . . *178*

. . . . *192*

. . . . *202*

. . . . *214*

. . . . *228*

. . . . *231*

. . . . *233*

. . . . *236*

. . . . *238*

Walking is the best way to gain an understanding of a place, to assimilate its rhythms and time scales. . . . Walking is the best way to know a place, perhaps the only way.

—Walking the Yukon:
A Solo Trek
Through the Land
of Beyond,
Chris Townsend

Introduction

My vicinity affords many good walks; and though for so many years I have walked almost every day, and sometimes for several days together, I have not yet exhausted them. An absolutely new prospect is a great happiness, and I can still get this any afternoon. Two or three hours' walking will carry me to as strange a country as I ever expect to see.

—"Walking," *Henry David Thoreau*

Bob Gaines

Why do millions of us flee the city when

the urge strikes and take a few hours or a few days for a hike in the mountains, the desert, the savanna, across a glacier? The answers are as varied as the people on and off the trail. If you're young, hiking may give you your first taste of open space and air and freedom, where the music of a river or a hailstorm brings home the authority and mysteries of nature. If you're older, walking and hiking may provide alternatives to more stressful forms of outdoor exercise, such as running and cycling—with the added boon of a backdrop more enchanting than a swarming bike path or noisy highway. We often think of walking and hiking as physical pursuits, but that's not the half of it.

I remember standing on the very brink, four thousand feet up on a great limestone apui in Brazil, where below and before me, rolling, mounting, sinking, rising, like swells in a huge green sea, the ancient rain forest fanned out to the edge of time. And I remember hiking toward Carstensz Pyramid in New Guinea, where miles in the distance, outlined one against the other, the crests of a high cordillera seemed shuffled like a deck of stony cards—brusque peaks, bluish dips and notches, beetling spires swaying and rising and falling in the harsh light, more inaccessible as we mounted on.

These were exotic sights forever scribed into my memory. And yet just a while ago I parked my car on the Pacific Coast Highway, hiked for half an hour up

a firebreak, and watched the sun dive into the Pacific. Sitting there on a big flat rock, gazing down at the ocean, I understood that the marvels of the jungle and the rain forest had nothing over what I saw and what I felt just then. Wherever you are, the power and simplicity of being outdoors is a therapy of a kind. For many of us, the greatest therapy.

West African tribesmen hold that certain of life's activities—too much work, grief, stress, marital friction, to name a few—can cause the soul to retreat from the body; sometimes just a few feet away, other times many days' walk away. Sometimes the soul drifts or bolts so far distant that it takes a strong magic to coax it back. But it can be accomplished.

Most of us are as happy and well-adjusted as the next person, or think we are; yet at times we can still benefit from a little magic and a little therapy. So we look to the outdoors, for there is great healing in nature, which pushes all things toward balance and integration. We might go for the exercise, or merely to get out of town, to be alone, beyond the reach of phones and computers and all the rest. But once we're outdoors and past the last road, our reasons for being there, and the chaos we've left behind, slowly ebb away as our experience becomes one of harmony between emotion and purpose. It might be a blinding strip of blue between two storm clouds, or a yucca in full bloom. Maybe a thundershower hunkers you down, cold and grumbling, beneath the limbs of a lightning-scarred oak. But the chilling wind and the sodden shirt and even the blisters on your heels all become grace notes in the song that calls the soul back home. And you don't need to fly three days to New Guinea or Brazil, or quit your day job, to hear the tune. A tent and sleeping bag, or even a pack, might not be required. Sometimes all you need is a spare day—perhaps just a few hours will do—and from any metropolitan area you can usually find yourself in the wilderness. And often as little as ten minutes on the trail will deliver you into prime terrain, because the fringe of a wilderness area shares at least some of the magic of the land's farthest reaches and most hidden nooks. The faces of nature are boundless, yet they are all of a piece, because you are just as much outdoors in the Santa Monica Mountains as you are in the middle of the Gobi Desert. And the song is often just as sweet. The trick, then, is to eliminate everything that may keep you from hearing it, and this breaks down into knowing what you're doing, and going prepared.

Great tomes have been written about wilderness travel. But barring technically difficult travel or extremely specialized terrain (like the arctic or trailless jungle), there is only a manual's worth of things you really need to know for 99 percent of the hikes you can take within the continental United States. And by the end of this reading, you'll know them all.

To enjoy time in the wilderness we need to stay as safe and comfortable as possible. Because mountain travel requires site-specific gear and methods—and the same holds true for desert, canyon and waterway, coastal, and forest hiking—there are many things to learn and consider. But focusing strictly on raincoats, maps, and walking sticks neglects the primal allure of a banyan grove or the thrill of

skiing down a scree field—the magical experiences that draw us outdoors in the first place. So in writing this book, coauthor Michael Hodgson and I tried to blend something of this magic with the hard knowledge every hiker should know.

The essays, stories, and anecdotes peppered throughout the text present regions (such as jungles and rain forests) that many hikers would likely never visit without reading firsthand accounts about the marvels they're missing. Though the face of the earth seems smaller every year, it's still a very large, unimaginably varied place. By offering not just facts and data, but also our experiences in various realms, we hope to expose readers to the world of possibilities. People who have hiked for years on regional trails should find valuable information if, for example, their interest is sparked by the chapter on waterways and they decide to trek away from the forests they know. We've tried to cover each topic and terrain from the ground up, so hikers from the novice to the old hand will find something to enrich their wilderness experience.

When we travel to the jungle in these pages, I'd encourage you to join us. Keep your mind open. Discard old myths and learn something true. The wilder an area is, or is perceived to be, the more danger and torment are ascribed to it, often falsely. Our stories and anecdotes strive to temper the many lies and groundless fears surrounding less-frequented environments, while uncovering both the actual trials and the majesty of those settings few outdoors people ever bother to taste. Don't rule out trekking through the Sumatran rain forest or tromping up Diablo's Canyon in Chihuahua, Mexico, before reading a hands-on account of what's involved. The truth might surprise you.

The Complete Hiker is not a manual, but a sourcebook and a testimonial that contains far more than Michael or I knew individually. Quite possibly, no two readers will use this book in exactly the same way. The wilderness buff might read it cover to cover. Others might surf through it, pausing to bone up on areas that catch their interest. Still others might study the chapter on mountains and cold-weather gear before heading for Alaska, or digest the section on boots before buying a new pair.

The opening chapters deal with issues encountered in most every climate and terrain; later the book dials specific areas into sharp detail, ending with a rundown on overnight and extended adventures. This enables a reader to use the book according to need or desire. When trying to get a feel for canyons, say, you might focus on the essay in Chapter 9. When you need specific, hard information, the table of contents and the index will direct you to particular subjects.

The Complete Hiker was not designed to be browsed, then retired to the bookshelf. It was styled as a friend, a reference for required information, a cradle for dreams, and most importantly a springboard for your own wilderness experiences. Enjoy it. Venture out and experience the rare and wild places.

1 First Steps

Afoot and light-hearted I take to the open road,

Healthy, free, the world before me,

The long brown path before me leading wherever I choose.

—"Song of the Open Road," Walt Whitman

Michael Hodgson

When I was a fourteen-year-old freshman,

a man named John Goddard showed up at our high school. He'd kayaked down the Blue Nile, trekked across Afghanistan, penetrated the darkest regions of the Amazon. There was talk that he'd eaten human flesh, and his crude home movies and embroidered lectures captured me instantly. For about three months I hitch-hiked all over Southern California, following Goddard on his lecture circuit, hounding him backstage after every show. I got to know the man in a casual way and copied his every move, even down to the way he spit. Like many kids raised in a cozy little suburb, with everything ordered and sugared and geared to make life easy, I was dead bored and jumpy as a cricket, so I couldn't get enough of Goddard's world. When I discovered that he wore a toupee and drove a Sedan de Ville, his image suffered. But I continued spending every weekend thrashing about the scrubby little mountains above our town, looking for my own Amazon.

I'd snag a friend off my baseball team, toss two days' worth of canned goods into a canvas army backpack, and head out cross-country. Soon we were marching through groves of poison sumac and stinging nettles, thrashing up bushy riverbeds, scrambling over moraine slopes and through brief forests charred black by annual fires, finally emerging above the tree line scraped, punctured, swollen, black as chimney sweeps. The mountains

above my hometown were not the Alps.

Eventually, I hooked up with a kid named Robles, who had boundless energy, the weak smile of the original fool, and my same lust to get out of town. We started trekking around the local mountains together, progressively tackling more direct lines up the local peaks, taking a fifty-foot yachting line along for protection on the tougher stretches of vertical dirt and man-zanita. We were inspired by the crackpot version of climbing served up on the big screen—the bold mountaineer teetering on a slim shelf below blank rock. He hurls the grappling hook, and though its purchase is something less than a frozen cobweb, he hand-walks up the line like it's tied off to a tugboat stanchion. A bad example to fol-low, and it's a miracle neither of us was killed trying to do so. Apart from dirt-climbing, most of our ventures took the shape of abandoning the many fine trails and thrashing through thorny herbage. After one such foray, when we both got sav-aged by wasps and two days later were cov-ered with poison oak hives over most of our bodies, we pitched the yachting line, took to the proper trails, and never looked back.

Over the years, my vista broadened. Maybe it happens all at once, but more likely as your career unfolds, the physical act of hiking becomes secondary to other factors. If you're fortunate, you'll experi-ence those flashes when you realize that what is inside your head and what lies

Taking your first step from the trailhead is a simple and safe affair. Just follow a few practical guidelines and you'll be stepping out with confidence and style.

- Wear comfortable footwear. Lightweight hiking boots that are well broken in, cushy socks, and maybe a dash or two of foot powder will keep your digits smiling and your steps light.

- Keep your pack weight to a minimum. You aren't heading out on an expedition, so don't pack as though you were. If your pack weight exceeds 10 pounds for a dayhike, you might want to question your packing choices.

- Pack along your favorite nutritious snacks.

- Don't forget the sunscreen.

- Experts recommend you drink between 3 and 4 quarts of water per person per day. With that in mind, you should plan on carrying 3 quarts of water per person or, if you know there will be natural water sources on your hike, pack along a means of treating water.

- Tuck a small first aid kit into your pack. A few Band-Aids, some essential moleskin (see page 54) should a blister begin to sneak up on your feet, an antibiotic, and a few other odds and ends depending on your personal needs and preferences.

before your eyes are of a piece. And there's magic in these moments, moments worth hiking after.

As young rock climbers, our little band of friends would hike up through the forest toward Tahquitz rock in Southern California. The trail was steep, and we'd usually stop at a certain fallen oak to rest, listening to the dead-soughing of the trees. It was always so quiet. Only the sound of wind, which carried with it the frank scent of bark and leaves and piquant red sap. The forest could bring all things to calm within me and make my mind strong and sure, when those eerie emotions trembling between wonder and sorrow used to shiver through me from head to foot. Squinting up through a brace of trees, we could see the distant white rock, and we would sit there for a while longer, wondering how we were ever made to be alive.

From early on, I was always aligned toward the radical end of things, and much of the walking and hiking I did (and continue to do) was to gain a mountain or a big rock, or to explore new caves, or to attempt the first crossings of arctic and tropical islands. But more than a few times injuries slowed me, and for weeks or even months I could do little but shuffle along the beach or thread a mountain path. Perhaps it wasn't till then that I came to appreciate walking and hiking as one of the simple pleasures in life. Not a spectacular or harrowing trek through primordial jungle, rather a simple two-hour affair along the shores of Mono Lake or up to the lip of Upper Yosemite

Falls. And while tens of thousands of people have walked these same routes for over a century, there are—in this country—thousands of times that number who have never left the pavement, who have never gotten beyond the sound of truck horns or out of eyeshot of a smokestack or a row of track homes. Many of us have been roped into the thick of it by our own hands.

Freedom has come to mean mobility, and the first major purchase for most Americans is a set of wheels. For many, going anywhere on foot means we are so broke we can't even come up with bus fare, an opinion that neglects the millions of years humans got about on foot. Jesus didn't fly to Jericho; he walked. In geological time, we humans have been riding in chariots, carriages, trains, and cars for mere seconds. But such is the modern world that if we were left to walk everywhere, most of us would starve to death. We have to keep moving, make things happen, and get things done. In the process the chasm between what we are obliged to do and who we are grows so wide that, at some time or another, most of us come to confuse our livelihood with our fundamental identity. That's not to say we can put in a couple of hard miles on a dusty trail and return to our routines wise as Moses, nor does the typical everyday hike unfold like a stroll through the Golden City. A swindle with some "outdoor writing" is that too much of it is composed from the window of a log cabin or is skewed by a "naturalist's" itinerary or the editorial edicts of a magazine. Here the sensitive outdoorsman flees the inhospitable and threatening world and "hikes" a half mile off the road in search of a lost pastoral haven. It's all hunting for echoes and prancing across rainbows with these people. It rarely rains on them. They never get sunburned or bullied by mosquitoes. Their shoulder straps never break, nor do their muscles ache, because they rarely cover any terrain, deluded as they are that playing in a landscape is as significant as exploring it. But the hiker who casts off into the wilds is sure to be downright miserable on occasion. Under the open sky with the dirt under our feet, we're dealing with our lives not as a commodity, nor in some airy philosophical way, but on a visceral level equivalent to the basic elements of air and sun and water and stone. And this is the surest way to find out how you feel—not what writers have told you to feel, or how you think you should feel, but how you actually feel. You might consider that discovering your real feelings about stinging nettles or deerflies is irrelevant to your "actual" life, but those nettles and biting pests *are* your life; and whenever you get the chance to experience anything directly, it carries over to the rest of your days. To many of us, the point is never truly driven home till we spend time with people whose lives are lived with the filters removed; and if these people have one thing in common, it's that when they want to go somewhere, it is generally on foot.

My initial taste of such peoples came during my first trip to Sarawak, Malaysia. In the process of getting to some ancient ruins (that, it turned out, existed only in the addled mind of a Chinese naturalist, now in jail for pandering), we spent time with some remote Dayak tribesmen. Straightaway I noticed the lack of distance between the people and their lives, though I couldn't see it as such at first. And I quickly realized that the intimacy these people enjoyed had nothing to do with the ignorant notion that "getting back to nature" is to return to simpler times, which might be true if you're a simpleton, but is not at all true otherwise.

We were hauling a dugout up the last reaches of an uncharted river. The outboard engine had exploded in flames the day before. The rice was almost gone. One of the chief's three wives had given birth to a fifth daughter the day before we'd headed off from the Punan village, and the chief was going to have to toss up new, expanded digs when he returned. He had a toothache as well, and we'd swilled through the medicinal gallon of borak—a sort of jungle moonshine—the first night. That evening, as a chilling drizzle wept through the jungle canopy, as the fire kept going out, while the chief fiddled with the five hundred pieces of the outboard motor spread out over a tarp, his tooth pounding in his head, no doubt wondering how he was ever to find the time to expand his longhouse, he mumbled that life was no simple affair. And I understood that reaching back to our first tentative slithering from the ooze, it never really has been. But out there, where the monsoon blows and the big trees are king, people have the chance to actually live their lives and feel the texture of them to a degree impossible in a mechanized world. Not to postulate existence, or dress it up in verse, or dissect it in any number of ways, but to actually *feel* it, tangibly and directly. And that, I think, is what we lose when we're locked in the city and into professional routines, and what we gain when we head outdoors and down the trail. If we're to believe the final opinion of Joseph Campbell, the highest purpose of all mythology is to make us feel alive. And if hiking has anything to offer, it is to affirm and extend our lives.

- If this is your first hike of the year, keep the trek to a minimum—no more than 6 miles. Experienced and strong hikers can expect to cover between 10 and 20 miles over an 8-hour day, depending on weather and terrain.
- Stay on marked trails and you'll have little need to use a compass; you will need a map.
- Take the time to stretch and limber up before heading out. Your body will thank you for it.
- Dress for the conditions you're likely to face, and dress in layers so you can add or peel off layers as needed. If properly outfitted, you'll enjoy a wonderful hiking experience no matter what the elements toss your way.
- Worried about wild animals? Don't be! Statistics show that most problems occur when humans encourage encounters: snakes bite when handled, bears bite when fed, etc. Stay alert at all times and remember that you are a guest in the animal's environment. If you encounter a bear, retreat slowly, avoid eye contact, and give it plenty of room. Should you run across a poisonous snake or one you suspect might be poisonous, give it a wide berth and never, never attempt to handle it. Snakes will not bite unless threatened.

STARTING OUT

The most common question coming from the aspiring outdoorsperson is: How do I get started? Many people have exaggerated ideas concerning the demands of even the most pedestrian dayhikes, as though they were setting out to reconnoiter some obscure planet rather than heading down a well-marked trail. Yes, there is plenty to learn, but this knowledge has been part of our collective wisdom since Day One. The value of easing into the game is not so much to safeguard against great mysteries (most of which you could overcome with common sense), but to calm doubts and to gain enough confidence that your outdoor experience becomes enjoyable rather than a nail-biter. And the standard way we all get started is to go hiking with someone who has had some experience.

Getting in Shape

Few of the wilderness areas I've visited have been on level ground, and if they were, there were swamplands, forests, glaciers, and a host of other natural elements to contend with. While most day-hikes follow trails of some kind, rises, bends, switchbacks, leg-pumping descents, stream crossings, scree, moraine, and boulder fields are a few of the natural obstacles encountered. The hazards are usually minimal; otherwise, the route would never have seen enough bootprints to have occasioned a trail in the first instance. While many popular trails are cakewalks, others are brutal. Many trails I've hiked in the Grand Tetons, Yosemite, and Zion National Park, for instance, feature withering altitude gains that have burned me right down to the quick. Likewise, I've hustled my kids along countless "nature walks" suitable for an old man on crutches. In all these experiences the only constant I've noticed is that as diverse as the terrain goes, so go the folks who are on it.

I once saw a tough in full Rambo gear, machete in hand, slinking along the paved "trail" wending through Hidden Valley in Joshua Tree National Monument; at over eleven thousand feet on one of the volcanoes in Mexico, I saw a tony señorita in a sequined evening gown, high heels in her hands, sitting on a rock and smoking a Delicado. There's no telling

Taking the First Step

Getting going requires no more effort than lacing up the shoes and heading out the door. Of course, sometimes a little motivation beyond the personal mantra of "I need to walk" is required, and that is where clubs, friends, and organizations come in. The following organizations are good places to turn if you are seeking to make that first step:

- American Hiking Society, PO Box 20160, Washington, DC 20041-2160; 703-255-9304
- American Volkssport Association (National Information Number); 800-830-WALK, or 210-659-2112
- Appalachian Mountain Club, PO Box 298, Gorham, NH 03581; 603-466-2721

Walking for Your Health

According to a 1991 study by researchers at California's Loma Linda University, individuals who frequently walk have stronger immune systems than people who exercise strenuously by running. Walking (read, hiking), it seems, activates the bloodstream in a manner that encourages the body's "natural killer cells" to function better in warding off germs.

what one might see, but one thing I've learned: The better shape I'm in, the more I *do* see.

From the very start I learned that my fitness level would determine what manner of hikes I could undertake. When I was in top shape, I had limitless options, and was quickly introduced to the world of "peak bagging." There is hardly a legitimate mountain range anywhere in the world that doesn't feature a slew of nontechnical routes up a slew of summits. Even those peaks, mountains, and sheer rock walls infamous for climbing epics often feature a passage along which a person in hiking boots can trek to the top. Believe it: Swiss guides have shepherded a Holstein cow to the top of the Matterhorn; Yosemite's Half Dome, grist for a billion postcards, has a cabled handrail running from the base of the wall straight to the visored summit. Years before I would ever climb the sheer walls of these monoliths, I learned that getting to the top by whatever route was not merely another day outing but an event. And it has been since the first person headed up the first slope. Hiking clubs award all manner of plumes

and widgets for each peak bagged, and checking off every peak of a given range is a rewarding endeavor.

Particularly with one-day jaunts, where it's car to summit and back to car, I've often found myself looking at twenty even thirty-mile days involving thousands of feet of elevation gain and many grueling hours of continuous going. Yes, there are psychological aspects involved as well, something I did not understand till I tried to "guide" a girlfriend up Mount Whitney and back in one long day. Naturally, a thundershower pinned us down on the summit and we had to bivouac, with no gear, starving and freezing in the rain, the girl—a charming debutante with a tongue like a paring knife—cursing me through the livelong night. No, not everyone who's fit wants to grind up and down a chain of exhausting peaks with dragging tongue and jelly legs. Such efforts are reserved for the few who require physical and psychological intensity. But for those with the fitness, need, and resolve, each peak bagged is a landmark on the road of personal history.

The point is, for the devout peak bagger, fitness is not a limiting factor. And

OUT

- Elderhostel, 75 Federal Street, Boston, MA 02110; 617-426-7788
- National Park Foundation, 1101 17th Street NW, Suite 1102, Washington, DC 20036; 202-785-4500
- Rails to Trails Conservancy, 1400 16th Street NW, Suite 300, Washington, DC 20036; 202-797-5400
- Sierra Club Outings, 730 Polk Street, San Francisco, CA 94109; 415-923-5630

Staying in Shape

There is no better way to get in shape for walking than to, well, walk. You will find it easier if you establish some sort of routine, although you don't want to get so routine that your "daily routine" becomes anticipated drudgery. Mix it up a bit, hiking for 30 minutes one day, 15 the next, an hour the next. Whatever you do, walk every day, rain, snow, or shine. I find it works best for me to fit in my

walks around errands and commitments—I walk my two dogs every day, for example. Before you automatically pick up the keys to the car, think about whether you could walk. Instead of driving to the grocery store a mile distant, I shoulder a pack and walk—the clerks stopped asking me if I want paper or plastic, and just load my pack. The bottom line . . . enjoy yourself.

because it is not, a peak bagger's options are virtually unlimited. This all goes to show that the better shape you are in, the more options you have. This is not to imply that peak bagging is superior to wandering along a flat trail. Everything depends on your aim, though that aim is usually revised as you square into shape. Though peak bagging is intense, it can easily take on all the aspects of a race. In some instances I've been so pressed by having to go fast that I didn't notice much.

Several friends of mine once conned me into stomping to the top of Mount Gorgonio (in Southern California) and back in one short, winter day, and try as I may I can't remember one thing about any of it except that it got dark about half a mile shy of the roadhead and our car. We lost the trail, naturally, and ended up postholing through waist-high drifts till about ten that night, finally stumbling out onto the road about six miles below the car. Whatever benefits can be ascribed to such a crackpot outing, enjoyment is not one of them.

There is a qualitative difference between surviving a hike and being fit enough to enjoy it. Few hikes are genuine burners, and even fewer hikers are keen on such efforts. Too many burners can, in fact, turn an outdoor experience into the harshest kind of job. But a degree of fitness will always enhance your enjoyment of hikes featuring authentic range.

Most of us are locked into professional routines and family responsibilities that limit our chances to work out on a daily basis. Yet even the president of the United States takes a jog every morning. I make it a habit to grab some exercise whenever I can get it. There are libraries full of books on how to get fit, but simply orienting yourself toward a more active lifestyle is always the first step. Whenever I have a chance, I walk instead of drive. And no matter what deadline I'm up against, I get some kind of exercise every day, no matter how minimal.

Bob Gaines, Bridalveil Falls, Yosemite National Park

If you think about how you walk and whether or not your body is in alignment, you will minimize the opportunity for aches and pains to sneak up and bite you on the knee, back, ankle, or neck. Your body was designed with balance in mind, and if you walk out of balance, you place added stress on the joints, muscles, and tendons that have to compensate to keep you upright. Use the following tips to keep yourself in line and add more power to your step.

- *Upper body:* Keep your chin up and eyes looking straight ahead down the trail. Your neck should be relaxed, your head centered between your shoulders. Relax your shoulders by lifting your chest—as if you are trying to fill your lungs with more air. Use your arms to maintain your balance by swinging them naturally close to your body. Stand tall with your abdomen pulled in slightly toward your spine.
- *Lower body:* Keep your hips loose and relaxed and watch that you do not lean forward at the waist (other than to compensate for the weight of a pack, of course). Extend your legs as you head into each stride, but do not lock your knees.

Shoes teach bad habits, not the least of which is forgetting to watch where one places one's feet.

Encased in protective rubber, fabric, and leather, a hiker can stumble and bumble over most surfaces with resulting noise that ensures only minimal and very tolerant wildlife are sighted. There is a better way! In Africa a number of years ago, I had the pleasure of watching my barefoot Samburu warrior friend, Partner, glide over the ground with only the slightest stirring of dust and certainly no apparent effort. I, on the other hand, struggled constantly to keep up in my leather boots, generating clouds of dust and making enough noise to unnerve a herd of elephants. Partner would only shake his head and patiently motion me to walk softer. How was Partner able to

Walking out of balance forces your body to struggle to keep you upright.

Stand tall, with your abdomen pulled in slightly toward your spine.

Brian Agnew (2)

walk so effortlessly and silently? By using a walking technique that Native Americans, Tibetan monks, African warriors, Australian aborigines, and others have employed for centuries—slowing the pace, adjusting the center of gravity over the hips, and placing each foot carefully on the ground before transferring weight to it. The idea is to shorten the stride dramatically so that the body never feels as if it is being propelled forward. Head up and eyes looking ahead, you step forward slightly, gently touching the ground with your foot or boot so that the heel, ball, and outer edge land at the same time. Roll the foot inward until the entire sole of your foot is on the ground—still unweighted. You should be able to feel what you are stepping on, without having committed your weight. Finally, shift your weight to the foot smoothly, in a flowing motion, and swing the next foot forward to repeat the action—no jarring, no puffs of dust, no noise, less fatigue. It takes a lot of practice—I still haven't mastered it as well as Partner—but it is worth the effort.

Saving Your Knees

Your knees take a pounding when you are hiking . . . especially if you are not sensitive to the ways in which they work. Take care of them, and they will take care of you. The

following guidelines will go a long way to making sure that your knees stay in good working order for many trail miles to come:

- Use trekking poles! Believe me, they do work. According to research, trekking poles reduce the impact on your body by up to 250 tons per day—that's a lot of weight! As a personal testament,

Your knees take a pounding when hiking. Trekking poles can reduce the daily impact on your body by 250 tons.

Michael Hodgson

during a 370-mile race by foot through the wilds of Utah, trekking poles saved my team's legs for sure. Other teams who opted not to use the poles weren't quite so fortunate and suffered knee and other pain measurably. Retired cross-country ski poles will work quite well too. (See Appendix 2 for sources of good trekking poles.)

- In loose terrain, when traversing or going up or down, sidestep. Roll the uphill edge of your footwear into the hill so that the boot edge cuts into the hill for added traction.

- Use your upper body to help your knees when climbing. Every time you step up, press down on your uphill thigh with your hands and use your arms and legs in tandem to lift your weight—not just your thighs.

- It is best to use small steps when heading downhill . . . keep your knees flexed to absorb the shock and move as smoothly as you can.

- When the going gets really steep on a descent, and if the terrain is not too rugged (meaning no cactus or sharp objects to rip and tear the skin), use a technique that employs your derriere—slide carefully down on your seat. It's hell on clothing, but you can replace that. It's not so easy to

Stretch your lower back, hamstrings, and backs of your knees with toe touches. Keep your knees bent slightly and feet planted shoulder width apart as you bend at the waist and reach for your toes. Go as far as you can without causing pain—it's fine if you don't actually touch your toes.

To stretch your inner thighs, hamstrings, and buttocks, find a rock or tree stump just below crotch height and swing one leg up on top of it, resting your heel. Slowly bend forward, reaching for the foot on the rock or stump to stretch the hamstrings and buttocks.

replace a blown-out knee.

• If your knees do get a bit sore after a long hike, try resorting to a cold compress directly on the affected kneecap—20 minutes on and then 20 off. You can also try wrapping your knees in an elastic bandage, but be careful to follow the wrapping instructions on the packaging and not to wrap your knee too tightly as it could lead to more pain and bigger problems. One other option is to take ibuprofen, an anti-inflammatory drug, to see if that helps. If the pain continues, see your doctor.

Don't Get Uptight

Stretch before, during, and after your walks if you want to prevent your body from becoming too sore, too

Brian Agnew (2)

To stretch your groin, inner thighs, and lower back, sit on the ground with your knees bent and the soles of your feet together. After a short while, cross your legs and lean forward at the waist with your arms reaching out in front of you.

Stretch your calves by leaning against a tree or wall and extending one leg at a time behind you. Slowly push your heel down to the ground while your foot on the extended leg is facing forward.

tight, and possibly injured from muscle pulls. Learn to relax, stretch gradually and comfortably (never to a point of pain), and don't bounce. The stretches shown on pages 14 to 16 will help you keep from getting too uptight when trekking down any path.

The Essentials

Some affectionately refer to this list as the "10 Essentials," as it was dubbed when it originated many years ago to highlight those items no one should be without in the backcountry. Actually, there are a few more items than 10 on the list, but the essence of essential cannot be overstated. Before you head out onto the trail, no matter how short the hike, ascertain whether you are carrying the following items in either a pack or fanny pack:

To stretch the inner thigh, turn your side to the stump or rock, keeping one leg up, and then bend sideways at the waist—slowly!

To stretch tight arm, shoulder, and chest muscles, reach behind you while standing and intertwine your fingers. Lift your arms slowly until you begin to feel the stretching and pulling.

Brian Agnew (2)

- Topographic map and compass
- Water and water bottle
- Extra food
- Extra clothing
- Fire starter (gel or candle)
- Waterproof/windproof matches

- Pocketknife (I prefer a mulitool such as those made by Sog or Leatherman)
- First aid kit
- Flashlight (it doesn't have to be big enough to illuminate New York City . . . just bright enough

to show you the way in the dark and compact enough to carry)
- Signaling device (mirror and/or whistle)
- Water purification system (chemicals or filter, depending on your preference; both iodine and

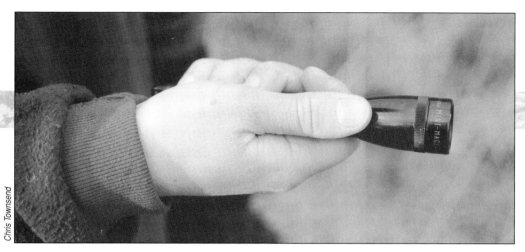

Nocturnal illumination is essential. Keep it small but bright!

Speaking of Water

A sign hanging at a ranger station in Arizona's Sycamore Canyon Wilderness states, "Water is Life!" Nothing could be simpler or more true. Because your body is approximately 70 percent water and your blood is 90 percent water, loss of water means loss of life. If your body doesn't have enough water, the blood thickens, blood pressure rises, and muscles seize up. Humans lose water at the average rate of 3 quarts per day through perspiration, breathing, and urination. Cold, altitude, and heat all increase the rate of water loss. When you are on the trail, you need to drink as if your life depends on it—it does. The human body must consume a minimum of 3 quarts of water per day up to 12,000 feet, up to 10 quarts above 12,000 feet.

chlorine have a limited shelf life once opened)

- Sunscreen (15 SPF or stronger)
- Sunglasses (must filter out UV rays)
- Personal medications (not your entire prescription but enough meds to carry you several days or so should an emergency arise)
- Emergency blanket
- Anything else that you deem essential to comfort and survival in an emergency. Keep in mind that what you select you have to carry, and the intent of this list is not to turn you into a beast of burden.

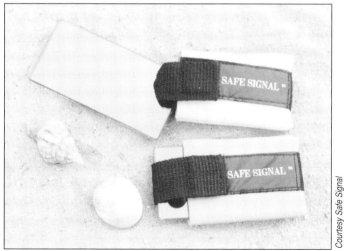

Signaling mirror.

ON HIKING ALONE

Many people have never spent a single day alone. Many more have not passed a day alone in the wilderness—a shame, as the rewards of solitude are boundless, and the outdoor arena greatly amplifies the proceeds. Many of us find that a little time alone is a chance for self-clarification and a lesson in self-reliance. Some have pushed this to a sort of art form, and our fascination with the man or woman alone remains a constant. The Daniel Boones and Amelia Earharts are long revered, for they seem to belong to no place and no person other than themselves. The city, and everyone in it, the thinking goes, can only corrupt the pure self of these solitary heroes. It seems they have overcome the profound human tendency to avoid self-knowledge, especially that which prowls in the basements of our psyches; and anyone who has

spent time alone knows that once you move beyond the distractions of the pack, the raw and naked stuff lurking deep bubbles to the surface soon enough. At the very least, time spent alone serves as a decisive means of getting in touch with ourselves. At the most it can remind us that no matter how onerous our situation seems, we are still fundamentally free.

Some of my sharpest memories have come when I've hiked alone, like the time Jim Bridwell and I were contracted by a now-defunct television show to perform the asinine stunt of rappelling down the 3,200-hundred-foot sodden face of Angel Falls, deep in the Venezuelan rain forest. From the tiny jungle resort of Canaima, we helicoptered to a small camp/clearing several miles distant from the gusher. Anxious for a better look, in the hope that we might recon where the hell we were going to descend the wall, Jim and I set

Famous Walkers/Hikers

John Finley was an editor of *The New York Times* and each year walked the 36-mile perimeter of Manhattan Island. There is an East River promenade named in his honor—to my knowledge the only civic monument in the country dedicated to a hiker.

Thomas Jefferson, who once was quoted as telling a family member, "Of all exercises, walking is best," might well be acknowledged as America's first walking advocate.

William Wordsworth was known to have walked 14 miles a day through his homeland, the English Lake District. It is estimated that he hiked nearly 185,000 miles in his lifetime.

Johnny Appleseed (John Chapman) wandered all over Ohio, Indiana, and Illinois for nearly 40 years, giving away apple seeds and tend-

ing to settlers' orchards along the way.

Supreme Court Justice William O. Douglas, a well-regarded mountain climber and hiker, helped save the Chesapeake and Ohio towpath for the public by organizing a 180-mile walk for press and politicians.

Henry David Thoreau, well known for his wandering ways, stated that people who walked were a class apart from all others: ". . . a fourth estate outside Church, State, and People."

Marco Polo is arguably history's most famous traveler. The Silk Route is a classic trek few have managed to duplicate though many have tried—*Danziger's Travels* is a book that outlines one recently successful attempt to trek from Venice to Beijing.

David Livingstone, best known from Henry Stanley's

out toward the falls following a narrow and muddy path. Night soon fell, and we left close jungle to ramble along the margin of a huge pool. A brilliant full moon, the moon of the ageless rain forest, flung its blaze over the pool, which even now appeared like a huge lagoon of good bourbon—this from the tannic acid leached from 10 billion surrounding trees. A light rain fell, and we moved back onto the muddy trail, pressed in from above and on both sides by aspiring thicket. Cicadas shrieked, and twice we waved through billows of flying ants that follow every rain. Though we could see barely five feet in front of us, we could tell by mulchy smells and viscous air that we walked in the middle of a great rain forest. For some reason Jim decided to turn back, so I pushed on solo. The stupendous falls, now thundering only a quarter mile away, coalesced into a stream running just to my right, which led straight back to the

clearing and our camp, so I wasn't troubled about getting lost. But I'd only gone a couple of minutes down the trail before the impact of absolute aloneness grabbed hold of me with all the force of that ancient realm. I burst into a clearing and in sharp moonlight looked up and saw great silver strands shooting off the lip and plunging three thousand feet into a magnificent bridal veil at the boulder-strewn base. The mist cooled the tropical swelter, and I moved over to a river boulder big as a locomotive, flat on top and splitting the stream. The thick mist clashed with fragrant purple orchids and sickly sweet festering offal matting the jungle floor, where new life, spawned by the dead, blasted through the compost and shot recklessly toward the light. The organic surge was primally indifferent to the very life it engendered, and nothing between Canaima and the next world could stop it. And then came the pelting

A L O N E

famous quote, crossed much of Africa, including the Kalahari Desert, discovered Victoria Falls for the European race, and searched for the source of the river Nile.

John Muir, whose wanderings through the Sierra Nevada, Florida, and Alaska fill the pages of many books, is most responsible for saving a large chunk of western real estate from the logger's ax and development.

Going Solo: Nuts and Bolts

Going solo means you are truly free to enjoy your hike on your own terms and perhaps experience things that would be impossible in the company of another. It also means there is no one around to help you if something goes wrong. For that reason alone, you must follow extra planning precautions to ensure safety.

• Know your limits and be able to gauge accurately your abilities in all situations. If the little voice in your head should ever suggest turning around or advise you not

Chip Kamber

rain—steaming, seething, breathless. For many hours I stood there in the swirling mist.

Another time I struck out from my sister-in-law's ranchero in El Tigre, Venezuela. After several miles hugging the bottom of a scorched arroyo, the bluffs slowly fell away on both sides, and I started descending into an everlasting grassland. Beyond me stretched hard greens and blues heaped on an unbroken horizon. Rippling with mirages, the whole vista curved with the earth, like open ocean from the bridge of a ship. Huge columns of light pierced high, boiling clouds and burned on great tracts of reeds and grasses that might be fifty miles off. The sharp scent of mint thickets, broom, and sweet Paraguayan pollen rose on arid winds that blew straight into my face. I turned, but the wind was still there. There was no other sound but the wind.

Quickly, the lonely vista exerted its

eerie drain on my mind. The Cariña Indians had a word for it, that shrinking sensation of being siphoned off and spread over the measureless plain. The effect so quieted the incessant babbling in my head that I had no thoughts to grab onto, nothing to keep my mind from soaring up amongst the ravens circling in the thermals.

I broke the trance by following a flawless chevron of red herons, winging east; next, staring at a knot of soapbark and mapora palms and the wasted shade they cast; and finally, watching a distant cowboy driving a few cattle. Each dale and bushy knoll looked unique, but this was a single land crisscrossed with a thousand different paths. I might turn off onto one of these paths and walk on for days, weeks even; but there would always be more *sabana* ahead. Always the *sabana*.

Empty as these experiences might be

to do something, *listen!*

- You have no business hiking alone in rugged country unless you are skilled in the backwoods in all seasons and conditions. You must know how to deal with severe weather as well as understand the consequences of traveling through the variety of terrain that weather can bring—fording streams, crossing snowfields, walking across deserts, . . . etc. Later chapters of this book will help.
- Carry emergency supplies no matter how short your intended hike—first aid kit, waterproof

matches, fire starter, signal mirror, whistle, flashlight, emergency blanket, emergency food.

- Understand intimately the terrain you will travel through, complete with all its environmental and wildlife hazards, as well as the topographical "lay of the land" so that you may accurately gauge the time and effort requirements of your trip. We'll show you how in this chapter.

Hiking for Mileage

Some people simply can't help themselves. Whenever they head out to place one foot in front of the other (or behind the other, as you will read), it is with the idea of setting a walking record or laying claim to a hiking feat, or feet, as it were (see "Fastpacking," page 128, for a new trend in backcountry powerwalking). Ever heard of Edward Payson Weston? I thought not. He lived between 1839 and 1929, reaching the ripe old age of 90 and proving by example his assertion that

for anyone else, they are forever burned into my memory, for by slowly walking alone, I was able to feel my life and the life around me with maximum intensity. It is a miraculous effect, how everything is heightened if you go it alone. Every doubt and fear and tinge of exhilaration takes on significance.

Hiking alone is something many people can appreciate only in small doses, if at all. Even in an individualistic society like ours, most people feel that activities should always be shared. To suddenly find that the vista, the river, every tree, and every ant are at once entirely theirs can hurl people into a funk, rendering the most treasured landscapes barren, bleak, and impersonal. Often this is a flash reaction, and even the most timid and rattled solo hiker will find peace in the surroundings given time to steady up and settle in. Perhaps the shrewdest approach is to ease into the business, starting with short walks over familiar trails. The trick, if it could be called one, is to keep walking past your last thought, for we all have a bent of mind that puts us at opposition to our surroundings and, paradoxically, to ourselves, as though "we" were separate and existing independently of everything around us. From this vantage we naturally feel insignificant against the magnitude of the natural world. Start slowly, on the smallest possible scale, and extend your forays as your confidence increases. Understand from the very first step the necessity always to play it safe and conservative, for if you wrench an ankle or wander astray, you are stuck. Before you decide to launch an extended solo trek, gain enough experience that you don't need to read a book about how to go about it.

he walked for health. During his lifetime, Weston walked 127 miles in just 24 hours—setting a walking record of 5.29 miles per hour. In 1867, acting on a challenge, Weston walked from Portland, Maine, to Chicago, Illinois, in 30 days, covering 1,326 miles. Forty years later, now 67 years old, he repeated the feat, but chose to add 19 miles to the distance while still managing to knock 29 hours off his original time. When he was 70, Weston still stepped briskly, walking from New York to San Francisco in just under 105 days.

Plennie Wingo of Texas gained fame for walking backward. In 1931, he attempted to set a world record by walking around the world backward. He might have made it too, had Istanbul constables not thought him insane and put a stop to his quest—one and a half years after he had begun. Apparently preferring his backward ways, Wingo completed a 500-mile, backward trek from San Francisco to Santa Monica, near Los Angeles.

Hundreds of people have officially been registered as "through hikers" on the Appalachian Trail, having hiked its 2,025 miles from end to end. Perhaps none is more famous, though, than Emma Gatewood, dubbed "Grandma." Gatewood hiked the entire trail in her late 60s with a denim sack full of supplies slung over her shoulder—perhaps she couldn't find a pack that fit?

TIMING YOUR TRIP

Getting stuck out for the night is not, strictly speaking, the same as getting lost, but both typically occur because you've miscalculated. And learning to make accurate calculations—particularly how long a given hike will take you—is a crucial part of the hiking game (especially with dayhikes, since you'll have no bivouac gear). Working out the details can get difficult only if you try to cut things so you arrive—you hope—back at the trailhead at the instant of absolute dark. Go conservative and it's pretty straightforward. A simple formula applies to almost all circumstances: Once the logistics have been worked out—per where you want to go—the first and fore-most thing to know is what time on that very day darkness will descend.

Depending on the terrain and season, pitch darkness can follow twilight in five minutes (in mountainous jungle during the monsoon) or half an hour, as it is at the beach in summer. So work your calculations to the falling of dusk. Any local newspaper has this information. By noting *when* you start hiking, you define a window of hiking time. If you start at noon and dusk falls at six, you have six hours of daylight.

The majority of dayhikes require you to travel out and back on the same trail. As in any other physical endeavor, you're going to have a lot more energy at the beginning. If you start at noon and darkness comes at six, it's best not to wait till

TIMING

Gauging Your Speed

Estimating your rate of travel is essential when determining the time required to traverse a route. It's no fun finding yourself only halfway home, out of fuel and food, on the third day of what was to be a three-day hike. You can estimate travel times as follows, with appropriate adjustments if you or someone in your group hikes a little faster or slower; hike at the comfortable pace of the slowest member of your group:

Hiking (boots)—on level ground with a light load and moderate elevation gain, 3 to 4 mph

Hiking (boots)—at 6,000 feet of elevation or higher with some hills, 3 to 4 mph

Hiking (boots)—bushwhacking or traveling cross-country without the benefit of trails, 1.5 to 2 mph

Hiking (boots)—steep climbing up ridges and mountain sides, 0.5 to 1 mph

Hiking (snowshoes)—on open terrain with gentle ups and downs, 2 to 3 mph

Trail Running—on level ground with a light load and moderate elevation gain, 6 to 8 mph

Trail Running—at 6,000 feet of elevation or higher with moderate elevation change, 5 to 7 mph

According to the US Army, a female walking 20 to 21 steps every 10 seconds or a male walking 16 to 17 steps per 10 seconds is traveling at approximately 3 miles per hour. Stepping out at 27 or 28 steps every 10 seconds as a female or 20 to 21 steps every 10 seconds as a male means you are blazing down the trail at approximately 4 miles per hour (obviously the distinction has little to do with gender—it's leg length that determines a hiker's stride). Of course, estimating your speed is one thing, and using it to determine how much time you need to get from point A to point B is another. For that you must factor in elevation gain and loss. To be conservative, most experts suggest adding 1 hour of time for every 1,000 feet of elevation change. If you hike at 4 miles per hour, a 4-mile hike with 2,000 feet of elevation change might take you as long as 3 hours.

three o'clock before turning around to charge down the trail. You may not get all the way back to the car that day—at least in daylight. Better to turn around at two or two-thirty, and allow for a slower pace. And don't push the envelope because the outbound hike is virtually all uphill. You may think the downhill return journey will require less energy, and most of the time this is so—but not always. I remember once when my baseball buddy Greg Martin and I hit the trail up San Antonio Peak, above my hometown. Snow and interminable switchbacks made for slow going, and all the way up I kept thinking about the fine sport we'd have dashing back down. We burned a normal day's hike worth of calories in three hours, fig-

uring to get back to the roadhead in half that time. The problem, of course, was that our legs were perfectly noodled from the steep trudging. And hiking downhill can be arduous on the legs, especially when the terrain is uneven, for your knees must absorb all the weight and shock. We started cramping after a couple of hours. In the end, it took us five hours to get back to the car, the last three in darkness, and I swear I barked my knees and shins on every rock, stump, bush, and tree on the entire mountainside.

Play it safe. If you need three hours to get there, allow at least four hours to get back—more if the going is tricky and you feel tired.

Y O U R   T R I P

Michael Hodgson, Kodiak Island, Alaska

SNACKS AND SUSTENANCE

No other aspect of wilderness education is so rife with half-truths, hogwash, and downright lies as the business of what a hiker is supposed to eat when traveling through the great outdoors. There are many oracles, all proposing the "correct" answer: the military; the traditional "wisdom" of woodsmen, mule packers, and antique backpackers; and perhaps most erroneous of all sources, companies that hawk victuals packaged specifically for consumption on the trail—shockingly pricey stuff often inferior to what you can grab off any supermarket shelf. Weight is always an issue, but the dayhiker does not face the extreme weight embargoes that are real concerns for a longer trip or expedition, where every ounce counts. No matter what grub you decide to tote, you can't metabolize more than three pounds of it (unless you start packing melons, which some people do), so anything beyond that is superfluous. The heaviest part of your food load should always be fluids.

I don't suggest you ape the habits of some of the more experienced outdoors people I have known over the years, but it can be instructive to look at what kind of food they normally take for a day outing.

Charles Cole takes a handful of energy bars, a half gallon of Diet Coke, and a quart of water. Clive Gerald buys Big Macs by the dozen and freezes them. He usually sticks four into his pack in the morning, and by the time lunch swings around they are thawed out—or nearly so. Kathy Sassan bones and skins an entire barbecued chicken and packs it in a Tupperware box. She augments this with five oranges, several muffins, bagels, and energy bars, a quart of energy drink, and a gallon of designer water. Mike Katz, the *ne plus ultra* of mountain trekkers, takes ten Baby Ruths, a six-pack of alcohol-free beer, and water. Climber and explorer George Hudson, who was so skinny he could shower inside the barrel of a .22, took nothing more than millet and sunflower seeds. He swore by these rations, but he died—some say from starvation—on the flanks of Aconcagua. Steve Goldfarb eats a huge breakfast and takes no trail food with him whatsoever—only water and sports drinks. I usually take a couple of deli sandwiches, some fruit, several energy bars, a quart of energy drink, a small poly bottle full of espresso, and of course, water (usually a gallon).

Some of these diets are eccentric, yes, but they pale against what I've seen folk eat in Asia. One time in Sarawak, Dwight Brooks and I were in a six-hundred-foot longhouse in primal jungle, bickering with a native headman about the porter's day wages. The headman, clad only in a breechclout, his mouth a blood bin of betel nut spit, was driving a hard bargain, when suddenly his arm shot out and he snagged a titanic purple insect from midair. He withdrew a Bic lighter from the waist folds of his breechclout, waved the flame a few times under the bug, then tossed it into his mouth. When the headman chewed, it sounded like sticks breaking. Another time

Dwight and I were thrashing through the Gulf Province, Papua New Guinea, when the natives held up and rolled from the flanking hedgerow a girthy rotten trunk, perhaps fifteen feet long, black and bloated and teaming with vermin. They laid into that trunk with an ax and split it lengthwise about a dozen times, each time finding six or eight writhing white grubs as big as your thumb. They tossed them down the hatch straightaway, live and uncooked. If their faces were any indication of the taste, these revolting larvae were in fact the choicest delicacy. Dani people in the Irian Jaya highlands have reduced mealtime to the fundamentals. As I witnessed and partook of every day during a month's trek, whenever hunger struck, several people would start building a fire while the rest of us fanned out through the surrounding bush in search of jungle tubers. The tubers, some the length and weight of a small boy, were chucked straight onto the flames. Once "done," they resembled a meteorite, but were slightly tougher to chew. But that's all we had.

Unless you've made a study of it or are with someone who has, grazing on natural herbs, berries, edible bark, and so forth can be trouble at best, fatal at worst. The first job I ever had was as a slave laborer for a raft outfit running trips down the Salmon River. One of the boatman—Paul something—was a self-styled woodsman, and once during a lunch break he led a bunch of us to a "natural" apple orchard about a half mile off the river. Paul nabbed a tart green apple off a tree and gobbled it

down with relish. The rest of us did the same. About twenty minutes later folks started turning poisonous green and throwing up. Later came the trots. We didn't listen to Paul much after that.

The people I mentioned at the beginning of this section are into "performance" trekking, where the priority is miles covered and the aim is sustained energy from whatever you eat. In that light, you can see how ludicrous are the trail diets of Katz and Hudson. If you're interested in grueling dayhikes, the surest way to go wrong is to read what's recommended in many backpacking books. One such manual flatly stated that for a dayhike, "Any menu will do." If you're out for an hour's casual stroll, the author is probably right. But if you really want to get down the trail, the knowledge is with the sports nutritionists.

These experts say you should refuel every couple of hours and never go more than four hours between snacks. By reducing your body's need to rely on its own short-term energy (sugar from muscles), frequent refueling helps prevent premature fatigue. The trick is to supply your body with enough of the right *kind* of fuel.

First, plan your food a day ahead of time so that you don't get caught snagging fast/junk food on the drive out. You need not go to a specialty store for a day trip. As mentioned, the local grocery probably has everything you'll need.

Eat a well-balanced breakfast before you leave. For example, a bowl of cereal, granola, or oatmeal with low-fat or skim milk, some yogurt with fruit or juice, and a couple of eggs. The eggs, milk, and yogurt yield sufficient protein, and the cereal and fruit are great carbohydrate sources.

The best way to pack for a long day is to bring a couple of substantial meals for longer rest stops, and two or three snacks that are light and carry well. Foods should consist of a good *balance* of protein, carbohydrates, and a little fat. For the main meals it's hard to beat sandwiches and fruit. Apples, oranges, plums, grapes (in a plastic container), and raisins carry well and are great for quick energy. Fruit contains fructose, a much better sugar source that the simple sugars found in candy bars and most trail mixes. The best carbo sources are not candy bars, but rather complex carbs such as fruits and whole-grain breads, muffins, crackers, and pretzels that give your body a longer sugar response and a slow, even energy level.

Make sandwiches on bagels or English muffins so they don't deteriorate in a day or fanny pack. Each should contain at least three ounces of protein. Good choices are canned chicken, sliced turkey, and other light lunch meats. Avoid mayonnaise, which spoils quickly, especially in summer heat. Mustard and catsup are better condiments.

Good carbo snack choices are granola bars sweetened with fruit juice, sports bars, low-fat granola carried in baggies, dehydrated fruit, and fruit strips. It's crucial to bring protein snacks to mix with your carbs. The result is more sustained energy. Beef or turkey jerky are favorites.

It cannot be overstated: Stay hydrated. Snack breaks are convenient times to drink plenty of water. Sugar-free drink mixes are easy to prepare and don't give you the energy crash that sugar drinks will. For each liter of drink mix, carry one liter of pure water as well. Electrolyte-replacement drinks are useful for grueling hikes, but should be diluted to half strength.

Whatever grub you settle on, never hike till you are hungry. Stop every

How Often Should I Rest?

 How frequently you rest is determined primarily by your body and how much rest it is demanding. Sounds simple enough. Still, there are guidelines to follow. First, keep your rest breaks short, no longer than 5 minutes. They should be long enough to take in fluids, have a snack, and slow down the heart rate, but not so long that the muscles begin to cool down and cramp. Second, if you require frequent rest breaks, more than two or three every 30 minutes, consider slowing your pace. Take time to smell the roses, and slow your steps enough to lift your eyes from the trail.

Trail-Tested Wisdom on Food and Water

Terrain and level of physical fitness both contribute to fatigue, but perhaps the biggest and most preventable contributor is lack of adequate fluid and food intake.

According to Buck Tilton, director of the Wilderness Medicine Institute in Colorado, "For maximum performance on the trail, your diet should be about 70 percent carbohydrates, 15 percent fat, and 15 percent protein. Consuming a high-carbohydrate diet for several days prior to a trip will double your glycogen stores and increase your on-trail performance as much as three times." Carbohydrates include dried fruits, bagels, muffins, rice cakes, energy bars, and cookies. Proteins are found in meats, beans, cereals, and nuts. Fats include cheese, butter, cooking oil, meat, and some nuts.

When I worked as a mountain guide, I used to constantly remind clients that the body is a factory in need of fuel. What this means is you have to keep feeding it when it's at work, starting with breakfast. Once

hour or so for a snack and water.

Most of us do not approach a dayhike like an athletic event, rather as an opportunity to get outdoors and stretch our legs and minds. As with virtually every other form of outdoor travel, provided you heed the nutrition fundamentals germane to vigorous exercise, the "right" food is an elastic concept. The majority of us will never require four-hundred-calorie-a-quart energy drinks or sophisticated (and costly) energy supplements. What food you *should* take is determined entirely by what you like and what you plan to do.

In determining a day's food, I ask myself a few questions: How distant is the destination? How many hours do I estimate to get there and get back? I calculate and take what I need. How much will you need for, say, a strenuous five-hour outing? Nobody can tell you that. In time you will know from experience. To start with, bring more than you think you can eat. Even if you estimate far too high, we're only talking about a pound or so.

Remember that you can work up a powerful hunger tromping up switchbacks, and for straight woe, going hungry is second only to going thirsty.

In years past most people would pack gorp, salami, and string cheese because everyone else did. This diet, high in fat and acceptable, but not great for long-term energy, caused problems for many, especially those who normally never ate gorp or greasy salami and didn't really like cheese. As long as your trail food has a good balance of carbos, protein, and a little fat, the closer it comes to what you usually eat, the better your system will deal with it. Your choices, of course, are limited to perishable grub, since no one hauls cooking gear on a day outing. Drink fluids. Snack at regular intervals. Experiment and learn what is best for you in a given situation.

Water Is Life

- Your body needs 3 to 4 quarts of water per day—more if it is hot and humid.
- Carry at least 3 quarts of water, unless you are certain of a water source along your hike.
- Always purify natural water you intend to drink by either filtering or adding a chemical treatment such as iodine or chlorine. (see pages 90–92).

breakfast ends, immediately begin snacking right through to dinner.

It is also critical that you keep drinking. Replacing lost water is an often overlooked dietary consideration; the body cannot metabolize nutrients efficiently unless it is well hydrated. A dehydrated body leads to thirst, fatigue, and headaches. You must drink a minimum of 2 quarts of water per day—the recommended intake is 3 to 4 quarts per day under normal conditions. Experts recommend that if you are a fast-paced hiker you should imbibe 1 cup of fluid for every 20 minutes of activity (see also pages 90–93).

Bob Gaines, Ryan Mountain Trail, Joshua Tree National Monument

HIKING WITH CHILDREN

Any parent understands that children are not at all interested in carrying out a predetermined itinerary. Experience is the game. Hiking from point A to point B so you can tell yourself you did so makes as much sense to a child as Whitehead's *Process and Reality*—and that's not much. So trying to herd kids along a path to some nebulous "destination" (like the end of the trail) is frustrating to all involved. If you have a concrete goal, like a waterfall or spectacular overlook, it can be used as incentive to lure the kids along. But you'd better be sure the payoff is pretty close or the kids will lose patience and want to stop and look for stinkbugs. Also, if a fantastic destination is used as bait, it best *be* fantastic,

because little Pepe remembers all. Next time you start up the switchbacks from hell, painting a picture of the dawn of creation with butterflies the size of condors and rivers of fruit punch, Pepe—not to be buffaloed twice—will flash back to last time, to the dusty boring precipitous trudge to a pissy little creek swarming with skeeters; getting Pepe's boots moving this time around will prove decidedly harder than inducing Baalim's ass to gallop the length of the John Muir Trail.

Hiking with kids is first and foremost a matter of the adult's attitude. Oftentimes, following a gruesome workweek, Mom feels she must get out of the house and into the hills or she may lose her mind. Grandma's in Terra Haute visiting relatives, and the babysitter's at traffic school. So if the folks are going to get out

Trekking with Little Ones—Nuts and Bolts

Children and the wilderness go together like peanut butter and jelly. If allowed, the wilderness becomes a natural teacher, educating your children about themselves and their world in an unhurried setting. Memories of a child gazing intently at a ladybug crawling on her finger and the uncontrolled giggling of youngsters searching for crawfish in a stream make hiking with children enormously enjoyable for me. Given the opportunity, I think you will find the same happiness.

When planning a hike with children, keep the following in mind:

- While many parents dare not embark on a hike until their children are "older"—say between the ages of four and five—consider that babies do adapt very easily to the outdoors. The rocking motion of being carried on a parent's back will lull them to sleep. They are easily fed (especially if breast feeding) and typically won't cry unless there is a real problem. Be sure to pack along a large plastic bag to carry out all the dirty diapers—burial is not a solution.

- There are many child carriers on the market. Choose one that is both within your budget and comfortable for extended wear. Remember that the carrier needs to be comfortable for both you *and* the child. Carriers that face the child forward seem to offer more security, but wandering hands and fingers in a par-

Michael Hodgson

With wide eyes and a keen imagination, children love to be outdoors.

ent's face get a little old. Be sure the carrier you choose has a security belt for the child and

David J. Mac Donald

A family enjoys an afternoon hike in the high peaks of Colorado.

C H I L D R E N

a kickstand that enables you to set carrier and child down without the whole package falling over. Tough Traveler, Kelty, and Gerry all manufacture excellent child carriers.

- I recommend tennis shoes for children up to age eight. There are hiking boots for children, but kids grow out of them far too quickly and seem to enjoy the freedom of tennies anyway. Once kids are old enough to carry some of their own weight, boots become more important. The Vasque Kids Klimber is one of the best boots on the market, although excellent alternatives are offered by Hi-Tec, Merrell, and others.
- Always pack extra clothes for the children. Mud, water, dirt, and

stains you didn't even know existed will magnetize toward your kids in layers. Bright colors will make it much easier to spot the little ones wandering through the trees.

- Plan your destination to be attractive and fun for all. Keep the hike fairly short, no longer than 5 miles. Keep the elevation gain and loss to a minimum—500 feet is about right. Scenery along the way, as well as interesting things to do and see, will spice up any hike and make the walk more fun. Always plan within the physical and emotional capabilities of everyone involved—both adults and youngsters.
- Favorite and nutritional snacks in addition to tasty meals are a

must: fruit, gorp (which, depending on whom you talk to, is short either for "granola, oatmeal, raisins, peanuts" or "good old raisins and peanuts," although most mixtures also include M&M's and other tidbits), cheese sticks, fruit juice in a box (fun because they are individually packaged and have a straw—be sure to buy the ones with fruit juice, not fruit-flavored drink), crackers, and other family favorites. Be careful when packing anything that is easily crushed or melted. Grapes and candy bars spread all over the inside of a pack aren't very appetizing.

- Carry the bare minimum in your packs. Make everything

of town, the kids must tag along. Fair enough. But if the kids are made to do what the adults want to do, to try to keep up, expect the worst, because you'll probably experience it.

Whenever you take kids into the wilderness, the kids must come first. It is their trip, and within reason the whole shebang should be designed around what they want. And what they want cannot be predicted. Kids are spontaneous, so you'll have to improvise once you get to the stream or mountains or wherever you are heading. Try to force a curriculum onto a child and you'll spoil his or her appreciation for the outdoors with bad experiences. Not the way to go. You want kids to treasure the mountains, the trees, and the myriad sounds and smells, and this is best accomplished on their terms. You are

along only to make sure Ruthie doesn't stick her hand into the beehive.

Practical considerations begin with age. How old is Pepe, and what are his physical capabilities? This is especially important if you plan to cover any ground. Most kids can motor around in atomic mode for hours, then suddenly will slump back exhausted. If this happens at your destination, be ready to carry Pepe home, because you'll probably have to. Regardless of how fit or game your kid(s) might be, don't plan to cover more than about half a mile an hour.

If Pepe is older, the way to discover where he stands is to start conservatively and go from there, always remembering that you're out there for his pleasure, not your own. The worst approach is to keep

count. Extra weight is not worth the pain. Children want to and should participate, even the younger ones. My daughter, Nikki, was carrying a small pack when she was just three. Granted, all she carried was a little teddy bear and a box of juice, but it was important to her to feel involved—and quite frankly, for Nikki the teddy bear and juice were essential.

- Everyone should carry a signaling device; I carry a signal mirror and a whistle. I recommend that every member in a hiking party, not just the children, carry a whistle and know when to use it. Teach your children never to blow unless they are in trouble. Also, teach them that signals in threes (three sharp and distinct

Michael Hodgson

Resting on a rocky perch, Nicole (at age 8) enjoys a snack she carried.

pushing the lad another half mile every time out, in an attempt to discover just how much he can take. Pepe might go along, particularly if he has to; but it's even money that twenty years down the road he'll be sitting in the therapist's office, weeping and raging in turn as he thrusts hatpins through pictures of dear old Dad. So-called character building is always best accomplished with a light touch and plenty of understanding of the youngster's needs. Start grafting your needs onto the kid and you reduce the magical outdoors to the point of dread—a condition any qualified child can make his parents share.

That much said, there are certain things an adult *must* make the kids do, and this starts with making sure they drink plenty of water, even if they don't want to.

Hanging around. A hike with a child opens up a smorgasbord of playing and exploring opportunity.

blows on the whistle) indicate someone in trouble and will alert anyone within hearing distance.

• Always have an emergency plan in place. You never know when a real emergency will arise, so it is best always to be prepared. Know where the nearest emergency room is. Involve your children in every plan you make. They are never too young to hear how to take care of themselves. Learn basic first aid and CPR; having no idea how to proceed or what to do in an emergency is a helpless feeling. The Red Cross is a good place to look for first aid instruction. No matter what, safety first!

• Sun protection is essential. A child's skin is sensitive, so be prepared with a good sunblock.

A hat and sunglasses are also important safeguards from sun and heat. Protection from insects is nearly as important as sun protection, but since insect repellent is such a noxious substance, I depend on long sleeves and long pants whenever possible. In the event insect repellent becomes necessary, read the instructions carefully and keep the liquid or lotion away from eyes and mouth. Insect repellent in the eyes is painful at the very least, and sometimes becomes a medical emergency. Always be sure the percentage of DEET doesn't exceed 10 percent (see page 194). Skeedadle, Cutters, and Sawyer all manufacture kid-safe repellents. Another alternative is to spray clothing with the chemi-

cal Permanone, which repels and kills mosquitoes and ticks.

• Children want and need peers with them. You will do well to bring a close playmate or another family along. The presence of a friend makes things much more fun for a child and, believe it or not, will usually make the hike smoother for you; you won't have to stage so much entertainment.

• Be prepared to get down and dirty with your children—experience the outdoors *with* them, not just over them. You need not get filthy to appreciate the outdoors, but don't let a little dirt come between you and your children.

• Patience and a sense of humor are musts. Without them, your efforts to share the outdoors with

The rest of your responsibilities are mainly a function of common sense, the rule of thumb: Be vigilant. Remember, most kids are extremely curious. Since they don't yet have an appreciation either of danger or their own capabilities, they must rely on your judgment to keep them safe.

Totally unforeseen things can happen in the wilderness, as illustrated by my friend Peter Williamson, who had taken his son and several neighbor kids for a three-mile trek up Malibu Creek to a big lagoon/swimming hole. I think the oldest child was eight. Peter had never been stung by a bee before. No sooner had they reached the swimming hole than Peter was immediately stung and went into anaphylactic shock. Luckily, an off-duty fireman was there with his kids, and was packing a first aid kit with Adrenalin (epinephrine).

Without such blessed assistance, Peter might have died, leaving the kids stranded and terrified. Three adults seem like the magic number. If one goes down, one can stay with the injured while the third goes for help. The likelihood of this happening is very small, but it does exist.

Great rewards accrue to adults who share their outdoor experiences with kids. Some of my fondest memories are of the little excursions I've taken with my wife and two daughters. Many of these happened in Venezuela. The most memorable was a canoe ride starting in Canaima, near Angel Falls, a small Indian settlement in the middle of the ancient rain forest where my wife once worked as a schoolteacher. We paddled almost an hour down the river, slow and wide, to gain another

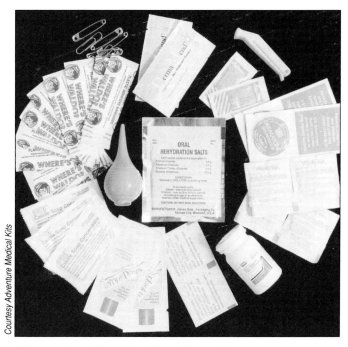

your children will be seriously hampered. Laughter, fun and games, silly pranks, and unexpected occurrences are part of being outdoors with children. Go with the flow and enjoy every moment. If you can learn to laugh off a mudrat expecting a ride home in the family car, you are ready to proceed as an outdoor leader. Good luck!

Youngsters have different first aid needs than adults.

Indian village, set back from the bank on a plateau of red soil, brick-hard from the tread of thousands of Pamons over nearly a thousand years. The poetic adobe and palm thatch huts were scattered over a couple of acres of cleared land. Naked, moon-faced kids rode bareback atop fat sows. Down at the river, under the vine bridge, shiny-skinned kids dove into whirlpools for sport, while lanky bystanders skimmed wafer rocks from one shore to the other. Several women trudged in from the surrounding forest, bark-thread bags harboring either an infant or husky ears of maize, swinging to and fro, a slow metronome of their tired dance. At the fringe, neatly parceled gardens extended well into the dark trees, hunchbacked men ever chopping the flinty earth with crude tools. We broke our thirst with cool spring water from thin bamboo tubes offered us by bronze-skinned beauties in their reed dresses, young women not yet marked by their certain descent into child-bearing and raw labor. My girls fell in immediately with the other kids, diving into the river and chasing after porkers. Not so long afterward I joined in as well, and immediately understood that by letting myself be carried away by the kids' native enthusiasm, I could return to a time when I was younger, much as the needle on a compass will naturally return to true north. Only with the simplicity of a child can we fully appreciate the majesty of the outdoors. We are their guardians, but they have much to teach us if only we can put our anxious itineraries aside.

Oh, the Games We Play

The following is a brief listing of activity/awareness games for you and your family to try in the wilds. Each activity, while fun, teaches your children vital natural awareness skills.

- *Forest/Swamp Crawl.* One of my favorites, similar to follow the leader. Lead your family on a crawl down forest trails, along animal paths, and even into wet, mucky areas. This encourages your children to become "involved" in the land, discovering things they might miss just walking through.
- *Blindfold Walk.* Teaches your children to use and focus all of their senses—you too! Lead blindfolded children on a walk through natural areas. Stop periodically to examine a rock, flower, tree, or animal track. See if they can identify what they are examining.
- *Night Sounds.* Encouraging children to tune into the world around them is important. Leading them away from the campsite to a preselected place where you all sit and listen to night sounds is a valuable experience and will go far in teaching them to respect, but not fear, the dark. Take time to explain the sounds you hear—or ask your children what they are: wind, a gurgling stream, an owl, squeaking mice, a coyote howl, etc.
- *Storytelling.* Nothing like sitting around the campfire telling stories and munching on s'mores (melted chocolate, toasted marshmallows, and graham crackers). I like reading aloud from a selection of Robert Service poems. Create your own family adventure so that everyone adds a part to the story. Use your imagination. One word of caution—tell ghost stories only to older children.

REMEMBERING YOUR WALKS

Recording your walks—whether poetically, experientially, or factually—is to fashion yourself a museum of memories. Unlike the bulk of our other experiences, with their hazy beginnings and ambiguous endings, a dayhike has a tangible start and finish, commencing the moment your boots hit the earth and finishing when, an hour or a day later, you point your car for home. From that first step you're as a weaver at a loom, knitting an experience of feelings, thoughts, sights, and sounds. You weave with windflowers and rattlesnakes, rainbows and blisters, with fogbanks, hailstorms, chiggers, and a lone hawk riding the thermals. When the day is done you've plaited a diverse tapestry unique as a snowflake, and can hang it in memory to admire at will. The problem is that as years pass, the pattern blurs and grows thin until everything fades except a few stitches forever etched into your life. The simple way to keep the articles of your museum in sharp relief is to record each outing. There are no rules, no fixed guidelines on how to keep a journal, but a few pointers might suggest possible directions.

Some people can make little if any sense of their experiences without recourse to "facts." That bird floating on the thermal means almost nothing—till it is verified as a dovetailed hawk who roosts during these months, eats this, does that. Then the bird takes on fabulous significance. The diary entries of this observer are bound to details, and her tapestry is apt to resemble a cold grid of learning with little emphasis on experience. This is science, not art. No harm in that, but what about encounters and memories? They should count for something. To this hiker I'd suggest trying to capture how you *feel* about the whole business, or about something—as little as

REMEMBERING

Watch Where You Step

In 1991, a college student walking on a field trip to Big Bend National Park in Texas alertly noticed something strange sticking out of the sand and notified the instructors. The "something strange" turned out to be the 2-foot-long left horn of an 80-million-year-old complete dinosaur skull from the three-horned Chasmosaurus—a 17-foot-long, plant-eating beast that wandered the Mesozoic marshes and ocean beaches of southern Texas.

the exhilaration felt when identifying the bird as a dovetailed hawk. And maybe push it a little. Sit down and write a poem about it. If it's doggerel, no one will ever read it but you.

Conversely, you may get so caught up in the passions that your journal writing becomes a forum for all manner of silly fluff and odes to earthworms. Unless your journal is grounded in the facts of the matter—if only barely—your tapestry will consist of so much gauze and air that in reading through it some years later you won't remember where you were or anything you saw. It is usually the manifest stuff—the mountains, lagoons, and sand dunes—that trigger the emotional fabric. A good balance is the best bet.

Of the many people I know who make a habit of or living from writing about wilderness experiences, most apply a three-step recording process. First, they carry a small notepad in the field, and scribble down whatever they feel like whenever it's convenient. I personally don't like to interrupt the flow of things, so I only jot down particulars I'm afraid I'll forget or won't remember in enough detail, especially place names. Step two is to write a summary shortly after the trip, when the experience is fresh and vivid. Here again I mainly stay with the facts and details. The last step is the attempt to relate the venture in experiential terms, which is where the real "writing" comes into play. Few people want to go this far with the thing. The most popular method is probably to jot down notes in the field, then later, using these notes for reference, commit the day's experience to a diary. It is astonishing to go back to a trip you might have taken ten or fifteen years before, to read what you wrote down and to see your tapestry jump back to life. To enjoy one's past is to live twice, and the easiest and most vital way to do so is to keep a journal.

Y O U R   W A L K S

Bob Gaines, High Sierra lake

Heading up into the local hills with your dog is a great way to spend a few hours. Not only does your favorite pet get a great opportunity to romp and play, but you will enjoy the walk too—beats laps around the block on a leash any day.

- Not every park welcomes dogs, however, and even in those that do, leash laws often place a restraining edge on your wandering freedom.
- In those parks where Fido is allowed to romp unrestrained (all parks require dogs to be leashed within parking, picnic, and camping areas), certain points of etiquette and safety must be considered.
- Not all dogs are good hikers. Like humans, dogs must be conditioned to the trail. Don't expect your pet to hike easily with you over hill and dale if the backyard has been the extent of exploration thus far. Remember that your dog will always try to keep up with you even if it is overheating or in physical pain.
- Be sure your dog's vaccinations are up to date. Rabies, parvo, heartworm (prevention pills can be obtained from any vet), and more await your unprotected friend.
- A good ID tag hanging from your pet's collar in case he manages to get lost is a must. A good friend got his dog returned, several days after the two were separated in the woods, because of an ID tag. A tag should have your name, the dog's name, and your phone number with area code engraved in it.
- Always clean up after your dog. Beyond the obvious fact that no one likes to step in poop, the smell drives off wild animals, it creates an urban aura for all who view it, and it is one of the problems that cause park administrators to crack down on dogs. If your dog brought it in, you carry it out—no exceptions.
- Do not let your dog chase wildlife. Reports of dogs chasing squirrels, deer, or other wildlife are reason enough for park officials to close a park to dogs.
- Dogs must yield to all trail users. Always leash up when encountering horses, cattle, bicyclists, and other trail users. Obeying leash laws is critical, because if citations stack up, the various boards and administrations may cancel dogs' rights to use the parks.
- You must carry water for both you and your dog—especially in the summer. Dogs do not tolerate heat as well as humans.
- Carry a first aid kit for both you and your dog. Treat your dog's cuts and bumps as you would your own. Nothing fancy needed—just clean and bandage if needed.
- Dogs will pass poison oak on to you if they manage to run through or roll in it. If your dog encounters poison oak, do not cuddle or pet it until you clean it. When you get home, put on rubber gloves and wash Fido with warm water and dog shampoo.
- Check your dog for ticks periodically. If you find one, grasp it close to the head with tweezers and pull out firmly. Check to make sure you have not left the head behind. If you have, monitor closely for infection. If you spot any, head to the vet. A good flea-and-tick spray, as well as a flea-and-tick collar, will help discourage ticks.
- In general, expect the following regulations regarding dogs: National parks—no dogs allowed except on leash within campgrounds. National forests—dogs allowed, but consult ranger stations governing each area for specific guidelines. State parks—no dogs allowed except on leash within campgrounds.

Michael O'Conner and Niji are inseparable companions.

Vicuna, Brutus, and friends enjoying a rest in a local park.

Problems associated with overuse or carelessness are visible in any wilderness or park setting. All you have to do is look—and not very hard at times. Scattered campfire rings; eroding gullies and trails; toilet paper and human waste littering a meadow; trees girdled by improperly tethered horses; food scraps and trash dotting a campsite; graffiti carved on trail signs, historical sites, and trees; vandalized park facilities; obnoxious and overly audible park patrons . . . the list goes on.

Land use and impact guidelines are established by land managers for the protection of the wilderness and to enhance each visitor's experience. Before any hiking, boating, mountain biking, or camping trip, or other recreational activity, check with the local Bureau of Land Management, United States Forest Service, national park, state park, county park, or regional district office as appropriate for minimum impact recommendations specific to the area you will be traveling in. Listed below are guidelines that are appropriate nearly 100 percent of the time. Most have been adapted from established policies and information provided by the Leave No Trace organization. A free, pocket-size, weatherproof card printed with specific guidelines, as well as booklets and other information on how to minimize human impact on wild

areas, may be obtained by calling 1-800-332-4100.

The following "rules," when coupled with common sense, will help to keep the wilderness we love pure and pristine.

HIKING/BACKPACKING/ HORSEBACK RIDING

- Planning your wilderness trips to avoid major holiday rushes is a first step in minimizing impact. Trailheads and campgrounds can become so packed with humanity that the water, air, and noise impacts are severe. Travel in small groups—four or fewer is ideal.
- On the trail, hike single file and in the center of the trail. Resist the urge to shortcut across a meadow or down a switchback; doing so will encourage erosion and trail damage.
- Take rest stops where your presence will not damage vegetation. Be careful to replace all gear in your pack—the most common place to forget gear or inadvertently litter is during a rest break.
- The perfect campsite is never constructed—it is discovered. Trenching, cutting branches, leveling, or removing vegetation can cause permanent damage. Look for a level site that has adequate drainage and is not in a sensitive area that will be dam-

aged by your presence.
- Whenever possible, select campsites that have already been used—this will eliminate the creation or expansion of unnecessary camping areas. Camp out of sight of others and the trail. Practice no-trace camping.
- Use a stove whenever possible. Campfires have romantic appeal, but they can degrade the environment in ways subtle and not so subtle. Beyond the obvious impacts, keep in mind that the dancing light from bright flames all but destroys your night vision, obscuring the larger world outside the boundaries of the fire. If you do make a campfire, use an existing fire ring and build it with sticks no thicker than your wrist. Make sure it is dead out and cold before leaving the campsite.
- Carry out all that you carry in—including fishing line, lures, spent cartridges, and cigarette butts. Bring an extra garbage bag and pick up litter as you find it.
- Never bury food scraps. They will be dug up and scattered. Burn or pack out all leftover food. Fish entrails must be burned, or packed out when campfires are not permitted. A consistent food source around campsites is an attraction to animals such as insects, rodents, and bears.
- Use established latrines when

Michael Hodgson

- Blend in with the environment. Save rowdy games for other places. Keep your traveling groups small and be considerate of other users.
- Horseback riders have trail priority over hikers, and both have priority over mountain bikers. Step softly to the downhill side of the trail and speak softly when encountering horses and riders.
- Let nature's sounds prevail. Avoid making loud noises. Boom boxes, tape players, portable TVs, and other electronic devices (other than those used for navigation and safety) have as much place in the wilds as a grizzly bear or wild boar has in your living room. In campgrounds where the boundaries between civilization and wilderness blur, keep the sounds of stereos and TVs within the limits of your campsite—if your neighbor can hear you, you're too loud.
- Where pets are allowed, they should be brought only if you can control them at all times so they will not disturb others or frighten wildlife. Otherwise, leave Fido home.
- Horseback riders and other trail users should not break off branches just to make it easier to pass. You could be killing a tree

they are available. Otherwise, dig a hole 6 inches deep and at least 200 feet from the nearest water source. Toilet paper does not break down readily, so it must be either packed out or burned—preferably in your campfire. If you must burn it at the hole, use extreme caution and be sure all flames and embers are out before leaving.
- Clothes, dishes, and your

body should be washed at least 100 feet from the nearest water source. Use hot water and a minimum amount of soap (avoid soap if at all possible). Boiling water will sterilize dishes and utensils. Soap residue can cause more harm than the odd speck of grease. Scatter dishwater after all food particles have been removed; pack out the food particles.

and leaving scars for others passing behind you. To duck or dismount is the best policy.

RIVER WANDERING

A river corridor is a thin strip of land and water where activities become highly concentrated. For that reason, minimum-impact techniques are of utmost importance to keep riverways looking pristine.

- All solid human waste must be carried out. A river or chemical toilet using an ammo can, heavy-duty plastic bags, a toilet seat, chlorine bleach, and toilet paper is required at most boat-in campsites on rivers and lakes. Although carrying out all human waste may seem unpleasant (it's actually not with a chemical toilet), it is far less unpleasant than mounds of human waste scattered along the riverbank. An option: close up a garbage bag at the end of each day and open a fresh one atop it.
- Pack out everything you pack in.
- Place a large tarp under the eating area to catch food scraps so beach areas do not become feeding grounds for rodents and massive communities of insects.
- Use a fire pan for campfires and use only downed wood—better yet, bring charcoal. Fire pans should be elevated so heat from the pan does not scorch the soil.

Michael Hodgson, Wind River Range, Wyoming

All ashes, once cooled and doused, must be carried out. A 5-gallon slush bucket is perhaps the easiest method. Ashes can be sprinkled on human waste in a container.

- Camp on beaches, sandbars, or nonvegetated sites below the high-water line. When the river floods, your passing will be washed away and the site will appear pristine to river runners who follow.
- Washing or bathing with soap must be done at least 200 feet from the nearest water source.
- Waste water from cooking should first be filtered through a fine-mesh screen to remove food solids, then poured into the river. Do not scatter waste water on the beach—it will attract flies and other animals.

ARCHAEOLOGICAL SITES

The single biggest problem for land managers and cultural resource persons is dealing with damage, both unintentional and intentional, caused by visitors. Even with extreme caution, impacts can and do occur. Use extreme caution and respect when visiting and traveling through the priceless resources offered by archaeological and historic sites.

The following suggestions will guide you through cultural sites with the least impact:

- Viewing the site from a distance, rather than entering it, will reduce the impact a site receives. Although there may be only one or two of you, thousands of other "onesies" and "twosies" visit a site each year—and that's a lot of foot traffic.
- Stop, look, and think before

entering a cultural site. Identify the midden area (trash pile) so you can avoid walking on it—middens contain important and fragile bits of archaeological information.

- Stay on a trail if one has been built through a site.
- Looking at artifacts is fine; picking them up and taking them is not. Leave all potsherds and other artifacts where they lie for others to enjoy.
- Camping is not allowed in or around ruins.
- Move nothing, including branches or rocks when scrambling around a site. Avoid touching plaster walls. Climbing on roofs and walls can lead to the immediate collapse of a cultural site that may have stood for hundreds of years.
- Enjoy rock art by viewing, sketching, or photographing. Never chalk, trace, or otherwise touch rock art, as any physical contact will contribute to the disintegration of the ancient figures.
- Graffiti is vandalism and a sacrilege.
- Never build fires in or around cultural sites.
- Finally, cultural sites are places of ancestral importance to Native Americans and should be treated with the respect and reverence they deserve.

WATCHING WILDLIFE

- *Keep Your Distance:* You can harm wildlife unintentionally by getting too close! Most wild animals react with alarm when approached by humans on foot or by vehicles. A panic reaction is stressful and causes the animal to use energy and food reserves needed for other activities. Repeated disturbances can cause animals and birds to avoid an area—even if that area offers the choicest food and habitat. Learn animal behavior patterns that will warn you if you are getting too close. Be advised that you will get your closest peeks at wildlife if you let them come to you. Never, ever use food to attract animals.
- *Use Spotting Equipment:* Quality binoculars (7 x 35 magnification as a minimum) or a spotting scope will help you observe wildlife from a safe distance. Use a telephoto lens (300 mm) and tripod to get close-up photos.
- *Take Your Time:* Rushing around is no way to watch wildlife. The more time you take, the greater your chances of observing wildlife that would otherwise be missed. Set up a base camp to spend a few days in an area. Wild animals are most often spotted at or around dawn and dusk.
- *Blend In:* Wear muted colors, sit quietly, and leave pets at home. Refrain from scented soaps and perfumes.
- *Research:* Spend time at local museums of natural history to learn about the wildlife in the area you are visiting. Natural history museums and organizations have books, brochures, maps, and displays to assist you. Learn to recognize an animal by its tracks, droppings, casts, and calls.
- *Carry Field Guides:* Local field guides pertaining to birds, mammals, animal tracks, edible plants, wildflowers, trees, rocks and gems, and more are readily available. Most major bookstores carry a selection.
- *You are too close to a bird* if it seems skittish, raises its head to watch you, preens excessively, pecks at dirt or its feet, wipes its bill repeatedly, gives alarm calls, flushes repeatedly, or gives distraction displays such as feigning a broken wing.
- *You are too close to a mammal* if it raises its head high, ears pointed in your direction, with raised hairs on the neck and shoulders; exhibits signs of skittishness, such as jumping at sounds or movements; lowers its head, ears back in preparation for a charge; moves away; or displays aggressive or nervous behavior.

EXOTIC? WHY NOT?

In later chapters we'll venture to the desert, the mountains, the forest, the edge of the sea, even the jungle. The jungle? How can I, you might ask, who rarely leaves Trenton, and who has no aspirations toward Ramboesque exploring, how can I realistically expect ever to walk through a primordial jungle? Isn't it true that all this forthcoming talk about great mountain ranges and rain forests is no more pertinent to my life and my prospects than is a ride in an Indy car or a trip to Saturn?

It is true only if you want it to be.

Very few people know how to go about getting to distant places, or know what to do once they've arrived. Much of this has to do with grandiose, even frightening expectations about what is necessary. So before we cast off for New Guinea and beyond, let's do away with some common false notions about "exotic" locales, and familiarize ourselves with general ideas about what is actually involved.

Once I had enough money to consider traveling, I looked close to home first. I was thinking the same thing you're probably thinking—that if I wanted to get to the far places of the world and live in at least moderate comfort, I'd need a stack of money. I was dead wrong. More than a decade would pass before I could afford a "normal" vacation to Disneyworld, or a motor junket to Mount Rushmore or wherever folk go on traditional vacations. In the meantime I went through three passports and visited more than fifty nations. So much for the first myth—that it takes big money to travel far and wide. In reality, a trip to the Costa Rican jungle or to the middle of the Malaysian rain forest costs about half of what a typical two-week vacation in the continental United States does—a little more if you're given to lavish rations and pricey liquor. Understand that air fares are as erratic as Sierra storms, but if you look around and become even a little fluent with all the chicanery that airlines pull to get your money, you can almost always obtain a moderate fare to most anywhere in the world. For example, it costs me about the same coin for a round-trip ticket to New York as it does for a round-trip ticket to Jakarta, Indonesia.

The second myth is that going to exotic locations means you're going to suffer and get violently ill from liver flukes or some other incurable disease. Perhaps you will even perish. This is a common preoccupation of the novice globetrotter, and there are ample stories—mostly exaggerated—to

EXOTIC?

Outstanding Trails of the World

- *Tour Du Mont Blanc* (Switzerland, Italy, and France): A 100-mile loop around the rim of the Alps with three language changes and unlimited scenic splendor traditionally reserved for mountaineers. A network of huts offers full dinners and rooms—hostel style.
- *Inca Trail* (Peru): This is where the world's trekkers come to walk when they want to wander in the footsteps of those who lived during the Andean empire.

Viewing glaciated peaks, walking through subtropical cloud forests, treading Inca cobblestone, and traversing the Sun Gate into the legendary ruins of Machu Picchu—reasons enough to visit.
- *Milford Track* (New Zealand): Sure the Milford Track's soggy, and, yes, you are bound to get soaked. But, as for everyone before you and all who are sure to follow, the stunning scenery will evaporate any damp memories quickly. Deep blue

support it. Provided you use common sense and observe a few basic health precautions, your chance of catching dengue fever or typhus is extremely remote. The Centers for Disease Control has estimated that upward of 99.6 percent of travelers' sickness comes from eating or drinking something that carried bacteria or a dangerous bug. There are many things you cannot control in wilderness areas or Third World nations, but what you eat and drink is not one of them. Start drinking tap water in Madagascar or eating from street vendors in Burma, and expect to get sick. Also know that you've done it to yourself. There are few places in the world where bottled water is not available, and even when it's not, small, personal water filters are now so effective they can virtually turn mud into mineral water. Food is a different matter, and deserves special study, but avoiding contaminated grub is relatively simple. I've been in some of the world's most notorious shit holes, and the worst "disease" I've ever gotten is dysentery.

As for the lack of creature comforts, you might not find a Hilton in every out-of-the-way place, but comfortable, even luxurious lodgings are obtainable in the vast majority of remote locales. Also understand that in every country—even ones like Haiti and Cuba—there are people with money. These people travel, and they need places to stay. That's where you can stay as well, usually for a quarter of the price of expensive tourist lodgings. Use such an accommodation as a base of operations for dayhikes. A whole new world often opens up for you if you are not insistent on a feather bed. You don't experience much holed up in a hotel room, nor do you remember much, because nothing much happens. But if you're willing to put up with a few geckos crawling across the ceiling or a shortage of hot water, you'll probably end up with experiences you'll never forget—most of them positive.

The last myth is that as a stranger in a strange land, you are meat for every pickpocket, thug, and grifter in the country. A stranger always does well to be cautious, but even in the most remote places there are always guide services, or at the least a guide who can take you on interesting day tours. Enlisting local expertise is crucial, and can generally be done by hotel personnel.

To reach and experience many of the world's most fantastic locations, all that's required are desire, common sense, some understanding about dayhiking, and around $1,200.

W H Y   N O T ?

lakes, snowy peaks, and a subtropical rain forest echoing with the wild cries of exotic birds are guaranteed to brighten even the cloudiest day.

- *John Muir Trail* (United States): A 211-mile trail that demands superlatives every step of the way through some of the most inspiring high country in the United States. Sunny days, misty waterfalls, sweeping granite faces, deep canyons, and wide-open vistas that peek over 13,000- and 14,000-foot mountaintops await you.

- *Annapurna Circuit* (Nepal): For many, this trek is their Everest experience—a 200-mile walk along an ancient trading path connecting Buddhist villages and faraway coastal towns. Everywhere along the route your eyes will be drawn to the enormity of the place—a continuous plunge of nearly 24,000 feet from ice-encrusted summits to the subtropical gorge.

2

Clothing
AND
Pack

What does he care if he hasn't got any money, he doesn't need any money, all he needs is his rucksack with those little plastic bags of dried food and a good pair of shoes and off he goes and enjoys the privileges of a millionaire . . .

—Dharma Bums, *Jack Kerouac speaking about Gary Snyder*

John Long

It would take many years of trial and error

before I understood the basic fact about functioning outdoors: that the "truth" of the trail is pretty elastic, and the ability to adapt to conditions is most often more important—so far as safety and enjoyment go—than sticking dogmatically to rules laid down in a book or magazine. This point was driven home when I started making exploratory trips to other continents. I learned, not only from native peoples but also from my partners, that the "best" way to trek through the jungle, across a glacier, or down a streambed does not exist. Nearly every adage is relative to personal tastes, strengths, and wants. There are inviolate rules, certainly. Only a madman or a fool starts across the Sahara without gallons of water and a hat as wide as a circus tent. But the "best" pace, route, rest schedule, and so forth is determined almost entirely by the individual.

Gear is a different issue. For dayhiking you need very few items, and if it's any consolation, understand that the competition for your greenback is so intense that the good stuff is very good indeed. Almost every aspect of gear is debatable, but whatever the argument, provided you have a viable product, the fine points are particular to the individual.

For instance, in 1983, I joined six others in making the first coast-to-coast traverse of Indonesian Borneo. I'd been in jungles before then, but this was the first time I'd had to *live* under the trees for

months at a go. Each of us had a different philosophy about footwear. Jim Bridwell went with tennis shoes; Stan Boer, army boots; Jim Slade, canoeing booties, etc. We'd given a pair of fancy Nike hiking shoes to the chief of the Dayaks, whose tribe we'd hired as porters and guides for the middle section through then-uncharted terrain. The chief wore his splendid shoes with vast pride as long as the trail, if there was one, proved easy going. It rarely did, however, and at the first sign of teetering log bridges, muddy ramparts, and the like, the chief stripped off his Nikes and ventured with bare feet. We first thought he was saving his new shoes, but later understood that he considered them a liability on dicey terrain. And they were—for him, as he had calluses like rawhide and feet as wide as swim fins.

The whole business about ultrahigh-tech gear having no low-tech match is not uniformly so. Before my first venture into arctic climes I went to a mountaineering friend (who'd spent most of the previous ten years kicking around the Himalayas) and had him rig me out for an ascent of Makalu in winter. A week later I stepped off a Nord Air D-9 and onto the frozen contours of Baffin Island. That afternoon I spent motoring around the frozen fjords in a snowmobile—an eighty-horsepower lightning bolt that an Eskimo and I took turns gunning upward of sixty miles an hour—and when I stumbled back to the lodge it was like the iceman cometh. On the advice of an Inuit friend, I pitched the high-tech climbing duds and pulled on some traditional seal and polar bear hides, and spent the next few weeks wandering over the ice pack in perfect comfort.

Wherever I go, my first care is to know the area. If I don't, I call someone who does or I read up to dial myself into the special demands of the place. It matters little that you're in fabulous shape if you don't know the local weather patterns, how much water to take, how to keep the bugs off you, and all the rest. Later chapters deal with special concerns relative to hiking and walking in desert, forest, and other terrains. For now we'll look at concerns common to all areas and climes, understanding that even the most comprehensive book can take us only so far. Again, it is the individual's task to familiarize himself with local conditions and necessities. Provided you go about your business as thoroughly as you'd go about picking a doctor to deliver your firstborn, you can generally calculate the requirements of any terrain with accuracy, and conduct your business accordingly. And if we can convey one thing, it's that systematic preparedness is the starting point for every adventure—be it a dayhike on the Oregon Trail or an exploratory thrash into the heart of Irian Jaya. Look at the preflight checklist of a pilot or consider what a sawbones goes through prior to a hip replacement surgery. These elaborate preludes are undertaken not so much to reiterate what the pilot or surgeon already knows, but to ensure that the basic and proven systems are squared away so when the unforeseen arises—as it often does—the boss is free to deal with it soberly, without nagging doubts that his or her arse is covered per the primary support systems.

Many gear manufacturers would have you believe you will perish ten paces off the highway if you are not rigged out in specialized gear. How so? Not so! The bulk of everyone's dayhikes—from world-class "fell" runners to Uncle Dinky, who goes five-foot-ten, three hundred pounds—follow well-marked trails, are done in mild weather, involve nothing more treacherous than tromping up a few switchbacks, and take no more than three or four leisurely hours to complete. Sports shoes (the old name was tennis shoes), shorts, T-shirt, sweater, two-dollar rain poncho, and book pack with water and rations are totally acceptable tackle. Once you start ranging into more rugged terrain or less temperate climates, such casual gear can get you into trouble. But to insist, for instance, that you must have the "right" gear to hike up to Yosemite Falls in mid-June is rubbish. Would a good pair of lightweight, all-terrain shoes and an eighty-dollar daypack improve your experience? Maybe. Maybe not.

In selecting gear I take three factors into account: environment, terrain, and conditions. Say I'm going into a desert environment. That tells me something, though not much. Then I learn that, unlike Joshua Tree National Monument, my desert is rolling with dunes and riven with chasms. Now I know that much more. And it's not summer, rather winter, with average daytime temperatures in the mid-forties. The combination of these facts gives me a reasonable idea about appropriate gear (provided you know what that gear is). The same formula holds for every locale in every corner of the world. Knowing precisely what gear to take comes from reading, talking with others, and, most important, from experience. Though certain generic equipment is functional in most places, gear selection is almost always relative to where you're going and when.

Another factor is budget. I did as much hiking and climbing when I was in college and essentially flat broke as I've done anytime since. My gear, if you could call it that, would have made Job seem well clad. I did have an expedition sleeping bag—which I bought secondhand for seventy dollars—but it was like a kiln anywhere south of Ellesmere Island, and for an entire summer I slept in an army wool blanket that a girlfriend sewed into a kind of sleeve. That blanket made trips up El Capitan, Half Dome, and Washington Column, up great rocks in Mexico and several in the Sierras, and it worked fine. There was nothing macho about this at all. The blanket simply did the job and did it well. I had a pair of platinum-stiff mountaineering boots I used on the rare occasion I climbed or ventured into snow, and for everything else—from volcanoes in Mexico to big rock walls deep in Sequoia—I went with sports shoes. My tent was a five-dollar plastic tube; I never had a proper one until my first expedition to Borneo. It wasn't till years later, when I had a little of the folding in my pocket, that I got all the tricked-out gear.

That much understood, let's look—from head to toe—at the components of a dayhiker's equipment list.

(text continues on page 52)

Bob Gaines, Hidden Canyon Trail, Zion National Park

No matter how large it is, you will fill it. With that in mind, the pack you choose should be as small and streamlined as you can possibly get away with. Between 1,000 and 1,500 cubic inches is about right for short day trips, when all you will be carrying is the "10 Essentials" (see "The Essentials," pages 15–17) and perhaps a few extra items. Look for a padded back, well-padded and -contoured shoulder straps, and a sturdy waist belt to keep the load from bouncing around. Some daypacks come with padded waist belts that add more weight and bulk than support. Buy what feels best on your back with a load in it. Ask the salesperson to fill the pack with about 10 to 15 pounds of gear so that you can get a good feel for the pack's comfort.

If you are heading out for a weekend jaunt or carrying gear for a large group including several children, opt for a weekend pack in the 2,000- to 3,500-cubic-inch range. Now, the suspension system becomes a little more critical to the comfort of the pack. Well-padded and -contoured shoulder straps with a sternum strap (which fastens across your sternum and takes some of the pressure off your shoulders by keeping the shoulder straps from slipping to the outside) are essential. Look for a padded back with a stiffening frame sheet to aid support and lend shape to the pack, and a padded, stiffened, and contoured waist belt.

If you plan on trekking overseas or heading out for multiday trips, a

A daypack should be 1,500 cubic inches or less and feature a padded back, padded and contoured shoulder straps, and a waist belt.

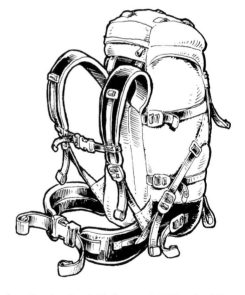

A weekend pack suitable for overnight trips should be around 3,500 cubic inches and have a suspension system that can handle the weight of your gear. Add a stiffening frame to the padded back, and a padded, stiffened waist belt.

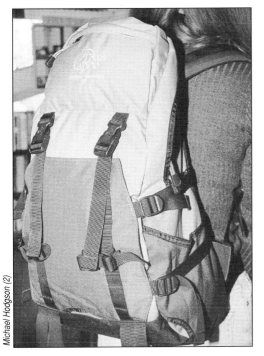

A daypack should hug your back and have a narrow profile that doesn't restrict movement or throw you off balance.

Some hikers prefer less cumbersome fanny packs that place all of the weight on your hips. Be sure to find one that fits well and is large enough to carry your gear but doesn't resemble a steamer trunk with straps.

more substantial pack with an internal or external frame is warranted. I prefer internal frames because they are easier to travel with, more flexible, and offer better balance—useful when ducking and weaving through trees or over loose scree. Sizes between 4,000 and 5,500 cubic inches should prove adequate.

Some people prefer fanny packs, which rest the load on your hips and are basically small packs sans shoulder straps. Their problem is their diminutive size, although I have used a Quest fanny many times for all-day trail runs when size and weight were critical and I was carrying only water, snacks, and a few emergency items. If you do opt for a fanny pack, look for built-in accessory straps on the underside (so that you can attach a jacket or other articles of clothing) and sturdy lash points on the top (for securing a hiking pole, camera tripod, or even a small insulated pad for sitting on).

Purchase your pack from a reputable specialty outdoor store whose staff is well versed in the styles available and probably even own one or two themselves. You will improve your chances of a good fit and the best pack for its intended use.

Operating Tips for a Hefty Daypack or Backpack

Perhaps you have experienced the minor discomfort or frustration of a backpack or heavily loaded daypack that doesn't fit perfectly or work quite the way you understood it would when you purchased it. Not to worry! Help is on the way.

- Establish a routine for adjusting your pack every time you put it on. Loosen the shoulder straps, load-lifter straps (the ones pulling off the top of the shoulder strap), and hip-stabilizer straps (running from frame to waist belt) slightly.
- Bend your knees, swing the pack up onto your thigh, slide first one shoulder into an available shoulder strap and then the other. Lean forward, hunch your shoulders to lift the pack slightly, and cinch the waist belt.
- Stand up, settle the pack on your hips, and pull the shoulder straps snug. Buckle the sternum strap (the strap across your chest between shoulder straps) if you have one—it should be snug but not tight enough to restrict breathing.
- Finally, tighten the load-lifters and hip-stabilizer straps to control the pack's penchant for swaying or pulling you backward. Ease some of the tension on the shoulder straps (placing more weight on your hips), and off you go.
- There is no such thing as a waterproof pack—despite what manufacturers may claim. Use a pack cover of some kind or your gear will get wet in a rainstorm. Specialty outdoor stores sell a waterproof nylon cover that is fitted to your pack, but budget-conscious hikers often prefer a heavy-duty garbage bag with slits cut for the shoulder straps.

Michael Hodgson (3)

Loosen the pack's straps, bend your knees, and swing the pack up onto one thigh.

Slide one shoulder into a shoulder strap and then pull on the other shoulder strap.

Lean forward, hunch your shoulders to lift the pack slightly, and cinch the waist belt.

- Never trust the flimsy split rings on many frame packs. Head to the hardware store and trade them for tighter, stronger split rings.
- Add extensions to the pack's zipper pulls to make opening and closing zippers with gloves or cold fingers much easier. Shower hooks, twist ties, or a split ring through the zipper-pull hole with a clevis pin hanging from it work well.
- If the pack is rented or borrowed, the waist belt may feel a tad too loose. Fill the gaps with small pieces of ordinary closed-cell foam. Should your waist belt become too loose because of the usual weight loss on an extended trip, "make do" with a rolled sweater or other soft material to fill the extra space.
- Some packs have accessory pockets attached to the waist belt, allowing ready access to snacks, maps, and water on the trail. If you don't have a pocket, don't fret. Simply wear a small fanny pack turned toward the front. When you take off your backpack, the fanny pack stays on, minimizing the chance of misplacing important gear. The fanny also creates an ideal carrying pouch for short jaunts.

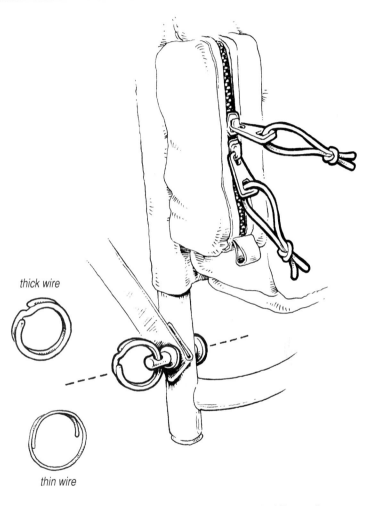

thick wire

thin wire

Add extensions to the pack's zipper pulls and replace standard flimsy split rings with tighter, stronger ones.

BOOTS

When the wilderness first captivated me twenty-five years ago, most "experts" insisted that big—make that massive—lug-soled, steel-shanked, shit-kicking mountaineering boots were the only viable footwear, no matter whether you were scaling Nanga Parbat or ambling along the beach in Monte Carlo. This opinion was due more to a lack of alternatives than to practical considerations. These were far too much boot for most people, and the rigid fit blistered the hell out of many a foot. In fact, more hikes are ruined by ill-fitting boots than anything else. The rugged ground and the load on your back—however small—conspire to place far more pressure on your feet than they are accustomed to, and the slightest pressure point or interior burr will rub a wound in minutes. Given moderate conditions, you can have the wrong hat, a ripped shirt, a thrift-store parka, wedge-dispensing shorts, socks full of holes, and meager grub and still enjoy yourself immensely. But if you have a pair of tight, cruel shoes or boots, you'll be ready to blow your brains out after the first blister wells up and you have no other choice but to push on. The boot or shoe *has to fit perfectly*, or you'll hate that your parents ever met. Believe it. I've seen the most grievous, weeping, open friction wounds from ill-fitting boots, and it's almost always the case that a person who

Happy Feet

Blistered and aching feet have, unfortunately, become an accepted nemesis for legions of hikers. Yet sore feet are preventable if you follow a few simple guidelines before and during a trek on the wilder side.

- Your hiking footwear must fit well or nothing you can do will save your feet from misery. When selecting a boot, wear the socks you will use hiking and use the insole you prefer. All too often, boots get purchased by hikers in a rush wearing thin socks. Your feet will swell when hiking. Check the width by lacing the boot firmly and rolling both feet alternately from side to side. If your feet slide or you feel discomfort in the toe area from compression, try another size or boot. Correct length can be assured if your toes don't bang the front of the boot when you slide your foot forward (good stores have an incline board for testing purposes). The heel must be snug enough to prevent up-and-down movement, but it should not pinch or bind. If your instep feels uncomfortable pressure, ask the salesperson to show you a boot with more volume.

- If the shoe fits, wear it. Don't get hung up on the printed shoe size. So what if you look like Dr. Frankenboot? On the trail, foot comfort is far more important than a fragile ego.

- Take the time to break in your new boots adequately. While lightweight boots feel comfortable almost from the moment you put them on, it will take a few days of walking around town to "mold" them to your foot's contours. Heavier boots made of leather require longer to break in adequately. The emergency method of soaking leather boots with warm water and then walking them dry does work, but only in a pinch—it's hell on your feet.

- Bring tennis shoes or sport sandals (such as Tevas) to wear around the camp. Extra shoes also become useful during a stream crossing when footwear should be worn for foot protection and you don't want to get your boots wet.

- When hiking through muck, loose dirt, gravel, water, snow, and other debris that always seems to find its way into your boot, try wearing ankle-high gaiters. Certainly not a fashion statement, but if your feet are happy, who cares?

is used to calfskin loafers laced up a pair of stiff mountaineering boots for a casual hike. It's hard to say what's worse—too little or too much boot. Remember, Emma Gatewood, a grandmother in her sixties, hiked the entire Appalachian Trail— three times—in a pair of canvas Keds. Nowadays there are footwear options for every terrain, so many that picking the right one is in some ways more confusing than before.

I spent so many years trudging up to cliffs wearing athletic shoes that I prefer the very lightest footwear I think I can get by with. Others with sturdy ankles and reasonable fitness will probably feel the same way. There's no getting around the old Marine adage that a pound on the feet equals five pounds on your back. If anything, this equation is understated.

I've seen some remarkable footwear in the wilderness—everything from knee-high Gestapo boots to Day-Glo spike heels—so it's hard to lay down inflexible laws about what to put on your feet. Most people, however, find that a well-fitting, lightweight hiker serves most needs pretty well. I have a pair of featherweight, cleated approach shoes that I have used from the muddiest nooks of the Solomon Islands to the lone and level sands of Death Valley. My other boots are for the Arctic, and I rarely use them because I hate the cold, but somehow seem to end up in it every couple of years. Most of us need a generic boot or shoe that will serve

Chris Townsend

Sport sandals are great for hiking when the weather is warm and wet. Michael packs along a pair for stream crossings.

us well in a variety of conditions and terrains; a ten-pound clunker model stripped off the foot of Frankenstein is one of the worst options.

Cashing in on sports-shoe technology, many companies presently make lightweight "all-terrain" or "performance" hiking shoes that are fundamentally beefed-up athletic shoes with a lug sole. (These are often referred to as "approach" shoes, de rigueur for weight-conscious climbers as the footwear to approach a cliffside.) A glove fit, cleated sole, and zero break-in time are pluses, but these are fair-weather shoes to be sure. The technology that has gone into some of these shoes is remarkable and oftentimes unnecessary. For instance, their makers have gotten carried away with composite construction, using leather here, nylon there, plus various "waterproof" materials. The waterproof angle is okay for rain, but in really wet conditions the water comes in through the top, and the waterproof exterior only keeps the water *in* the shoe. Plus, waterproof materials are not nearly so rugged as synthetic leather. But if you've got more than a hundred dollars to experiment with, you can always buy a pair and draw your own conclusions. Tens of thousands do.

Anyway, for mild conditions, athletic trail shoes, performance hikers, approach shoes, or whatever you want to call them are the first choice for many—especially the fit and experienced. Most come in both

- Attend to hot spots on your feet before they turn into fluid-filled monsters. Use molefoam, moleskin, 2nd Skin, or any other product (some hikers swear by duct tape—ouch!) that will eliminate friction at its source.

- Keep your feet dry. Use liberal amounts of foot powder while on the trail, and take time during rest breaks to let your toes wiggle in the sun. If your feet are prone to perspiring heavily, plan on a sock change at lunch or any other time you can enjoy an extended rest break. Dry socks will help keep your feet and boots dry, and dry feet are less apt to blister. Hang wet socks from your pack to dry.

- Even if your boots fit well, a long hike over several days can swell feet sufficiently that the toe area becomes a little tight. If your boots feel cramped in the toe, try trimming a little off the front of the boot's inner soles to loosen up the toe box. You can always replace the inner sole. This won't work if the boots fit improperly to begin with.

Creative Lacing for Better Fit

Sure, you learned to tie your shoes as a mere tyke, toddling across the earth on uncertain feet. But it's time

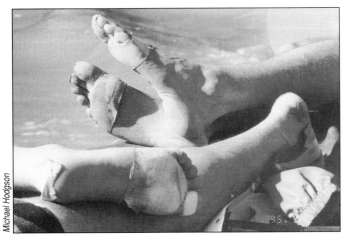

Michael Hodgson

Attend to the hot spots on your feet, and don't be afraid to slap moleskin anywhere they require it.

An approach, or performance, hiker is a souped-up athletic shoe with slightly more support and, if it is a true approach shoe, a sticky sole for grip.

to add more lacing options to your shoe-tying repertoire if you wish to guarantee the best fit for your trail-trekking dogs. To maximize your options, be sure that when you purchase your footwear there are no sharp edges on the eyelets, D-rings, or speed hooks that will fray your laces. Also, toss the round laces and install flat nylon laces instead—they hold knots much more securely.

- *Triple Wrap:* Wrapping the laces three times around each other will allow you to adjust the tension of the lacing both above and below the triple wrap.
- Sometimes, you may encounter a pressure point or hot spot on the top of the foot along the instep. You can alleviate the pain by tying a double or triple wrap below the trouble spot, skipping the eyelets or D-rings at the trouble spot, and then tying another double or triple

wrap above before resuming your normal lacing.

- Are you having trouble maintaining tight laces as you secure your boots? It's a common problem

with an easy solution. Tighten your laces up and over speed hooks. By effectively wrapping each hook, you maintain enough friction for easy tightening.

Triple-wrapping your laces (wrapping them around each other three times between speed hooks) enables you to adjust the tension of the lacing both above and below each wrap.

Clothing and Pack **55**

A good midweight hiking boot provides adequate ankle support, a lug sole, a footbed with a cushioned midsole, and a steel shank that runs ¼ to ½ the length of the boot.

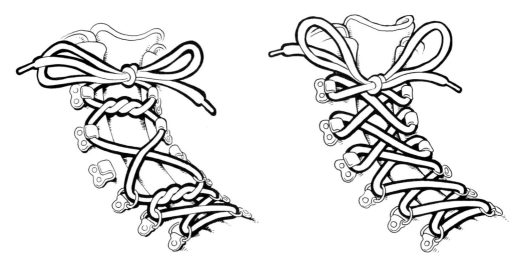

If you develop a pressure point on the top of your foot, you can often alleviate the pressure by tying a triple wrap below the spot, skipping the eyelets over the troubled area, and then tying another triple wrap above it.

To really snug down your laces and secure your boots to your feet, bring the laces down from the top of each speed hook and then around before crossing them. This technique prevents the laces from slipping and the boot from loosening up over time.

high-top and low-cut versions. The high-top design is said to give greater ankle support, which it probably does to some degree. But most models are not high enough, and even if they are, to attain significant ankle support you have to cinch the top snug enough to cut off the circulation to your foot. The advantage of high-tops is less in the support, real or imagined, than in their ability to keep pebbles, burrs, sand, leeches, and such outside your shoes.

Somewhere between the performance hiker and the mountaineering boot is the midweight boot. The need for something more substantial than the performance hiker comes from the demands of cold weather and heavier loads. This boot comes into play when you expect to encounter rough terrain or snow. There is no need to go with a stiff mountaineering boot unless you intend to use crampons.

Boot Care Tips

For the ultimate foot protection, more and more people are returning to all-leather boots. With leather, however, comes an increased obligation to take care of your boots. Cleaning is essential to preserve leather. A stiff suede brush, a little elbow power, and a few drops of water are all that is needed. If your boots get wet, take the time to dry them slowly and properly. For best drying results, pull the tongue open, the insole out, and air-dry the boots where there is lots of ventilation but no heat. Stuffing with paper at home or several bandannas in the field hastens the drying. After any good soaking, and at regular intervals even when dry, use a leather dressing to restore lost oils and waxes. Each salesperson has a favorite leather conditioner, so ask around. I prefer Biwell or a new product called Nikwax. Seams and glued joints are a boot's weakest points, most susceptible to abrasion and leaking. Armor them with a good welt-seal.

Chris Townsend

Leather footwear needs regular reconditioning.

SHORTS AND PANTS

It's astonishing how many different pants are available for the hiker. If you don't like any of them, you can always follow the way of the Dani people, in Irian Jaya, and go with a koteca (penis gourd) for the men or "ass grass" (a thatch of kunai grass secured with a rattan belt) for the ladies. Otherwise, you have two options: shorts or pants. To get the best of both worlds, and to safeguard against weather, I usually wear shorts and pack a pair of lightweight pants for warmth, and nylon wind/rain pants just in case. A loose-fitting, sturdy pair of nylon shorts have always been my preferred trail duds, particularly those that have nylon underwear stitched in. Loose nylon doesn't bind or get clammy like cotton or canvas, and for day-hikes, I'm not so worried about a pair having to last—a real consideration on longer trips. Best of all, nylon dries quickly. There are many "hiking" shorts on the market, usually canvas. These have been around so long they *look* like hiking. I hate them. They always bind at the crotch and look so dowdy I could never bring myself to wear them. Loose nylon trunks are far superior.

I learned the drawback of shorts the hard way by wearing them in the Sierras. It started snowing, and by the time I'd stumbled back to the roadhead, my legs were blue and tingled for a week afterward. Another time, in Colombia, I went with shorts and got devoured by mosquitoes. Without a pair of wind pants to pull on, I just had to endure it. Same thing

goes with heavy bushwhacking. One time we were trying to raft a river in Mexico but were forced to give up on the second day when the river plunged underground. All we could do was try to gain a farm road the map showed about ten miles east. I was in shorts, naturally. We sloshed over wet ground for five miles, not minding it so much. But after cresting a hill, the wet dirt turned to mud, ankle-deep for a mile, then knee-deep for two more. I had to plow a trough through the ooze. The sun beat down hard, and I kept thinking the mud would turn to quicksand. About noon, the mud gave way to waist-high thicket, each branch bristling with hooked thorns. No use trying to avoid the barbs, since getting free from one meant getting snagged by another. Within ten minutes thorns were tearing into my flesh. Soon, the shrub grew so thick I had to drag myself over the top on all fours. Branches snapped, dropping me into thorns that slashed my face and arms. My shorts hung in bloody tatters. From that day on I've always packed a pair of sweatpants and a pair of sturdy wind pants.

The choice is tricky when it's blazing hot but you need, or want, the protection of pants. One option is to wear shorts till you can't hack it any longer, then slip on wind pants. I despise the feel of wind pants over bare flesh. They never breathe as well as the ads claim, so my legs sweat and the pants stick and feel so creepy I want to tear them off and take my chances. My preference is loose, lightweight cotton/spandex sweatpants. They pick up every burr and bramble around, cost too much, wear out fast, and are no good when wet. But in moderate conditions, I still prefer them. Others swear by wind pants. Worn *over* sweatpants, wind pants are marvelous, and I've found this combination works brilliantly when temperatures or activity warrant the use of dual clothing layers.

Wind pants are available in water-resistant fabrics (they are called *waterproof*, but few actually are, and these don't stay completely waterproof for long) and in various thicknesses—some sheer, others insulated with everything from Thinsulate to Chinese goose down. The "proper" density is determined completely by the conditions. In anything under about fifty degrees, I switch the sweatpants for synthetic-fabric britches. Colder still, and I start layering synthetic long underwear and pile/polypro pants, with the wind pants as the last layer.

SOCKS MANTRA

Pick the wrong pair of socks, and say hello to a packload of misery. A sock's fit, ability to wick moisture, cushioning, and compatibility with your boots are critical to your hiking pleasure. The things I have learned over the years must work, since my feet remain blister-free even during the hardest hikes. Use the following tips as a guide to hosiery heaven:

- The traditional school still holds that two pair of socks are best, preferably a good rag wool sock lined with a thin synthetic sock woven of polypropylene or polyester (such as Capilene). This helps minimize friction, reducing the possibility of blisters. With the advent of sport-specific socks, however, the two-pair philosophy is not a hard-and-fast one. I now clad my feet solely (sorry) in sport-specific socks (such as those woven by Thorlo), and my feet have never been happier. Utilizing a variety of weaves combining synthetic and (sometimes) natural fibers in various thicknesses, sport-specific socks are like golf clubs—one for optimum performance and comfort in each particular combination of activity and conditions.

- Whatever sock or combination of socks you choose, be sure the socks are woven well, with no lumpy seams or loose fabric to bunch up under toe or heel.

- Sock sizing is bizarre. I'm convinced the sock czars met in Zurich one year and decided, after imbibing far too much good European beer, that instead of sizing socks to match shoes, they would come up with a method no one can understand. Read the sock size labels carefully. Socks should fit snuggly, but not constrict or place pressure on the toes.

- Change your socks frequently. I change socks two to three times during an 8-hour hike. It is a simple matter to sit down at a rest break, put on a fresh, dry pair of socks, then hang your damp pair from the compression straps on your pack to dry. Your feet will love you for it.

- Bring your boots when you try on socks, and vice versa. Socks can affect the fit of a boot by as much as one whole size.

Chris Townsend

FABRICS AND FIBERS:

Like death and taxes, changeable weather happens. If you are out pushing the aerobic limits, staying comfortable can be a challenge, unless you understand the finer points of layering. The theory behind layering suggests that as your body temperature fluctuates or the weather shifts, you simply peel off or add available layers as needed. Simple? Well . . . it used to be, until manufacturers introduced so many confounded layer thicknesses and fabric weaves to the mix. Like a set of Ginsu knives, some of these wild fabric concoctions will do just about anything, including shed wind, wick away moisture, keep you warm, keep you cool, and even dice a carrot—well, maybe that's stretching it, but not by much.

While the basic concept of beginning with a base layer, then adding insulative layers as needed and topping it all off with a protective layer to shed wind and rain still holds, the lines between the categories have definitely blurred.

Where underwear ends and outerwear begins is no longer clear. Today's designs go both ways just as easily. With all the blends of synthetic fibers and fabrics, as well as different weights (most common are lightweight, midweight, and expedition weight), the aerobically inclined can turn to one, two, or more layers of underwear. Some

creative weaves and constructions even offer wind-stopping properties, usually sewn or woven into the front panels—ideal for sports such as skiing and mountain biking, since speed and wind can accelerate thermal loss and lead to chilling.

Bicomponent knits work to provide wicking and insulative properties in one layer. The side facing your skin is water-hating, and the side away from your skin is water-loving and pulls body moisture through. You'll stay dry and happy even with only one layer on, something not possible with older, single-function weaves.

Stretch fleece and microdenier pile provide crossover applications too, working equally well as base layers or for around-town sweaters or functional insulative add-ons for cross-training needs. I love microdenier pile, as it can be worn alone or layered under or over other pieces, and it has excellent wicking ability as well as more windproof potential than expedition-weight base layers.

Even that most important of fabrics to runners and bladers, Lycra, has not been immune to weaving and designer wizardry. Products such as Therma Fleece, Drylete, Dry-Fit, and Ultrasensor (it used to be Fieldsensor) combine Lycra with moisture-wicking synthetics that offer thermal properties.

In putting together your "ideal layering system," you seek to

combine elements of breathability, wicking, rapid drying, insulation, durability, wind-resistance, and water-repellence in a lightweight combination that offers the necessary freedom of movement—all with just a few garments. Which articles of clothing you choose on a particular day will depend on your intended aerobic level and the anticipated weather conditions.

The intent of a base layer is to manage moisture. By definition, your base layer will be the first article of clothing you put on, and the last to come off. Since your skin will be churning out perspiration, the goal of this "second skin" is to dissipate moisture while trapping your body's heat. Unblended, 100 percent cotton should become a part of your base layer only if you wish to keep cool, not warm, such as in a hot, desert climate where evaporative cooling becomes your friend.

To add to the base layer, you will want an arsenal of insulative layer choices. The goal here is a familiar one—to provide warmth by creating dead-air space, which slows the loss of body heat, and to continue to the dissipation of moisture begun by the base layer. Since insulation requirements depend on body size, weight, and fitness level, there is no universal formula for success. In general, the more options you have available, the more fine-tuning you can do and the more comfortable you will remain.

For the initial layer or two I prefer pullover garments, but for that final just-in-case insulative layer, I opt for full-zip every time. You'll find a full zipper maximizes ventilation fine-tuning and makes this layer much easier to put on and take off. I make sure that my layers have roomy sleeves so I can push them up or slide them down. I also prefer zippered T-necks because they ventilate superbly when open, yet insulate well when zipped up around the neck. A chest pocket is a worthwhile feature too, as this provides a place to tuck a snack, a notebook, or some sunscreen.

Finally, you'll top the entire ensemble with a thin, windproof, water-resistant layer. You want this layer to breathe like crazy, yet not be so porous that rain runs through it like floodwaters through a leaking dike. I always look for jackets that are bright as well, since chances are you will be wearing them on dark and stormy days. I really appreciate the fact that a driver might see me before impact if I am at least making a loud visibility statement.

When selecting a shell jacket and pants, be sure they offer enough room to accommodate layers underneath. The roomier the cut, the better the ventilation possibilities—no need to wear a garment that looks as if it could house the entire city of Los Angeles, however. You don't want loose fabric that will flap around, and that goes double for the hood. For my active wear, I prefer a jacket with a thin hood that can be stowed into a zip-closed collar. When I'm hiking, running, blading, or mountain-biking, I rarely use a hood anyway, and I doubt you will either unless the weather turns really ugly.

Ease of use cannot be stressed enough. If your layering system is a pain to put on and take off, chances are you won't adjust the layers as frequently as you should, and that defeats the purpose of layering all together.

The Seasonal Art of Aerobic Layering

Sunny, Hot, and Dry

Base layer: Long-sleeved, light-colored, loose-fitting cotton/synthetic-blend shirt.
Base layer: Lightweight and loose-fitting nylon shorts with built-in mesh brief.
Added protection: Light-colored, brimmed hat with built-in sweatband.

When the sun is beating down and the temperature soars into the 80s and 90s, the layering strategy for aerobic comfort is fairly simple—keep cool. This is the only time cot-

Dressing for sunny, hot, dry weather.

ton is appropriate, since it holds moisture fairly well, trapping it near your skin and cooling you as it evaporates. Of course, cotton has inherent weaknesses—it gets cold and clammy when the aerobic level drops and can chafe when wet. For that reason, I love a blended weave

Dressing Well: The Basics

- To get the best of both worlds, dress in shorts and pack lightweight long pants.
- Clad your feet in sport-specific socks or in cushy wool outer socks with a thin synthetic liner.
- Footwear should be light and comfortable, and it should fit well. Lug soles add traction, but typically, the more lug, the heavier and stiffer the boot. Our favorite shoe for dayhiking is the so-called performance hiker, or approach, shoe.
- Dress in layers and be prepared for the weather to change. The time you forget to pack a wind shirt or lightweight waterproof/breathable jacket is the time you will need it.
- Choose light, loose-fitting, long-sleeved shirts for comfort and versatility.

of cotton and synthetic fibers designed to wick moisture away from the skin, pulling and pushing it into the outer layer where it evaporates—such as that found in Sierra Designs' Ray-T-ator. This system kept me pleasantly cool during a blistering California afternoon run and yet never got so wet that it hung on my torso like a wet rag, a common ailment for T-shirts of the 100 percent cotton variety. Too, long sleeves provide more protection from the sun than short sleeves. You can always push the sleeves up if you get too toasty. Whatever shirt you select, be sure it is light-colored and loose-fitting.

Depending on my mood and the intended speed of travel, the choice becomes a little more complex. For aggressive aerobic activity, I opt for a Lycra short or even a loose running short, but for all-around outdoor frivolity, I favor baggy nylon shorts with built-in mesh briefs, since they dry quickly and allow plenty of movement. Stay away from cotton underwear—it chafes.

You'll want to keep a cool head, and there is no better hat for that than the Desert Rhat. It has a built-in sweatband, a reflective sur-

face inside the upper mesh, a wide bill to shade your face, and plenty of ventilation, and it is all-white for maximum sun reflection. When I am going for the day, I carry a wind shell of some kind in a fanny pack, just in case the weather takes a turn for the worse or I get caught out at night. Sure, it might be 90 degrees now, but in the desert or other arid yet mountainous parts of our country, it is not unusual to experience wide temperature fluctuations . . . in the 50s by nightfall.

Sunny, Warm, and Windy

Base layer: Mesh, sleeveless vest.
Optional base layer: Lightweight, long-sleeved synthetic zip T-neck top.
Base layer: Lightweight synthetic sport tights.
Thermal layer: Midweight synthetic pullover.
Protective layer: Lightweight, highly breathable, full-zip wind top.

When pushing the aerobic edge in mountainous conditions, where the temperature hovers between 60 and 70 degrees in the sun, layering is a little more difficult than it might appear. In the sun you will be warm, but as you go from sun to shade, the temperature can swing wildly. Further, if your activity level

should drop, your heat output will cease and you will begin to chill rapidly in the wind, even at 60 degrees. It is essential that you stay dry and not generate too much per-

Dressing for sunny, warm, windy weather.

spiration and that you have several other layers in a fanny pack, available to put on as you need.

I start off with a sleeveless stretch-mesh-fabric construction that wicks outstandingly well and dries very quickly if it does get damp. This fabric is not the familiar fishnet construction; rather, it resembles a very soft burlap. Most often, I find that wearing the sleeveless top with thin and quick-drying tights is all I need when out running the trails. As a just-in-case base layer, I pack a lightweight synthetic underwear top that fits snugly over the vest so that wicking is enhanced. Although color is not too important, I prefer lighter colors. Dark colors tend to absorb the sun, adding heat I don't need when my aerobic level is high.

As an option, you can combine the two layers into one by eliminating the mesh sleeveless and going with a polyester/cotton blend such as Sierra Designs' Ray-T-ator or Patagonia's Go-T. This will work for those who find themselves more concerned with staying cool than keeping warm—even in cool temperatures.

If I never stopped moving, I wouldn't need any other layers, but realistically, that is never the case. For that reason, I tuck a microdenier fleece into my fanny pack along with a bottle of water and the odd snack or two. During rest breaks or unplanned stops and also during my warm-down, I'll slip on the pullover. The microdenier fleece top continues to assist with moisture transfer, actually wicking perspiration from the inner layers into its own fabric for eventual evaporation. The fleece is a tight weave, making it fairly wind-resistant, but I wouldn't count on this alone as adequate wind protection. For this layer, I choose darker colors that absorb the sun; then solar energy helps my layering system keep me warm and also assists in drying out this layer if it gets damp.

Since changeable weather in the mountains is a sure bet, only a fool would leave a wind shell behind. This shell should be a microfiber construction with a naturally tight weave that sheds light moisture without difficulty, stops wind dead in its tracks, and allows water vapor (sweat) to escape easily.

One of the toughest times to figure out an ideal layering system is when the rain is coming down, the wind is swirling, and the temperature hovers between 45 and 55 degrees.

Dressing for wet, windy, cool weather.

Wet, Windy, and Cool

Base layer: Midweight synthetic zip T-neck top.

Base layer: Lightweight or midweight synthetic tights.

Thermal layer: Midweight synthetic Polartec 100 pullover.

Protective layer: Breathable, highly water-resistant, windproof, full-zip shell.

Protective layer: Breathable, water-resistant, side-zip pants.

In these conditions, you are going to get damp, one way or another. The challenge is to assemble a package that will keep you reasonably protected from the rain, assist you in dissipating the copious amounts of perspiration you are sure to generate, and keep you comfortable—not too hot, not too cold. It is not an easy bill to fill, and I have yet to discover layering nirvana where all layers worked together in complete harmony and all was well and dry with the world.

With a synthetic (Thermax, Capilene, Driclime, Lifa, Polartec 100 are common fabrics) zip turtleneck as my base layer, I maximize insulation potential, wicking ability, and versatility. If I get too hot, I unzip and roll up the sleeves. Too cold and I zip up the neck and slide down the sleeves. I opt for a Lycra-synthetic thermal-blend tight since it will help to keep my legs warm and won't absorb moisture, allowing it to pass through and evaporate. Evaporate? In a rain? Okay, it will need some help and air space, and that is achieved on both my upper and lower body by wearing highly water-resistant and breathable shells.

Patagonia's Velocity shell has long been a favorite of mine. Its outer fabric is DWR-treated (a durable water-resistant finish), and

the coating is by Gore—Patagonia calls it Pneumatic (Gore now calls it Activent; Marmot, Moonstone, and North Face all offer their own versions). Though condensation will still build up inside, it manages to get rid of enough moisture, and that performance has kept me from turning into one giant overheated prune time and again. For pants, I like a soft and supple microdenier fabric with a cut that is roomy without making me feel like a flagpole with banners flapping in the wind. Untreated microdenier fabrics are not as water-resistant as the Velocity, but on the legs, you'll worry more about wind protection and breathability.

As my just-in-case layer, I pack a pullover made of stretch Polartec 100, a polyester, highly breathable fleece that aids in moving moisture away from my body and serves to keep me quite toasty even in a deluge (Lowe and Marker make two of my favorite pullovers). One final word of advice: Always bring along a warm hat for those times when you need to seal in warmth—you lose a large percentage of heat through your head.

Cold, Breezy, and Drizzle/Fog

Base layer: Mesh wicking, vest-style underlayer (fabric resembles a soft burlap) with windproof front panel.

Alternative or additional base layer: Lightweight, long-sleeved synthetic zip T-neck top.
Base layer: Lightweight synthetic briefs with windproof front panel.
Additional base layer: Midweight synthetic sport tights.
Optional base layer: Lightweight synthetic gloves.
Thermal layer: Midweight synthetic pullover.
Alternative thermal layer: Midweight full-zip vest.
Protective layer: Lightweight, water-resistant, windproof, breathable, full-zip top and pants.

Brrrr . . . the temperature is hovering around 35 degrees, it's drizzling, a slight breeze is stirring the air, and you had planned to go for a trail run. Call it quits? Not a chance! As long as the layering system works to shed the wind, seal out the drizzle, and move the inevitable sweat storm from inside to outside, you'll be a happy camper.

The key to happiness is the judicious use of wind-blocking garments and a water-resistant, extremely breathable protective layer. I absolutely love Windstopper by Gore, and a number of garments, such as those made by Hind, use it to create windproof panels in the

Dressing for cold, breezy, drizzly/foggy weather.

base layers. While you might chuckle at the thought of windproofing your underwear briefs, you'll be singing a different tune once you've tried them on. Eliminate wayward

breezes and you stop evaporative heat loss, staying much warmer with fewer layers. What a concept! Of course, the base layer still needs to wick, and it will, since the Windstopper is combined with synthetic fibers to pull moisture away from the body. Over the briefs, as protection for the legs, I prefer a Lycra blend such as Therma Fleece, Drylete, Dry-Fit, or Ultrasensor. One pair of Ultrasensor tights I tested refused to absorb much moisture even on long jaunts, somehow managing to keep my legs from feeling wet and drying out within minutes when the drizzle stopped—a Lycra first in my book. Performance like that ya gotta love.

Over the mesh vest underlayer, you will want a zip T-neck top, which helps insulate your upper body, is somewhat windproof, wicks moisture well, yet won't trap so much heat that you turn into a sauna. The top will continue to work with your mesh vest to disperse moisture buildup if it is kept reasonably dry from the outside.

For that reason, I toss on a jacket of microfiber construction, such as ClimaGuard, which sheds light drizzle well and breathes superbly. Most models do not come with pit-zips (underarm zipper openings) though, which is beyond me—the added ventilation would be wonderful.

Whether or not you use rain

pants too is up to you. Most times I find in these conditions that pants are just too much and only serve to make the experience clammier.

When you need a thermal layer, add a microdenier pullover, the goal being a soft, wickable, not-too-thick insulative layer that you can pull on "just in case." I prefer freedom of movement and most often reach for a vest before a pullover, especially if my aerobic level is high. At this temperature, with these weather conditions, you have two choices, depending on your metabolism. If you want more insulation, grab for a vest that is soft, warm, and seals around the neck nicely. If it is light and windproof I seek, especially when mountain-biking, I reach for a vest with a windproof front and a moisture-transporting stretch knit over the back, such as Mountain Hardware's Aquaduct Vest. With these extra layers, you may find you're carrying instead of wearing, and that's just fine because it is better to be safe than cold and miserable. For really active use, thin, liner-type gloves will suffice to keep the digits and hands comfortable even in rain.

See Chapter 7 (page 152) for details on truly cold-weather clothing.

RAIN GEAR

It happened one summer in Yosemite Valley. Jim Bridwell—high lama of American rock climbing throughout the seventies—woke me up one morning and said, "Pack a bag. We're hiking up to Mount Watkins to scout a new climb." I squinted up at the growling gray sky. "Looks like rain," I said, "and I don't have any rain gear." "I got your rain gear," Jim promised. "Let's go." And we did.

We first heard the rolling thunder about noon, followed by pattering rain. Finally it hammered down like buckshot and I said, "Jimbo, let's break out that rain gear of mine." Jim reached into his pack and withdrew a couple of gigantic plastic trash bags he'd gotten from a wine steward in the hotel. We hunkered down under a ponderosa pine and pulled the trash bags over us as the storm raged into a perfect deluge. Every twenty minutes or so I'd peek from under my "rain gear" to get a little air and clear the sauna-like atmosphere. This did not present a problem for

Waterproof/Breathable Jackets: Nuts and Bolts

If the perfect all-around jacket seems like an idea too far-fetched to attain, you're right. First and foremost, the jacket must be able to shed the deluge coming down outside while dissipating the perspiration generated inside. A good waterproof/breathable (WB) jacket should keep you smiling whether a light mist is floating down or Noah's ark is sighted just outside your tent flap. It should be stuffable and light enough to carry without an extra thought. The ideal jacket should be sturdy enough to shed the mild nip of a late fall wind, but not so heavy that a summer's heat leaves you feeling as if you had spent the day in a portable sauna.

There is no such thing as an absolutely 100 percent waterproof and breathable jacket. If you want waterproof, you buy waterproof and forget breathability, expecting to drown in your own sweat if you are too active. Conversely, if you demand breathable, you buy a water-resistant jacket and pray you don't get caught in anything more severe than a drizzle.

Even with the best WB jacket, if you stand in the rain long enough, you will get wet. How long that takes depends on how well the jacket is designed and constructed, whether or not the outside fabric has a repellent coating, and which WB materials are used on the inside.

The engine of a WB system is in the coating or laminate, designed to repel water droplets from the outside while passing water vapor from the inside. Gore-Tex, probably the most recognized name in WB constructions, is a laminate with a strong track record. A number of companies are using proprietary WB coatings (typically a polyurethane concoction) that work well—some better than others, of course.

The secret to good WB performance in inclement weather is not just in the coating or laminate, however. It's in the durable water-resistant finish applied to the outer fabric. Without DWR, any jacket, including a Gore-Tex one, will soon feel like a wet dishrag and be about as pleasant to wear.

Whether a jacket is laminate- or coating-based, you will encounter both two- and three-layer constructions in your search. The difference between them is significant. Three-layer constructions look like one layer, but essentially are a sandwich—an outer fabric shell, a WB layer, and a wicking (to pull moisture away from your body) inner facing. Three-layer constructions are typically lighter, less warm, more breathable, less bulky, sometimes more durable, but stiffer than their two-layer cousins.

Two-layer constructions have one outer and one inner layer. The outer layer is a combination of a WB coating or laminate bonded to an outer fabric. The inner layer is a free-hanging, wicking liner in either mesh or taffeta. Two-layer constructions feel comfortable because they drape well—a better fashion statement, if

Jim, however, for he'd burned a little bullet hole into his shelter from which issued a continuous stream of smoke from his perpetual Camel cigarettes.

Jim Bridwell is not the only person to ad lib a solution to staying dry—or trying to. I've seen natives the world over use palm fronds and colossal leaves, conch shells, strips of tin, hardwood bark, even swine fat smeared onto their pates and shoulders. Provided the temperature is warm, it can refresh a hiker to get wringing

wet—but nobody wants to stay soaked for long. You get clammy and chaffed, and stuff—like leaves and peat—sticks to your skin. Unless you're suffering a continuous downpour—when only an umbrella works—the reason you stay wet after the storm is that your clothes get drenched and it's too humid for them to dry out. Hence, a standard practice in tropical climes is to *remove* all your clothes and pack them

G E A R

you will. The free-hanging liner does add warmth and minimizes clamminess, but it can also reduce your jacket's ability to breath efficiently.

A WB jacket is only as good as its more subtle features, with those that provide ventilation being most essential. Ventilation is the key to happiness. If you can't vent your body's heat and moisture to the outside, rather like a chimney, you're going to get damp and disgusted, even in a jacket made of the best materials. Ventilation pockets and adequate pit-zips will allow you to maximize airflow, minimize heat retention, and reduce moisture buildup. I also like storm flaps that close with Velcro or snaps, because you can leave your jacket's zipper undone and still secure your jacket against the rain while allowing passage of air.

Hoods are not just afterthoughts. For me, it is essential that a jacket feature an attached hood that can be tucked or rolled out of the way using a Velcro tab or snap—this prevents the hood from becom-

Bob Gaines, the Virgin River, Zion National Park

If the rain is really hammering down, the only way you're going to keep dry is with an umbrella.

away until the rain stops, then put them back on.

Once temperatures drop below about seventy degrees, the task is to keep the rain from soaking the clothes you don't dare take off. This means donning a rain shell and/or parka and pants, or going with garments that have a waterproof outer layer. An absolutely waterproof (plastic) poncho is another alternative, but is really just a variation of the trash bag—far better than nothing, but unwieldy.

One time on Prince Albert Fjord I was staying with an Inuit friend whose sister got her snowmobile stuck on an icefall a few miles from their arctic village. My friend and I motored out there and, in minus-thirty conditions, dragged the snowmobile onto the flat icepack and motored back home. I'd gone out wearing a coated rain shell over an expedition-weight down parka. Back inside the house, I peeled off the coated shell and found my down jacket was half soaked through with perspiration.

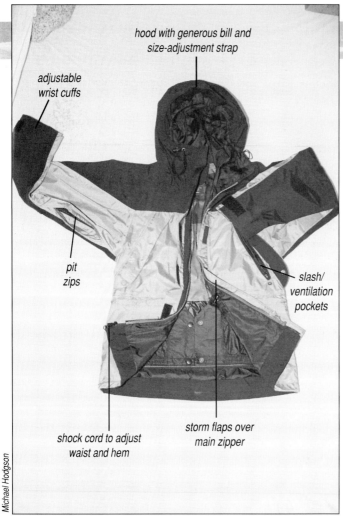

hood with generous bill and size-adjustment strap

adjustable wrist cuffs

pit zips

slash/ ventilation pockets

shock cord to adjust waist and hem

storm flaps over main zipper

Michael Hodgson

A waterproof/breathable jacket.

ing a collection point for rain, snow, and other debris when not in use. Some jackets offer hoods that roll into the collar, but most often this results in too stiff a collar and a hood that is a pain to access when you need it most.

Since you should expect your jacket to shed wind and keep you sheltered from the rain as well, other features are important when considering value and performance. Adjustable waist and hems using easy-to-operate cord locks and shock cord are good, since they allow you to batten down the hatches when the weather turns ugly. Factory-sealed seams (usually taped) keep the water from migrating inward, which it will otherwise do.

You won't be happy with your jacket unless it fits properly. Look for generous and fully adjustable wrist cuffs that open wide, allowing you to slide the sleeve up your arm if desired, tuck the top of a glove under the cuff, or cinch the cuff tightly around your bare wrist to seal out wind and rain. Your jacket should

This presented little problem in a well-heated room, but outside, the jacket would never have dried. It would have frozen stiff as a board the moment I stopped moving, reducing a full-blown arctic parka to the insulation value of a sweater.

Folks have been getting rained on since time began, so what did we all do before Gore-Tex? We got by with palm fronds. In cold, rainy conditions, you'll simply have to resign yourself to getting a little wet. You can't leave anything open or unzipped without the rain pouring in. What you can do, however, is leave the garment loose around the wrists and waist. A last consideration is to make sure to size any nonbreathable garment a little big, which allows trapped air and condensation to circulate and hopefully escape wherever it can.

feel roomy, without making you feel or look as if you just climbed into a family tent with sleeves. Remember that you should be able to layer clothing underneath without testing the stretch limit on the jacket's shoulder seams. I also prefer hems that stop around the upper thighs to a waist hem, because a longer cut allows marvelous protection even without rain pants—a feature you will appreciate when urban wandering or mall-hopping.

Since not all heads are created equal, be sure the hood of the jacket has a size-adjustment strap on the back to complement the standard drawstring on the front. Also, when you cinch down the hood and turn your head, a good hood should turn with you. If all you get, however, is an inside view of the side of the hood, select another jacket.

Little things make the difference between a serviceable WB and a truly fine one. Zippers should be two-way, allowing you to vent from the bottom as well as undo from the top. Chest pockets that feature two-way zippers are especially wonderful. I look for bar tacks (reinforced stitching) at all the key stress points—pocket corners, where the zipper attaches to the bottom of the jacket, etc. Pull tabs on all the zippers, microfleece or tricot lining in any waist pockets for hand warmth, stuff sacks or pockets that turn into stuff sacks, and reinforced elbow and shoulder patches are all nifty touches. Finally, being a glasses wearer, I am especially sensitive to good bills on hoods. Wimpy bills or token awnings that redirect rain to drip incessantly onto my face or glasses just won't do!

The Founder of Lightweight Travel

According to *Camping and Woodcraft,* written in 1906 by Horace Kephart, the founder of lightweight travel was the Scotsman Macgregor who, in 1865, built a canoe named the *Rob Roy* and cruised rivers and waterways with only a small black bag measuring 1 foot square and 6 inches deep. "Featherweight camping in 'civilized' fashion began with the *Rob Roy,* progressed with the flotillas of British and American canoeists who followed its skipper's example, was refined by the squadrons of cycle tourists and the pedestrian campers who scour the highways and byways of all Christendom in their yearly holidays."

Tom Stick, Kodiak Island, Alaska

F I R S T   A I D   F O R   Y O U R

Murphy's Law has an uncanny way of asserting itself when you travel in the wilds. Leave your raincoat at home and presto, a downpour. Forget your stove-repair kit and, you guessed it, your stove decides to take an untimely vacation from work. Of course, the best cure for the Murphy syndrome is good planning and a good field repair kit. Granted, bringing a repair kit on a dayhike may not seem critical, but if you do head out overnight, trek in remote areas abroad, or hike into the backcountry, you'll want to carry a repair kit.

During my years as a professional mountain guide, in search and rescue, and as a product tester, I have put together a basic repair kit of essential items as follows:

- Duct tape (for hole patching, tent-pole splinting, boot-repairing, and myriad other jobs)
- Leatherman Tool (available from REI and other specialty stores; it features a knife, pliers, and other necessary tools for repair purposes in one compact kit)
- Sandpaper (for roughing up surfaces that have to be glued)
- Seam Grip (a waterproof urethane rubber compound that works as a seam sealer and a patching compound)
- Spare flashlight batteries and bulb
- Miscellaneous stove-repair parts

- Waxed thread (such as dental floss)
- 1 medium-size and 1 leather needle for leather and webbing repairs
- A spare 1-inch nylon strap with buckle
- A tent-pole sleeve (a standard 3-inch, heavy-gauge aluminum tube that fits over broken tent poles and serves as an effective splint)

As each trip demands repair items specific to that trip (a backcountry ski trip requires ski-binding parts, pole-splint material, and a spare ski tip), I evaluate the basic kit and make necessary adjustments. As for the weight of the kit, I try to

G E A R — R E P A I R   K I T S

keep it around 1 to 1½ pounds. Not light by any means, but I'll take a pound of prevention over a ton of misery any day.

A friend of mine, Mark Jenkins, Rocky Mountain editor for *Backpacker* magazine, suggested some additional items that, from his extensive experience, might come in useful on any prolonged trip into the hinterlands. Jenkins urges packing a 5-inch-square patch of mosquito netting for the one time a hole appears in your tent screening. Add 5 inches of 1-inch-wide Velcro strips with adhesive on the back for repairing a jacket or sleeping bag should the zipper give out. Also, pack several hose clamps for

splinting a broken pack frame.

Many repair-kit lists include rubber bands for securing things. I used to pack several heavyweight ones myself. Pat McHugh of MPI Outdoor Safety Products suggested I substitute a large balloon for a rubber band, and he makes a good case. The elasticity of a large balloon makes it usable for lashing poles together for emergency shelter or repair, or as a tent tie-down line, or to secure gear to a pack or canoe. Partially inflate the balloon and use it as a makeshift outdoor pillow. Hunters, a balloon stretched over the barrel of a gun or scope protects it from debris and moisture. Inflate several balloons to cushion

fragile gear during transport over rocky terrain or rapids. The list of uses goes on in almost as unlimited a manner as Pat's imagination.

Assemble a repair kit to meet your needs. Use your imagination and the basic guidelines offered here to plan for the unexpected, because you can bet that the one time you aren't ready for the unexpected is the one time the unexpected will occur. In the wilderness, after all, you can't call for a repair person . . . you will have to make do yourself.

3

Staying Safe
AND
Found

What joy it is to feel the soft, springy earth under my feet

once more, to follow grassy roads that lead to ferny brooks

where I can bathe my fingers in a cataract of rippling notes,

or to clamber over a stone wall into green fields that tumble

and roll and climb in riotous gladness!

—The Story of My Life, *Helen Keller*

Chris Townsend

A century ago, in *The Private Papers of*

Henry Ryecroft, George Gissing said, "For the man sound in body and serene of mind there is no such thing as bad weather; every sky has its beauty, and storms which whip the blood do but make it pulse more vigorously." I'll wager that when Gissing wrote this, he was turned out in a smoking jacket and huddled by a log fire. As he gazed out a mullioned window at the winter storm, the leaden sky appeared all art and majesty. But switch George's tweeds for Levi's and a tank top and chuck him outside, and that regal sky becomes his mortal enemy. Within ten minutes he'd start shivering, get hypothermic, and the whole business would become a medical emergency. Quickly.

In the wilderness, weather, safety, and health issues are all interrelated. Consider my first trip to the desert sandstone monoliths outside Moab, Utah. We went climbing at high noon in the dead of summer. I wasn't wearing a hat, hadn't applied sunscreen, and hadn't brought enough water. When my partner and I started seeing double—after only forty-five minutes—we rappelled to the ground and collapsed. The road was close by, but by the time we gained it both of us were throwing up, feeling like the tops of our heads were going to blow off. A passing motorist stopped, pulled us into his motorhome, and covered us with wet bath towels. Half an hour passed before my head quit spinning and my heart stopped pounding. The next day I

was so weak I could barely walk.

Once, above the mountain hamlet of Idyllwild, in Southern California, I drank straight from a stream frequented by thousands of hikers, got dysentery, and was gushing from both ends before I knew what hit me. Truly, dysentery is as enjoyable as having barbed wire dragged through your intestines. In Yosemite I disrupted a hornet's nest and got stung upward of twenty times. I didn't have Adrenalin on hand; had I gone into anaphylactic shock, I'd have been finished.

Oftentimes it has been the mistakes we've made—and the misadventures we've heard or read about—that provided the hard information that follows. The aim is to prevent you from securing an outdoor education through trial and error, learning things the hard way. Many aspects of wilderness travel are matters of opinion, but weather, safety, and health issues are not among them. Drink bad water, you get sick. Scramble onto a loose cliffside, you risk disaster. Get caught in a snowstorm without suitable gear, you'll suffer at the least, die at the worst. Intestinal bugs, shattered rock, blinding snow—these natural occurrences are not affected by our opinions. Knowledge, sticking with safe practices, and being prepared for mishaps—these are the keystones to remaining safe and sound in the wilderness.

Thousands of books have been written about weather, wilderness procedures, and first aid—three subjects coinciding with our keystones. The topic of weather is big as the sky, and ten thousand books couldn't exhaust the subject. The same goes for safety and health issues.

The following information covers the essentials of health and safety and related details we thought useful. Each topic deserves study. The trick is to develop a firm grasp of the basics and to acquire the philosophy that knowledge and prevention are what ultimately keep us secure in the wilderness.

BASIC NAVIGATION

Two basic tenets for any dayhike are: Know where you are going; and as you go, know, or be able to determine, where you are. That said, it is often the case that you neither know where you are going nor have any possible means of knowing exactly where you are at any given time. Many short hikes are spontaneous. You spot a trail or a stream and decide to cast off and see where it takes you. Whenever you "head out" like this, make sure that whatever marks the way—a trail or creek, etc.—is distinct enough to be retraced. Heavy weather and darkness are two factors that can greatly compromise your ability to get back safely.

Perhaps only a fool goes hiking in pouring rain, but it's sometimes fun to be a fool. Also, some areas are so inclement that if you were to wait for perfect weather, you'd never go hiking at all. Heavy weather is a given in alpine and tropical climes, and marching through it can be at once spectacular and miserable. Be aware that heavy rains can wash out trails and swell creeks, and snowstorms can bury the deepest tracks and stop you dead in the drift. So a very good idea when venturing onto new terrain where logistics might be a problem is to backtrack quickly if nasty weather moves in. A good rule of thumb is to avoid challenging yourself at more than one skill at a time—which is exactly what I did once, and spent two days, dead lost, thrashing around Mount Baldy above my hometown in Upland, California.

We were operating on the "straight-shot," or "line-of-sight," method, a school of hiking that has gotten more people lost than perhaps any other. We wanted to climb the North Face of Mount Baldy, a steep hike topped by a paltry, thirty-degree snowfield leading to the rounded summit. It was said that a bold hiker could attack the terrible snowfield directly, provided he or she had an ice ax. My friend and I had just purchased two secondhand ice axes at a close-out sale, and decided to tackle Mount Baldy for the simple reason that we wanted to try out the axes. A glance at a topographic map—had I known what one was—would have shown several long-established trails switchbacking up the peak. But since anyone with eyes could see from twenty miles distant that a prominent gully led straight to the terrible snowfield, we didn't bother with maps or trails and hacked straight up the gully. The thinking behind our approach was as simple as it was erroneous—it was no more possible to get lost in the gully than it would have been in a railroad tunnel. A tunnel, like the gully, has a start and a finish, and unless you bored your way through the living rock of the tunnel, or grappled out of the gully, you couldn't possibly get lost. All tunnels lead to the light on the other side, and our gully led straight to the snowfield. Simple as that.

Well, not quite. . . . The gully turned out to be much wider than we reckoned—perhaps half a mile at its widest—and within its walls lay a labyrinth of steep chutes, mud cliffs, waterfalls, and so forth. In perfect daylight we easily wended our way around all obstacles, and by early afternoon were tromping up the terrible snowfield (ice axes were unnecessary). Then the wind picked up. And it started snowing. We turned around, glissaded the snowfield, and started blazing down the gully. Within an hour, visibility was down to twenty feet. Naturally we could no more retrace our route than we could see our car several miles below. First we stumbled onto—and almost over—a small cliff, and had to backtrack through hateful snowy hedge to gain another chute. That one led to a waterfall. More backtracking. And more. When night fell we hunkered under a rock and suffered.

By the next morning we were soaked and freezing. If anything, visibility was worse in thick fog. For most of that day we thrashed up and down that horrible gully and could never quite get free of it. On our last attempt we'd descended nearly the entire length of it, only to run into yet another steep cliff bank. Finally, through a perilous and jackass combination of clinging to icy roots and shimmying up rickety trees, we clamored out of the gully and onto the western ridge, stumbled onto a trail the size of a Third World highway, and made our sorry way to the car with about ten minutes of daylight to spare.

I'm not the only one to be defeated by the straight-shot school of orienteering. Two close friends, both expert outdoorsmen, tried to descend a forgotten canyon in a wild and rarely visited part of the lower Sierra Nevada. They *did* refer to a topographic map, and worked out a strategy accordingly. About eighteen miles into the twenty-mile trek, they learned that several seasons of storms had radically rearranged the terrain. The canyon was plugged with giant, teetering boulders, huge mud banks, extremely quick sand—in the form of silt banks—and a riot of uprooted trees. It was too steep and scaly to climb out of, so my two friends had to turn tail and thrash back the eighteen miles.

It is unlikely that such misadventures would ever happen to a casual dayhiker, but they illustrate the shortcomings of the straight-shot method, which everyone follows at some time or another. To really learn how to stay out of trouble, you must acquire basic navigational skills that use not only your head, but tools of the trade as well.

Sure, packing along a topographic map and a compass fulfills the "10 essentials" (see pages 15–17) mandate, but what good are they if you don't know how to use them? Not much! You might as well pack a world atlas or AAA road map, because without map and compass skills, a road map will be as useful as a topo in the backcountry.

There is an art to staying found that involves using one's head, staying observant, and applying map and compass skills properly. The skills required for simple navigation are not hard to acquire. What follows is a basic guide to staying found with diagrams, courtesy of compass makers Brunton and Silva, to help you choose the right tools, learn how to use them, and stay on course, or for the purposes of this book, the trail.

WHICH IS THE BEST COMPASS FOR ME?

That depends on your intended use and how much you wish to spend. The three most common brands of compass are Silva, Suunto, and Brunton. Each company offers numerous models, each with a specific purpose and different features but all with essentially the same role—to help you determine direction, plot a course, and stay on it.

As a minimum, your compass choice should feature a rotating bezel with a 360-degree dial in

2-degree graduations, a clear baseplate with inch and millimeter scales, a direction-of-travel arrow engraved into the baseplate, and a rotating magnetic needle mounted in a clear capsule filled with liquid to reduce shake and movement. Orienting lines should also be engraved or printed onto the bottom of the rotating capsule. A basic compass costs around $10.

Additional features such as a sighting mirror, adjustable declination screws or imprinted declination

scales, clinometers, or a magnifying glass will add to the cost. For maximum accuracy, you will want a compass with a sighting mirror, which enables you to hold the compass at eye level, line up a landmark in the notched sight at the top of the mirror, and read the compass bearing using the mirror. The accuracy of your sightings goes from approximately 5 degrees of error using a simple compass to about 2 degrees of error or better with a mirror.

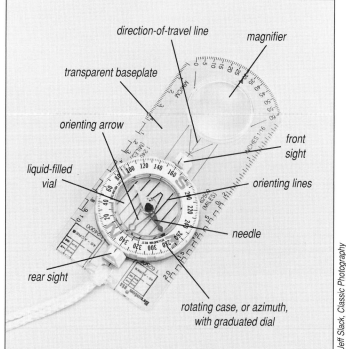

direction-of-travel line

magnifier

transparent baseplate

orienting arrow

liquid-filled vial

front sight

orienting lines

needle

rear sight

rotating case, or azimuth, with graduated dial

Jeff Slack, Classic Photography

A baseplate compass.

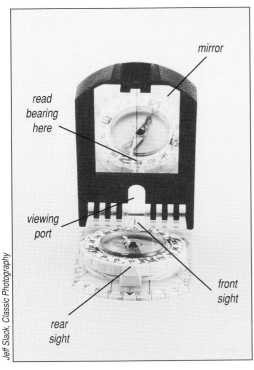

A baseplate compass with a sighting mirror.

Labels: mirror, read bearing here, viewing port, rear sight, front sight

Jeff Slack, Classic Photography

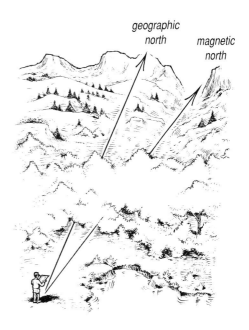

Labels: geographic north, magnetic north

If you don't account for declination, you can end up well away from your intended goal in only a matter of miles—on a steep mountainside instead of in the valley, for instance.

WHAT IS DECLINATION?

The difference between the north shown on a topographic map and the north indicated by the magnetic needle on your compass is known as *declination*. Declination is either west or east depending on which side of geographical north the compass needle points. On US Geological Survey topographic maps, declination is indicated by arrows printed on the bottom margin of the map. The arrow with a star above it indicates true or geographical north. The shorter arrow with MN above it indicates magnetic north (refer to the diagram provided courtesy of the USGS), and the written number indicates the amount of declination. If the MN arrow is on the left side of the true north arrow, declination is west and you will add the indicated number of degrees to correct your bearing. If the MN arrow is on the right side of the true north arrow,

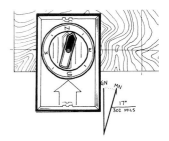

The printed side of a map is always oriented to true north. The declination arrow shows the correction necessary to account for the magnetic variation.

declination is east and you will subtract the indicated degrees to correct your bearing.

Say what? It's really not as hard as it sounds. If your indicated heading is 80 degrees after taking a map bearing, and the map declination is 15 degrees east, you will turn your bezel 15 degrees east, subtracting the degrees, to leave you with a corrected bearing of 65 degrees. Some find it easier to remember when to add or subtract by using the following: "West is best (+) and east is least (−)."

Why is this important? In the example given, if you did not correct for declination and set off hiking on an 80-degree bearing, you would be off course by approximately one-quarter mile for each mile traveled—no wonder you can't find that freshwater spring!

Keep in mind that declination changes; the degree correction indicated on a map is only accurate for the year the map was printed. To obtain the most accurate declination correction, call the USGS at (303) 273-8488.

WHAT IS A TOPOGRAPHIC MAP?

A topographic map is a one-dimensional piece of paper that represents the three-dimensional lay of the land. It does this by using contour lines to show where hills, mountains,

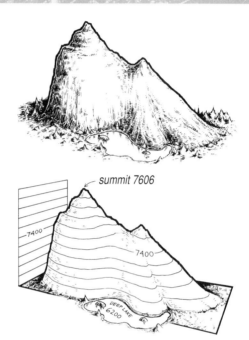

Contour lines represent points of equal elevation, enabling a one-dimensional map to represent a three-dimensional image. If you were to slice through a mountain with a saw at regular intervals (in this case, every 40 feet), each cut would represent a contour line. Every fifth contour line is labeled with its elevation and printed double-thickness; this is called an index contour.

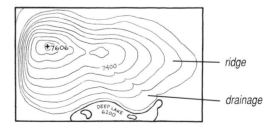

A map of a mountain as seen from above. As the circles formed by the contour lines become smaller, the elevation increases. V-shaped contours that point away from the peak indicate ridges; those that point toward the peak indicate valleys or drainages.

valleys, and canyons are located—a trained eye will see the three-dimensional images. Topographic maps are printed in color, with green areas depicting forest or vegetation and white indicating open terrain. Contour or elevation lines are printed in brown. Blue indicates water—lake, river, stream, or ocean. Black is used for man-made features such as trails, roads, and buildings. Man-made features on USGS maps are suspect as many have not been revised in more than 20 years; privately printed maps (such as those from Trails Illustrated, DeLorme, Earthwalk, Harrison, etc.) are more reliable. Other map symbols depict mines, ghost towns, marshes, swamps, waterfalls, caves, and so on. They are not explained on each USGS topographic map, but rather on a separate sheet that can be obtained free from the USGS (see Appendix 2).

ORIENTING YOUR MAP

Since a map represents the lay of the land, you must accurately orient your map to the land if you wish to match the geographical picture with its map image. You can do this by picking out landmarks and then spinning your map to match those landmarks—assuming your map-reading and geographical-interpretation skills are good enough. Or, you can use a compass to be sure that the top of

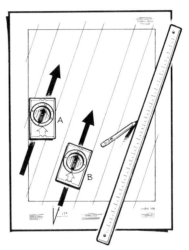

You can easily orient your map by drawing magnetic lines across it and then placing the baseplate along the edge of the lines (compass B). A more difficult alternative: adjust for declination on the compass dial manually before orienting the map (compass A).

your map is pointing north. Don't forget about declination, however. Nothing like having your map point 15 degrees in the wrong direction to really foul things up. Since the map is printed with its edges aligned with true north, you will have to account for declination when aligning your map with a compass.

A common way to ease this process is to use a pencil protractor and a yardstick with a very straight edge to project lines marking the declination across the entire topo. Pick a point, preferably near the center, along the printed base of the map. Place the protractor on the marked point and measure the decli-

nation using the written degree angle. Draw your first line connecting these two points. Then, using this line as a guide, you can draw magnetic-north lines parallel to the first, each the width of the yardstick apart. Now, take the compass with the orienting arrow pointing due north, place the edge of the baseplate along one of the magnetic lines, and spin the map until the magnetic arrow is centered in the orienting arrow—now your map, your magnetic needle, and the orienting arrow are all speaking the same language.

No magnetic lines on your map? Adjust your compass for the declination, place the edge of the

Gentle slope

Gentle ridge

Obvious ridge with cliff

Saddle or pass
between two summits

Summit with steep slope to the
west and moderate slope east

Lake in a steep cirque with a
river draining downhill

Ridge with obvious
pinnacles

Bench between two cliff systems
with a path on level ground

Contour lines show you the terrain you will have to hike through, over, down, and around. The closer together the lines are, the steeper the terrain; the wider apart, the more gentle the slope.

baseplate along the printed edge of the map, and then spin the map until the red end of the magnetic needle is centered in the orienting arrow. Your map is now oriented to magnetic north.

WHAT ARE CONTOUR LINES?

Contour lines are the brown squiggly lines on a topographic map that appear rather confusing at first glance, but are really precise representations of geography in the area the map represents. Each contour line connects points of equal elevation. The line with a darker shade of brown, usually every fifth line, is called an *index contour* and usually has the elevation printed on it.

To correctly read the severity of the terrain's ups and downs, you must determine the contour interval, printed at the bottom of the map. The contour interval indicates the elevation change between adjacent contour lines.

In general, widely spaced contour lines indicate a gradual slope. Closely spaced contours may mean a cliff. Contours that roughly form circles, with each one getting smaller as elevation is gained, indicate hills or mountain peaks. Those that bend into a "V" represent either a canyon or a sloping ridge. If the V points uphill—toward a point of higher elevation—it represents a canyon; if it points downhill, it's a

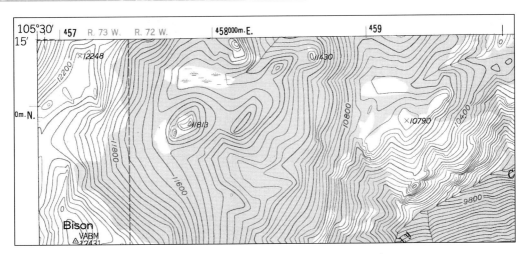

A small section of a topo covering the Pike National Forest, Colorado, at 1:24,000 scale
(1" = 2,000'). These large-scale 7.5-minute-series maps show a small area in great detail.

ridge. It stands to reason that a
stream in a V would indicate a
canyon (see diagrams).

HOW DO I TAKE
A FIELD BEARING?

Imagine you are hiking toward a distant mountain peak that is presently
visible from the ridge you are on but
which you know you will soon lose
sight of in the woods. How can you
be sure of staying on course? Hold
your compass level at waist height
and point the direction-of-travel
arrow at the mountain peak. Rotate
the compass housing until the orienting arrow boxes the red end of
the compass needle. Your bearing
may be read in degrees at the center index line.

Navigate to a distant summit by taking a field bearing and then hiking along
the bearing to get to the summit. The tree is along the line of sight, so you'll
hike there first, take another bearing, and then continue to the summit.

To follow that bearing, pick the first major landmark in line with the direction-of-travel arrow, say a large evergreen—one that you will not lose sight of when you're in the woods. Also, look over your shoulder and select a major landmark (say a rocky outcrop) directly behind you—again, one you will not lose sight of. Do not touch that compass dial! Walk directly toward the evergreen and don't worry that you can no longer see the mountain peak. Once at the tree, hold the compass level once again, turn your body until the north end of the compass needle centers itself exactly inside the orienting arrow, and then find another landmark in line with the direction-of-travel arrow. Before you head out, take a back bearing by turning around, still holding the compass level, until the white end of the compass needle is centered inside the orienting arrow. Do you see the rocky outcrop in line with the direction-of-travel arrow? If so, you're on course for the mountain peak as planned. Turn around and head directly to your next selected landmark. Repeat the procedure until you arrive at your selected destination, the mountain peak.

A hiker takes a bearing on a tall tree in line with the summit he is targeting (top). After crossing the gully and reaching the tree (bottom), he can't see the summit, but he can see the point he stood on before. So, he takes a back bearing to ensure he is still on course.

HOW DO I TAKE A MAP BEARING?

Oh, oh. You still want to head to that mountain peak, but this time you are enshrouded in dense fog. How are you going to get there? Get out your map. Place the edge of the baseplate like a ruler with the direction-of-travel arrow pointing in the direction of your destination. The edge of the baseplate should connect your current location and your intended end point. Rotate the compass housing until the orienting arrow points to magnetic north and the compass housing's orienting lines parallel the map's magnetic-north lines (if you've drawn these on your map). Without changing the bearing indicated by the compass, stand up holding the compass level at your waist and rotate your body until the north end of the compass needle centers itself exactly inside the orienting arrow. Your course is indicated by the direction-of-travel arrow. Follow the navigation directions given in the section on taking a field bearing (page 81).

WHEN YOU SUSPECT YOU'RE LOST

It has been rumored that famed outdoorsman Daniel Boone was never lost, although he did admit to being "mighty disoriented for several days in a row." In this age of search-and-

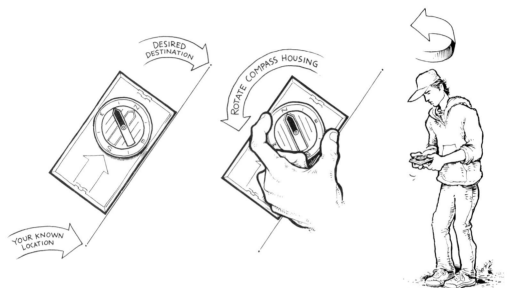

How to read a compass bearing to an intended destination from a topo map: Using edge of baseplate, connect your known location on map to desired destination. Rotate compass housing until orienting arrow points to map's magnetic north. Hold compass at waist level, rotate body until north end of needle centers inside orienting arrow, and hike in the direction the compass's direction-of-travel arrow indicates.

rescue teams, maps, compasses, and high technology, "lost" most often means you will be late for dinner, or at worst that someone else will find you. The following tips can help you and your loved ones stay found:

- Always tell a family member or close friend where you are going, when you will be leaving, and when you plan to return—and then stick to your plan.
- Be prepared for the worst. You may be heading out for a day-

hike under sunny skies, but don't assume you won't be forced to spend a night out in adverse weather. At a minimum, carry the "The Essentials" (see pages 15–17). I also carry a lightweight survival kit—see "Gearing Up a Survival Kit" later in this chapter.

- Don't just carry a map and compass, become proficient using them. Join a nearby orienteering club if you want added instruction.
- Pay attention to your surround-

ings. Staying on the correct path and then being able to find your way back again requires 360-degree observation. Make mental notes of landmarks as you walk toward and then away from them.

- If you do get lost, don't panic. Recognize the problem and then rationally work your way through it. Most often, if you sit down and calmly reflect for a few minutes, mentally retracing your steps, the solution becomes clear.

- If you conclude that you are definitely lost, stay put! Drink plenty of water. Your body can do without food for a few days, but it cannot function without water. Signal your position by building a smoky fire. If you run out of food, don't eat anything you find unless you are sure it is edible.
- Shelter from the elements as best you can. Use the tarp in your survival kit to fashion a lean-to. Use dry leaves and other dry plant debris (not poison oak or stinging nettles) to insulate yourself from the ground and prevent heat loss.

Waterproofing a Map

There is nothing fun about trying to navigate while clinging to a soggy map in a downpour. Right before your eyes, the route home begins to turn into a greenish brown papier-mâché clump. Your only hope is that your memory of the route doesn't wash out with the map.

Making a see-through, waterproof cover for your maps is an easy way to prevent soggy-map syndrome. All you need is a large, freezer-weight, plastic zip-top bag and a few sections of sturdy, waterproof tape like duct or packing tape.

Simply cut the tape into a strip long enough to adhere completely to one edge of the bag from top to bottom. Press one half of the tape, lengthwise, onto the bag, leaving the other half hanging over the edge. Flip the bag over and fold the loose tape down onto the other side of the bag. Repeat each step two more times, once for the bottom and once for the remaining side. You now have a wonderful waterproof map container reinforced on three edges.

Other ways to waterproof a map include:

- Covering it with clear self-adhering paper (like Con-Tact)—making the map waterproof but very stiff and leaving no way to write on it.
- Painting on a product called Stormproof, available at most map and outdoor specialty stores. The clear chemical coating renders the map waterproof and flexible, and the map can still be written on.
- Applying a coating of Thompson's Water Seal or another brick and masonry sealant. This will make a map water-repellent, but not waterproof.

Folding a Map

Map folding is an acquired skill. Combine a blowing wind, a little rain, and a sprinkling of fatigue and what you get is an irresistible desire to jam or crumple your trail map into the nearest pocket and forget the idea of folding.

There is a better way—one that results in an easy-to-use, accor-

Natural Navigation on the Trail

Staying on course when stepping a lively beat down a trail is relatively simple—just follow the trail and read the signs. Off trail, especially on snowfields, ice floes, and desert sands, route finding is an entirely different beast. A compass is an invaluable aid, but so is an observant eye. When confronting miles of trackless terrain, take note of the prevailing wind direction and the resulting textures it leaves on the land. On tundra and sea ice in the Arctic, systematic drift patterns in the snow—*sastrugi*—offer a valuable directional clue. Use a compass to check the directional formations of these patterns and remember them. The same is true of sand drifts in desert environments. These physical directional clues are invaluable when a sand- or snowstorm limits visibility and impairs the taking of compass bearings. In such limited visibility you can use sand drifts and sastrugi underfoot to aid in staying on track and keep from wandering endlessly in circles.

dion-style configuration. This technique is taught to British Boy Scouts—my cousin from England can fold a map like this in his sleep.

This method allows you to look at any portion of the map without having to open it fully, which is ideal in windy or wet weather. Further, the accordion configuration collapses to pocket size with ease. Once you've established the creases, any map will open and fold almost without effort.

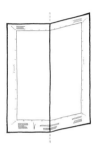

Step 1: *Lay the map flat, printed side up.*

Step 2: *Fold it in half vertically to establish the first crease (make this and every subsequent crease clean and sharp).*

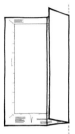

Step 3: *Open the map and lay it flat once again. Working with only the right half of the map, fold the right side in half toward the center, to make quarter-folds.*

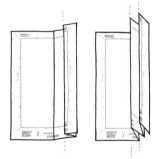

Step 4: *Fold the outside quarter-fold back to the edge, producing an eighth-fold. Use this fold as a guide and fold the other quarter the same way—trust me, it's easier than it sounds. Half the map should now have four accordion-style folds.*

Step 5: *Repeat steps 3 and 4 on the map's other half so that you end up with a full accordion of eight folds in a long, rulerlike shape.*

Step 6: *Finally, fold the map in the shape of a Z so it's in thirds.*

Voilà! Now you can look at any section without having to completely unfold the map, and it snaps into place almost by itself.

Keeping a weather eye skyward is important if you wish to remain safe and hike in relative comfort through the wilds. Woe to the traveler who ignores nature's signs and gets caught unprepared by severe weather. Although it is always wise to prepare for the worst when traveling on foot—keeping in mind seasonal averages for the area you are in—learning to anticipate weather changes will aid you tremendously in trekking along the path of least resistance.

FORECASTING CHANGES IN WEATHER WITH AN ALTIMETER

An altimeter is, in essence, an aneroid barometer, capable of reading relative changes in barometric pressure and, with the addition of a scale inscribed on its face, changes in elevation (see also page 167). Because of its compact nature, an altimeter is not ideally suited for reading the minute changes ($\frac{1}{100}$ inch) used by the National Weather Service, but the standard $\frac{1}{10}$-inch increments are adequate for amateur use.

The innards of an altimeter consist of a vacuum chamber that contracts with high pressure (found closer to sea level) and expands with low pressure (pressures get lower the higher one climbs). Through the intricacies of gears and gizmos, the information is trans-

ferred and displayed by a needle (or in the case of electronic altimeters, digitally) on the face of the altimeter.

In general, when the weather report refers to a falling barometer, a lowering of the atmospheric pressure, the altimeter shows a rise in elevation. Conversely, a rising barometer, a rise in the atmospheric pressure, is read on the altimeter as falling elevation.

How does this relate to changes in weather? A rise in barometric pressure, demonstrated by a drop in your elevation reading while you remain stationary for several hours, indicates improving or continued good weather. A drop in barometric pressure, shown by a rise in the elevation reading, is a precursor to deteriorating weather.

Be warned that any rapid change in barometric pressure, up or down, promises a change in the weather. Slow changes usually indicate a stable weather pattern (dry or wet) that will last a while.

Learn to use wind direction and your reading of the altimeter's fluctuations of elevation when stationary to anticipate possible weather changes. The following information has been adapted from National Weather Service data detailing average conditions within the United States.

Winds from the NW. When winds are from the northwest and the weather has been clear, you can anticipate 24 hours of continued clear weather if your altimeter is steady or shows a slow drop in ele-

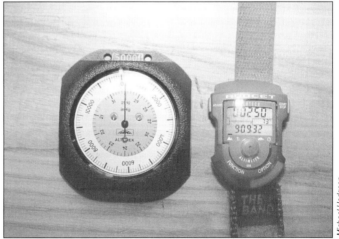

An altimeter is a useful navigation tool and a serviceable weather station.

Nature's Weather Signs

Through the centuries, humankind has devoted great effort to anticipate weather changes. Long before the advent of sophisticated weather paraphernalia, people studied weather by reading all the available signs. They listened to the animals, the plants, the wind, the earth. They used their eyes, ears, nose, and taste. Not surprisingly, records show that these "ancient ways" are frequently as reliable as modern methods for making short-term forecasts. Arm yourself with weather tools if you will, but don't close your eyes and ears to the signs of nature all around.

- *Morning or Evening Sky:* "Red sky at night, sailor's delight. Red sky in morning, sailors take warning." This means that if the clouds take on a reddish hue in the morning, one can expect rain by the end of the day. If the evening sky is red, the weather will probably remain clear the following day.
- *Coffee:* Grizzled outdoorspeople swear by the "bubbles in the coffee" method. Perhaps this explains why so many of them spend hours staring into a steaming mug of java? For coffee forecasting to work, the brewed coffee must be strong. Instant won't do because it doesn't have enough oil to create satisfactory surface tension. Pour the coffee into a mug (vertical sides work best; venerable Sierra cups don't work as well). Give the coffee a good stir or two and watch the bubbles form. If they scatter this way and that and then form near the center, fair weather. If they cling to the sides, a low-pressure system is setting in and rain is possible.
- *Hair:* Although not everyone is affected in quite the same manner, hair does react to humidity changes. Like rope, hair tends to contract when damp and to relax when dry. Straighter hair means dry weather. Wavier or curlier hair means wetter weather.
- *Halo around the Sun and/or Moon:* In the summer, the sight of a hazy halo, or corona, around the sun or moon is a good indication that a change in the present weather pattern, most often to rain, is in the forecast.
- *Frost and Dew:* The presence of heavy frost or dew early in the morning or late in the evening is a fairly reliable indicator that up to 12 hours of good weather can be expected.
- *Colors of the Sky:* Tints and hues of green, yellow, dark red, or grayish blue indicate precipitation and quite often accompanying winds.
- *Cattle:* For years, farmers have looked to their cattle for reliable indications of changing weather. Cattle herd together in lower elevations and off exposed hills when the weather is about to take a shift for the worse. To some extent, the same is true of deer and other grazing animals.
- *Wind:* "Wind from the south brings rain in its mouth." Low-pressure systems create cyclonic winds that rotate counterclockwise. Since low-pressure systems are frequently associated with rainstorms, the rhyme proves quite accurate. Along the leading edge of a low-pressure system as it advances west to east, the wind blows from the south. Thus, frequently, southern breezes mean a low, with its rain, is on the way.

    High-pressure systems are often associated with clear or clearing weather, with clockwise-rotating winds. Be aware of wind directions and you will keep your finger on the weather's pulse—is it beating fair or foul?
- *Campfire Smoke:* By observing the smoke from your campfire, you can discern whether a low- or a high-pressure system is in the area. If the smoke from the fire hangs low to the ground and dissipates into the firewood, a low-pressure system is here and rain is possible. If the smoke rises in a straight, vertical column, high pressure rules and fair weather can be anticipated.

vation (a rise in barometric pressure). If it has been raining and you read a drop in elevation, the weather should clear in several hours. In all cases, expect lower temperatures. If the altimeter shows a rise in elevation (a drop in barometric pressure), expect it to remain clear for 24 hours if it has been clear or expect the weather to change if it has been stormy.

Winds from the SW.   When the winds are from the southwest and the weather has been clear, you can anticipate continued fair weather for 12 to 24 hours if your altimeter shows a drop in elevation (a rise in barometric pressure). If it has been stormy and you read a drop in elevation, the storm should pass in 6 hours. If the altimeter shows a rise in elevation (a drop in barometric pressure), you may predict rain within the next 12 hours if the weather has been clear, or increasing rain with possible clearing after 12 hours if the weather has been stormy.

Winds from the SE.   If the weather has been clear and winds are from the southeast, you may plan on continued fair weather if the altimeter shows a drop in elevation (a rise in barometric pressure). If the weather has been stormy, anticipate clearing weather to follow soon if the altimeter shows a drop in elevation.

A rise in elevation shown on the altimeter during clear weather indicates impending rain within 12 hours and possible high winds. If the weather is already stormy, a rise in elevation indicates an increase in severity of the storm followed by clearing within 24 hours.

Winds from the NE.   When winds are from the northeast and the weather is clear, expect continued fair but cool weather if the altimeter shows a drop in elevation (a rise in barometric pressure). If the weather has been stormy, expect it to clear and the temperature to drop. If the altimeter rises in elevation while the weather is clear, expect stormy weather within 12 to 24 hours. If the weather is stormy, expect very heavy rain coupled with severe gale-force winds and much colder temperatures.

A Hot Seat: Dealing with Lightning

Roy C. Sullivan, a former Shenandoah National Park ranger, is the only human being known to have been struck by lightning on seven separate occasions and live. Sullivan lost one big toenail and his eyebrows, had his hair catch fire twice, and was admitted to a hospital once for chest and stomach burns. No explanation has been offered for why Sullivan

was so attractive to lightning.

How can you avoid becoming a statistic in an upcoming edition of *Guinness*? By following a few basic guidelines: If in a group, spread out so a single bolt won't zap everyone at once. Sit on your foam pad if you're carrying one, or other nonconductive object (pull out the foam padding at the back of your daypack if possible), and make yourself as small as possible. Avoid bodies of water, high or wide-open places, tall or metal objects (aluminum pack frames and ice axes come to mind), and low, damp places. Sitting near a grove of trees is a good, safe bet—just don't sit under a tree. If you're caught on a mountain summit, get off quickly. Hunker down on the slope, below the highest point, and pray.

avoid tall trees

avoid rocky pinnacles

avoid obvious high ground

avoid caves

avoid all metal gear

avoid low drainages

find a low area away from hazards

avoid water

If a lightning storm catches you unaware on high ground, take immediate steps to ensure your safety.

GOOD HEALTH, GOOD WATER

Staying healthy in the outdoors normally breaks down to five key points: common sense, experience, fitness, gear, and preparedness. But there are no guarantees. Sudden storms, lightning, potholes, hornets, etc. care nothing for your comfort and are all part of the adventure. And so is an occasional dose of grief. Stick with the casual trails and your chance of getting sick or hurt are remote. Venture afield and the potential for trouble increases. Spend time above 14,000 feet or in extreme temperature zones such as equatorial jungle or polar regions, and

your body will almost certainly balk a little (this varies from person to person). Although the effects of severe conditions can quickly strike the unprepared, given suitable readiness and appropriate gear the dayhiker can avoid many problems that the expeditionary will face, particularly sickness.

Before heading up the Kapuas River in Kalimantan, Indonesia, a veteran of the area guaranteed me that at least one of our party would go down with typhus, malaria, blackwater fever, or any number of other grim illnesses. As promised, about a month into the expedition, Rick Ridgeway, veteran of Everest and K2, shriveled into a fetal knot, gushing from

Water Filters

Drinking untreated water straight from a backcountry source is a bit like rolling dice; maybe you'll be lucky, maybe not. In the United States, protozoa such as *Giardia* and *Cryptosporidium* potentially lurk under the surface of almost all available water, even the most seemingly pure high-mountain runoff. A drink from the wrong source can lead to misery—nausea, diarrhea, and vomiting. The obvious precaution is to purify every drop of water you drink either by boiling (too time- and fuel-consuming for most), chemical (iodine or chlorine) treatment, filtration, or a combination of chemical treatment and filtration.

A hand-held filter is the most convenient method of field water treatment I've used—just pump and drink. Filtration physically strains out microorganic contaminants and parti-

cles, rendering the water clear and somewhat pure. How pure depends on the filter. Manufacturers use a mind-bending blur of technical terminology and references to depth, maze, or screen filtration. The upshot is that all filters with a pore-size efficiency of 2 microns or smaller will remove *Giardia* and *Cryptosporidium* as well as parasitic eggs and larvae. Filters must have a pore-size efficiency of less than 0.2 micron to claim meaningful bacteria removal. No field pump that relies entirely on filtration can yet guarantee 100 percent virus removal—although some claim they can. You'll want to be able to eliminate viruses if traveling in Third World countries and anytime drinking water might be contaminated by sewage.

To rid drinking water of viruses, a number of filters use either iodine resins or include iodine tablets in the packaging as an extra bit of protection. Because iodine has an

unpleasant taste and presents possible health risks to some people, filters often contain a carbon element.

Activated carbon elements remove organic chemicals such as pesticides, herbicides, and chlorine as well as unpleasant flavors from filters. The Achilles' heel of the carbon element is that once it has reached its limit to "adsorb" a particular chemical, the filter will no longer remove that chemical, allowing it to pass undetected. Stick to the manufacturer's recommended replacement schedule.

A good filter should be compact, lightweight (more than 20 ounces, forget it), simple to use, and easy to clean or maintain. At the very least, buy a filter that will remove protozoa and bacteria. A number of cheap, pocket-size filters remove only *Giardia* and *Cryptosporidium*. That, in my book, is cutting corners to save money and threaten your

both ends: typhoid fever. And during a sea kayaking trip in the Solomon Islands, I saw an entire German expedition leveled by dengue fever—the scene resembled a page out of *Night of the Living Dead*.

As a dayhiker, if you catch a bug or virus you'll be back home by the time it truly hits. But that doesn't mean you won't suffer, so the key is to avoid exposure to intestinal bugs (far and away the most common ailments picked up by dayhikers) in the first place. The safeguard is simple: Watch what you drink.

The transmission of most stomach bugs is fecal-oral—you get sick by consuming water containing human or animal waste. Don't let a pristine-looking stream or lake fool you. With the traffic many wilderness areas currently see, you have no idea what has leached into the water. When water runs straight from a mountainside, down a cliff, or bubbles from the ground, it's okay. But many springs are polluted, and the remoteness of a creek or stream doesn't guarantee that the water is kosher. Ron Fawcett and I once spent an entire morning thrashing around the steep slopes above the Cookie Cliff, in Yosemite Valley, looking for a certain infamous climb. It was ninety in the shade, if you could find any.

GOOD WATER

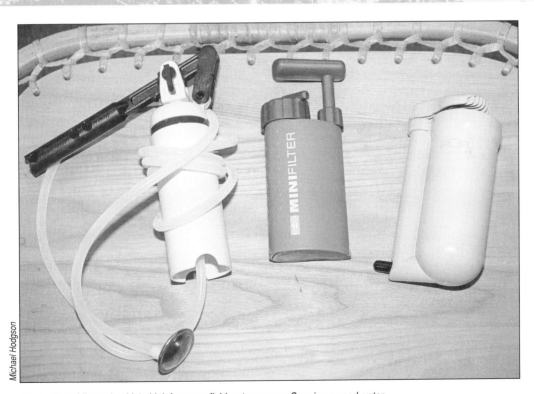

Michael Hodgson

These days, hikers shouldn't drink from any field water source. Carrying a good water filter is essential.

We didn't bring enough water. We never found the climb. Hiking back to the road, I was thirsty enough to drink seawater. We stumbled across a small creek. The water looked a little dark, smelled strange, tasted worse, so I drank just enough to slacken my throat. Ron didn't drink. That night I was just settling into my sleeping bag when my works started to churn. Then came the light sweat all over and the queasiness and malarial trembling that assures you you're shortly going to throw up for real. I grabbed a gallon jug of water and, in only a pair of nylon gym trunks, headed off behind camp to a moraine about a quarter mile away. It was pitch black—I fell and wrenched and barked this or that, and barely made the moraine when I started to retch. Hard. Then came the diarrhea. It went on for hours, and it trashed me for several days. Never again.

Water is heavy, and you need plenty of it if you're humping along a trail. The safest bet is to pack water with you—which seems ludicrous if you're hiking beside a flowing stream. But if you get roaring sick from stream water, the extra pounds will suddenly seem immaterial. Go light, and suffer. Staying hydrated is crucial, and there's a saying I always keep in mind: Wait till you are thirsty and you have waited too long. I don't know the

health. Seek out filters that offer a flow rate of at least 1 liter per minute. Any less and your lips will pucker while you wait for drinkable water.

All filters will eventually clog. Some filters can be backwashed or even scrubbed clean to extend their life—a big advantage in cost and convenience. If the filter has a pre-filter, use it. It will prolong the filter's usefulness dramatically. Always follow the manufacturer's instructions to the letter. Never try to force water through a filter that is difficult to pump; most likely you will end up injecting a load of microbiotic nasties into your bottle—yech!

Drink to Your Health

Your body is approximately 70 percent water. The river of life, your blood, is 90 percent water. Water carries oxygen and nutrients your body needs, and helps flush out contaminants your body doesn't

need. Water helps lubricate joints, regulate body temperature, and aids digestion and metabolism. If you are like most people, you don't drink enough water. Think about it. When did you last drink pure H_2O? Experts recommend you consume between 3 and 4 quarts of water a day, or around 0.5 ounce of water per pound of body weight.

Do you wait to drink until your body says, "Gee, I'm thirsty"? If so, you are about 1½ quarts low. Take stock of your daily routine, your physical condition, and your ailments. Chances are, if you were drinking the correct amount of water, you would feel better. Fatigue and mild headaches are signs that you are becoming dehydrated. Too little water and your energy output drops.

If your water needs are reaching critical, your urine will be dark yellow. It should be relatively clear. You may even become irritable and

feel completely exhausted; your mind may wander and be unable to focus on anything meaningful.

In medical jargon, there are three levels of dehydration:
- *Mild Dehydration:* your mucous membranes dry out, your pulse is normal, your urine is noticeably yellow, and you are mildly thirsty.
- *Moderate Dehydration:* your mucous membranes are extremely dry, your pulse is weak and rapid, your urine is very dark, and you are very thirsty.
- *Severe Dehydration:* your mucous membranes are completely dry; you are disoriented, drowsy, and tired; you are unable to urinate or make tears; you are in shock (rapid, weak pulse; rapid breathing; pale skin).

Should you drink water or should you drink sports drinks? Although some people argue the benefits of one over the other, the answer is that both are

physiology, but once you are dehydrated it takes some hours to recuperate, no matter how much water you swill at one time. This is especially important for dayhiking, when you can't pitch a tent and relax with a gallon jug, but have to push on. An Israeli army officer once told me the troops did maneuvers on the banks of the Dead Sea in the most demonic heat and never had problems with dehydration. All soldiers were ordered to keep their bellies full of water (They could quaff an astonishing ten gallons per person per day!) at all times. The Dumba tribe in Papua New Guinea's Gulf Province had no such standing orders, but they follow the same doctrine, drinking every time they come across good water—five, even six times an hour. I spent a month with the Dumba, drank when they did, and never once got dehydrated—despite hellish temperatures and greenhouse humidity.

Resistance to heat prostration varies from person to person, but no one can hike indefinitely under a cruel sun and not pay the devil for it. One hour's brisk hiking under overhead sunlight is ample to flatten you—if you don't have water on board. Make a conscious effort to drink water at regular intervals—whenever you stop to rest or adjust a strap. Keep your stomach full and you'll avoid the problem.

good. Sports drinks provide energy, maximize fluid absorption, and replace minerals lost during activity, which pure water cannot do. However, your body needs pure water to help filter out contaminants your body builds up during activity. The bottom line is that you need to drink. If the only way you can feel good about drinking is by flavoring your water with Gatorade, All Sport, CytoMax, Recharge, or any other of the host of sports drinks out there, go for it. Just don't forget to supplement your intake with at least a quart or two of pure, simple H_2O . . . your body will thank you for it.

Michael Hodgson

With a water filter, all you do is pump and drink, as Michael demonstrates here.

First Aid and Emergency Kit

Before you read on, keep one thing first and foremost in your mind: A first aid kit is only as good as the person using it. When I taught wilderness first aid, I told my students that the best thing they could put in their kit was a brain filled to the brim with common sense. Never forget the first aid creed: Do good if you can, but do no harm.

Antibiotics
Antiseptics
Acetaminophen (such as Tylenol)
Ibuprofen
Antihistamine (such as Benadryl)
Tincture of benzoin
Sterile gauze pads
Gauze roll
Nonadherent dressing
1-inch-wide adhesive tape
Steri-Strips
Ace wrap
Large compress
Moleskin
2nd Skin
Tweezers
Bandage scissors
Irrigation syringe (In a pinch, you can make an irrigation syringe out of a plastic baggie with a pinhole poked in one corner. Fill the bag with water, squeeze, and aim the water

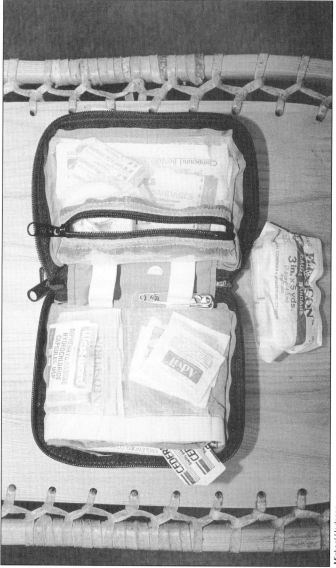

Michael Hodgson

A first aid kit doesn't have to be big to include the things you need to deal safely with minor cuts and bumps.

stream into the wound to flush out debris.)

Low-reading thermometer

SAM splint

Space blanket

Sawyer Extractor snakebite kit

Epi Pen (epinephrine, also known as Adrenalin, to prevent allergic reaction to bee stings; available by prescription)

Emergency report form

Pencil

Emergency phone numbers and money for a phone call

For information on a first aid clearinghouse, see Appendix 2.

The Doctors Say

Doctors Howard Donner and Eric Weiss, both active members of the Wilderness Medical Society and highly respected medical doctors with vast emergency room and backcountry emergency experience, were asked to comment on items found in first aid kits to help clear up possible confusion. This is what they had to say:

The Survey Says

Several studies have been published recently that examine and better define the first aid needs and health issues of backcountry travelers. A field survey published in *The Journal of Wilderness Medicine* assessed the risk of injury and illness of backcountry hikers in Yosemite National Park. It found that 15 percent of backpackers had to shorten their intended trips at one time or another for medical reasons. The most common problems listed were insect bites, wounds, blisters, and sunburn. Acute mountain sickness, asthma, allergic reactions, and lacerations were the most common of the serious medical problems. It was also found that on average, backcountry travelers carry only 48 percent of the recommended first aid supplies.

Todd Schimelpfenig, safety and training director for the National Outdoor Leadership School (NOLS), recently published the results of a 5-year study of the types and severity of injuries and illnesses encountered during NOLS-led wilderness programs. He found that 56 percent of their medical incidents involved sprains, strains, and wounds to soft tissue. Fractures and dislocations accounted for 4.6 percent of all injuries. Nonviral syndromes and diarrhea accounted for 60 percent of medical problems related to illness. Eighteen cases involved dental problems. In 43 percent of the cases, the patient required evacuation.

Gloves. Yes, vinyl gloves are cheaper, but they leak more readily, making them less valuable as a protective device for the user. For that reason, the recommended gloves are latex.

Splints. SAM splints are the way to go for orthopedic injuries of all kinds because they can be cut and molded to fit any extremity, can be fashioned into a usable cervical collar, are reusable, aren't affected by temperature extremes, and are X-ray–permeable.

Rehydration. Salt tablets were the standard for oral rehydration needs, but what a lousy standard. Salt tablets are virtually impossible to digest and frequently induce vomiting—not what you want when you are trying to achieve rehydration. World Health Organization oral rehydration salt packets (which dissolve more readily in water) for treating diarrhea and dehydration are the standard in most good kits.

Wound Management. Since the old days of traditional 4 x 4 gauze pads, wound dressings have gotten more sophisticated and feature nonadherent designs and hydrogel dressings such as Spenco 2nd Skin. Cleansing a wound is now best performed via a high-pressure irrigating syringe. Gone too are the butterfly bandages, replaced by more effective wound closure strips. Be sure your kit has tincture of benzoin in them, which, when spread on the skin on either side of a wound, helps tape and bandages adhere—useful when the skin is sweaty or dirty.

Snakebite Kits. Ice, electric shock treatment, constriction, and those tiny kits with razor-sharp blades and miniature rubber suction cups are not safe and can do much more harm that good when treating for a snakebite. The Sawyer Extractor is the only snakebite kit that is actually acknowledged as useful in certain situations. The recommended first aid? Get the victim to a hospital where antivenin may be given safely.

Medications. Acetaminophen (Tylenol and others) will reduce fever and relieve pain, but it does nothing for decreasing inflammation that can occur from a sprain or strain. Ibuprofen (Nuprin, Motrin, Advil, and others) is the preferred choice for reducing inflammation. An antihistamine (commonly Benadryl) is often included in today's kits as a treatment for mild allergic reactions, but if you are a frequent traveler in the backcountry you would be wise to add epinephrine (Adrenalin) in the form of an Epi Pen to treat serious allergic reactions that might otherwise be fatal.

Taking Care of Blisters.
Typically, a blister is caused by friction (your boot rubbing against your foot) or by pressure (a wrinkle in a sock). Either causes the outer layer of skin to move back and forth over the inner layer. Eventually the layers separate and fluid fills the space. Prevent blisters by keeping your feet dry, applying moleskin to hot spots before they fill with fluid, and wearing socks and boots that fit properly.

Should a blister happen, and they do happen to even the most careful hiker on occasion, wash the site carefully with soap and water and sterilize it with alcohol, then puncture the blister near its base with a sterile needle. Gently work out the fluid, taking care not to damage the roof of the blister—leaving it in place will encourage healing. Cover the site with a 2nd Skin, secured in place by moleskin. Use tincture of benzoin around, but not on, the blister site to help the moleskin adhere to your foot.

Special Considerations for Children

According to Dr. Barbara Kennedy, pediatrician, NOLS graduate, member of the Wilderness Medical Society, mother of four, and author of Adventure Medical Kits' mini-guidebook *A Medical Guide to Traveling with Children*, children need special consideration.

- For family use, standard first aid kits must be adapted to meet infants' and children's special needs. The specific items to be carried vary depending on the ages of the children, preexisting medical conditions, length of travel, specific environments traveled in, and the knowledge the parents have of first aid.

- Infants can develop infections and become hypothermic, hyperthermic, and dehydrated more rapidly than adults or older children. Carry a digital thermometer and the appropriate lubricant for monitoring rectal temperature. Temperatures 100°F and over in a child younger than four months require immediate medical attention. A bulb syringe is useful because it can suction mucus from the throat and nasal passages of infants, flush foreign bodies from ears, and administer enemas.

- Most children under five cannot swallow pills. Chewable medications are preferred. If a chewable is not available, a liquid will work, but liquids add weight and can leak. Most children can chew tablets once their first molars are present—usually around 15 months. For children who cannot chew, chewable medications can be crushed and mixed with food.

SUN PROTECTION 101

Many major newspapers around the country list "burn times"—when the sun begins to beat down—and for good reason. Skin cancer death rates are soaring. How should you protect yourself when you head outdoors into the land of sun and fun? The following are suggestions from the Skin Cancer Foundation:

- The sun is strongest between 10 A.M. and 2 P.M. (11 A.M. and 3 P.M. during daylight saving time). Minimize exposure during this period.
- Apply sunscreen with a sun protection factor (SPF) of 15 or higher before every exposure to the sun. Reapply frequently and liberally every 2 hours as long as you stay in the sun. Always reapply sunscreen after perspiring heavily or swimming—even if the product claims to be waterproof.
- If you are taking medications or birth-control pills or using certain cosmetics, you risk an increased sensitivity to the sun and a possible allergic reaction when using sunscreen. Check with your doctor or dermatologist for advice.
- Clothing does not guarantee protection from the sun. Loose weaves allow dangerous burning rays through. Wear loose-fitting pants and long-sleeved shirts made with tightly woven materials. Fair-skinned people should apply sunscreen even under their clothing.
- On overcast days the sun's rays are just as damaging—sunscreens are still a must.
- Be happy with your natural skin color. Tanning parlors can increase your risk of skin cancer.
- The higher you climb, the more intense the sun's rays become since there is less atmosphere to diffuse the damaging rays. Pile on the sunscreen.
- Sand, snow, water, and even concrete reflect the sun's rays. Protect yourself completely from sunburn by coating the underside of your nose, ears, chin, and other less-accessible body areas.
- Take advantage of sunscreens formulated just for children, such as Summer Stuff's colored lotions with wild names like Green Slime, Pink Pizazz, Whacky White, and Blue Blast. The more kids enjoy applying it, the more likely they are to use it and not duck and run every time you come near them with the bottle.
- What should you do if you get a sunburn? Cool the area with cool compresses. Try aloe gel and even a moisturizing lotion. If blisters form, you've scored a more serious burn than simple first aid can take care of—see your doctor.
- The Skin Cancer Foundation publishes and distributes a free newsletter, "Sun & Skin News." For a free copy, send a self-addressed, stamped business envelope to Skin Center Foundation, PO Box 561, Department Sun and Skin, New York, NY 10156.

HYPERTHERMIA

Overheating is yet another malady that hits outdoor adventurers—but it shouldn't. With the right precautions, heat cramps, heat exhaustion, and even heatstroke are completely preventable. If the going gets hot and the sun is bearing down, be sure you don a hat and loose, airy clothing. If you are not used to a hot climate, take a day or two to acclimatize before heading out on a strenuous hike. Moisture intake is key: Best is a regular mix of water and electrolyte replacement fluids. Watch your urine. If it is not relatively clear, your fluid intake is too low and you are becoming dehydrated, which can lead to heat illness.

Heat cramps are the body's first signal that you are overheating. Painful muscle spasms are caused by excessive sweating and heavy salt loss. Rest, electrolyte replacement fluids, and water will solve the problem.

With *heat exhaustion,* the next

stage of your body's rebellion, the symptoms to expect are weakness, dizziness, nausea, and cool, clammy skin. The body is unable to shed heat efficiently. At this stage, more aggressive action is needed: get out of the sun, drink cool water and electrolyte replacement fluids, eat a salty snack or two, and rest for at least several hours.

Heatstroke is the final stage—and it is life-threatening. The core temperature increases until the body is literally cooking its brain. Confusion, headache, dizziness, and hot, flushed skin that is dry to the touch are common symptoms. Rapid cooling is the required first aid. Place cold packs or cold compresses (cloth soaked in cold water) at the neck, armpits, and groin; if possible, soak the entire body in cool (not cold) water. Seek medical help immediately.

HYPOTHERMIA

When your body cannot generate enough heat to replace the heat being lost to the elements, your core temperature will begin to drop—a process called *hypothermia*. Fatigue, shivering, uncoordinated movements, and slow speech are all symptoms of mild hypothermia. Replace wet or damp clothing with

warm, insulative clothing. Get into a sleeping bag. Drink warm liquids. Build a fire. *Severe hypothermia* is much more serious and requires medical attention. Symptoms are cold, pale skin; lapses of consciousness; lethargy; and apathy. Perform the same first aid as for mild hypothermia with the addition of warm water compresses (made from a bandanna, or by adding warm water to your water bottle) applied to the groin, armpits, neck, and hands. Evacuate the victim immediately to an emergency medical facility.

THE TRUTH ABOUT SNAKEBITES

Contrary to what you may have heard, very few snakebites are fatal. According to statistics, of the 8,000 or so annual bites in the United States that involve venomous snakes, only 12 are fatal. Nearly one-fifth of all rattlesnake and one-third of all copperhead and cottonmouth bites are dry—no venom is injected.

Despite the unlikelihood of getting bitten in US deserts, swamps, and mountains, it is important to know appropriate first aid should a snakebite occur. Dr. William Forgey, a trustee of the Wilderness Education Association, member of the Wilderness Medical Society, and author of numerous books on wilderness medicine, states, "Ice and tourniquets should never be used as

they have potentially serious and debilitating side effects and are of questionable value in saving a life."

Forgey recommends that one first treat for shock, which in many cases can be more harmful than the bite. Make the victim lie down, keep him or her warm, and elevate the extremities. Clean and dress the wound as you would any cut. Then, evacuate the victim. According to Forgey, evacuation is the single-most important first aid step. If you are alone, walk out. A group should try to carry the victim out as long as this doesn't significantly slow the group. In either case, you have one to two hours before the venom begins to affect the body.

Should you be more than several hours from medical help, making field first aid necessary, wilderness medical experts, including Forgey, and other medical experts familiar with snake poisoning recommend only one form of mechanical first aid—the Extractor manufactured by Sawyer Products. If suction is applied within 3 minutes, scientific studies have shown that the device will remove up to 30 percent of the venom.

Some people still cling to an archaic notion that electric shock treatment neutralizes the venom, but medical experts deem this practice ineffective and potentially harmful.

What of the other snakebite

kits on the market? Surveyed doctors who are acknowledged experts in wilderness medicine unanimously regard those tiny kits that include a tiny razor-sharp blade, a cord for constriction, and rubber suction cups for venom removal as archaic and potentially dangerous.

To be fair, some experts stand by the "cut and suck" method. Andrew Koukoulus, director of the Ross Allen Reptile Institute for many years and consultant for treatment of snakebites in Florida (he is not a physician), believes doctors recommend against cut and suck because they strongly believe that a layperson will cause additional tissue damage. "The cutting is not as deep as doctors state; you are only cutting the first few layers of skin in order to enlarge the opening and place suction over the wound. I carry a Cutters kit with me and I have treated over forty-three snakebites with it," says Koukoulus.

Still, the fact cannot be overlooked that not one doctor or wilderness medical expert I contacted would side with Koukoulus. Do yourself a favor—learn the appropriate first aid, carry a Sawyer kit if you feel it is necessary, and leave the "slicing and dicing" to the doctors.

AVOIDING THE STING

Hornets, bees, wasps, and yellow jackets are the bane of many an outdoorsperson. Just when you thought you were sitting down for a nice picnic lunch or a midhike snack, in come the buzzing squadrons. The fear of a sting motivates most people to swing and swat wildly, and yet that is the worst thing you can do. Avoid attracting undue attention by following a few simple guidelines:

- Dress in light-colored clothing. Black, red, and blue are more attractive to bees and their stinging cousins because they see in the ultraviolet spectrum.
- Don't wear perfume or cologne as the smell attracts insects of all kinds.
- Don't bring fruit, red meat, sodas, and food packed in heavy syrup—it's like ringing a dinner bell.
- Resist the urge to wave and swat should a stinging insect make frequent flybys through your personal space. Instead, use a gentle pushing or brushing motion to deter the incursion. Wasps, bees, hornets, and yellow jackets don't react kindly to quick movements.

What should you do if stung? Cool the area with a cold compress. If you were stung by a bee, scrape the stinger out with the edge of a knife (don't cut yourself) or your fingernail. The Sawyer Extractor works very nicely to suction the bee venom and stinger. Do not attempt to grab the stinger and pull it out—you will inject more venom into the skin by compressing the venom sack. If pain persists, add a topical ointment such as benzocaine to numb the site. An over-the-counter antihistamine (such as Benadryl) will alleviate some of the swelling and itch. If the allergic reaction goes beyond mild swelling or if there are numerous stings to the face and hands, seek medical attention quickly. A serious allergic reaction with massive swelling is life-threatening. First aid requires the use of an Epi Pen (epinephrine) to control the allergic reaction.

POISON OAK, IVY, AND SUMAC

"Leaves of three, let 'em be . . . berries white, then run from sight" is the mantra taught to campers and backwoods hikers all across the United States. Poison oak and ivy are not the most serious maladies one might encounter on a visit to the woods, but they are probably the number one reason people head to the doctor afterward. The itching can drive you crazy. The problem is the oily substance, called *urushiol,* that coats the plants. Get it on yourself and, if you are like nearly 85 percent of the population, you will break out in a bubbly, blistering rash. The best first aid is avoiding the stuff in the first place, but plowing through a batch of

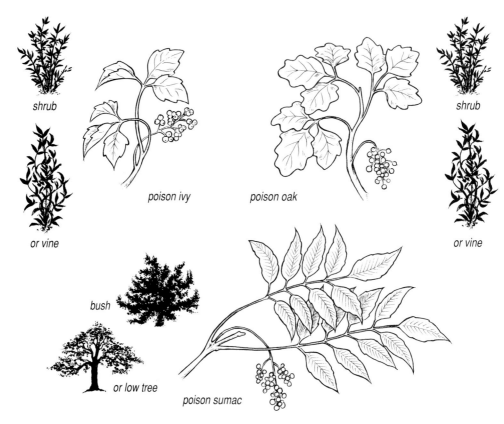

shrub

or vine

poison ivy

poison oak

shrub

or vine

bush

or low tree

poison sumac

Learn to identify these plants by sight—you are certain to run into one or more of them if you hike frequently. Don't touch, and you'll be fine.

the nasty leaf is sometimes unavoidable. If you know you have touched the plant, be sure to remove your clothes and wash them as soon as you get home. Wash yourself in cool water with a liquid soap called Tecnu, designed to remove the plant oils. In a pinch, wash yourself with a mixture of 1 gallon of cool water to several tablespoons of chlorine bleach. It's hell on your skin, but it does strip away the plant oils. If you develop a rash, a number of over-the-counter remedies offer relief. If the rash gets too much to handle, head to your doctor.

TICKED OFF

The very thought of walking through a valley infested with ticks makes most people's skin crawl. Perhaps it is because of the tick's predilection for attaching itself firmly to its host and then draining a seemingly prodigious quantity of blood from those dark and moist places we would rather not have something alien nibbling. Over the years, ticks and their disease-carrying capability have pushed our worry to illogical, near mythological proportions.

When in tick country . . .

- Wear long pants tucked into your socks and a long-sleeved shirt tucked securely into your pants and held with a belt.
- Wear light-colored clothing, which makes ticks easier to spot. A tight weave deters them from hanging on.
- Use the buddy system to perform tick checks regularly, especially in those dark, moist areas and crevices around the waistline, knees, breasts, armpits, ears, and crotch.
- Insect repellents containing DEET are far more effective than alternatives. Use percentages under 10 for children (see page 194).
- Apply a permethrin spray tick repellent, sold under the name Permanone, to clothing, tents, sleeping bags, and other surfaces—except the skin. It kills ticks (and mosquitoes) on contact, lasts up to 14 days, and won't wash off in water.

If you find a tick on yourself or a partner . . .

1. Get as close as possible to the tick's head and slowly pull the tick away from the skin without twisting or jerking. Sawyer's Tick Plier is recommended by experts because the user can slide the jaws beneath the body and extract the tick without squeezing or cutting it.
2. If it is too difficult to remove the tick by pulling, apply a safe pesticide such as permethrin (spray a cotton swab with Permanone) directly to the upper and lower surfaces of the tick. Wait 15 minutes and then try pulling out the tick again. Pesticides relax the tick, making it easier to remove.
3. Wash the bite area with soap and water.
4. Apply an antiseptic to the wound.
5. Try to identify the tick. If it is a lone star or deer tick, place it in a vial or plastic bag with a cotton swab of alcohol to preserve it for analysis if disease or infection sets in.

The two most common diseases in the West are Lyme disease and Rocky Mountain spotted fever. Rocky Mountain spotted fever occurs in all parts of the United States but is most common in the Appalachian region. Its symptoms are headache, fever, severe

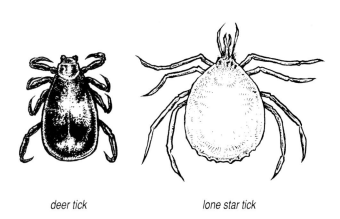

deer tick   lone star tick

Consummate bloodsuckers, ticks can carry debilitating diseases.

Taking the Cramps Out of Camp

- Do not share bandannas, toothbrushes, razors, water bottles, eating utensils, etc.
- Wash and air-dry all community kitchen gear.
- Keep anyone who is ill or appears to be ill out of the kitchen.
- Wash your hands before preparing meals and after you go to the bathroom— every time.
- Filter all drinking water using a chemical treatment or by boiling.

muscle ache, and a rash on the palms of the hands and the soles of the feet that spreads to other parts of the body. It must be treated with antibiotics.

Lyme disease has occurred in every state except Alaska and Hawaii. It causes fever, flu-like symptoms, a target-shaped rash at the point where the tick attached, and soreness and swelling, most significantly in the joints. It also must be treated with antibiotics.

BACKCOUNTRY HYGIENE

"Although wilderness visitors are placing more and more emphasis on concerns like the water-borne protozoan *Giardia lamblia,* they downplay their contact with other humans and other sources of disease in the outdoor environment," reminds Buck Tilton, coauthor of the book, *Camping Healthy: Hygiene for the Outdoors* (ICS Books).

"As increasing numbers of Homo sapiens show up more and more often in backcountry areas, the presence of humans, even if only for a short while, builds a community of disease possibilities," states Tilton.

One of the most obvious, but underappreciated, means of

staying healthy is to wash one's hands after bowel movements, before attending to wounds, and always before preparing and eating food. Roughly 25 to 40 percent of all food-borne illness can be traced to the hands.

For maximum clean, but not 100 percent bacteria removal, use water that is almost too hot to touch—100 to 120°F. Soap up and work the lather into your skin and under your nails for at least 30 seconds. Rinse thoroughly with hot water. Re-soap, re-rinse, and dry. Drying is one of the most overlooked and yet most important steps because washing alone will leave some bacteria suspended in the droplets of water clinging to your skin, enhancing the possibility of a chance migration from skin to food.

Of course, in the backcountry, hot water is a rare thing indeed, unless you pack copious volumes of fuel. For wilderness use when hot water is a luxury, Tilton recommends a germicidal soap, such as Betadine Scrub, Hibiclens, or Klenz-Blu Gel. Wash hands as described above.

"Sure, washing your hands so meticulously is a bother, but so is getting sick," says Tilton. "Remember most of all, however, that even plain old unscientific hand washing beats no hand washing at all."

GEARING UP A SURVIVAL KIT

Outdoor safety is an exercise in preparation: Know your limits, understand your environment, prepare the right equipment, and be knowledgeable. Knowledge and equipment must go hand in hand. It is useless to carry an arsenal of kits and gadgets but not know how to use them.

According to John Street, president of Woods Walker, Inc., in Florida, and an outdoor expert who has taught outdoor awareness and survival for 29 years, "Outdoorspeople need to understand that with today's equipment and the advanced techniques of search and rescue, most emergencies involve only hours and not days or weeks. With basic equipment and an understanding of how to use it, most situations should end up happily."

Most outdoorspeople don't know how to put together an emergency kit, however, and end up heading to the store or thumbing through a catalog to find "canned" survival kits (packaged in plastic or metal boxes). Are these "survival in a can" kits gimmicks or legitimate tools that might save a life if the need ever arose?

"The first thing an experienced outdoor professional would say is, 'I would hate to have to depend upon this,'" says Street, "but the other side of the issue takes into account the beginner. The purpose these kits serve is that they may be better than nothing, and with the proper education will serve as a springboard to help assemble a more complete and appropriate kit."

What do outdoorspeople need to consider when assembling their own kit? Patrick McHugh, vice president of MPI Outdoor Safety Products, advocates learning five outdoor survival skills (first aid, signaling, fire building, obtaining food/water, making shelter), understanding the seven enemies to personal safety (loneliness, fear, thirst, fatigue, pain, hunger, temperature), and determining which of the five basic weather conditions you might encounter (temperate climate, snow, ice, tropical climate, desert). McHugh asserts that anyone can put together an effective personal outdoor safety kit with nothing more than a rudimentary working knowledge of his "5-7-5 will help you stay alive" plan.

Street is quick to point out that even without adequate training, a little common sense goes a long way, provided the individual in trouble has followed a few universal preparation guidelines.

"Mother nature is not forgiving, she does not revise her plan because poor John Q Public is inadequately prepared. Smart outdoorspeople always carry some basic emergency equipment with them," says Street. "The essentials—knife, waterproof matches, fire-starting materials, map and compass, and whistle and/or signal mirror should always be in your pockets—not stashed away where they could be forgotten."

In addition to the items listed in "The Essentials" (pages 15–17), Street suggests that the following be assembled in a separate compact kit:

- Kit container—something that you can cook in that also compactly holds all the listed items
- Needle and thread

- Fishing kit with two types of line—mono and a heavier one—a variety of hook types and sizes, and an assortment of artificial lures
- Parachute cord or some type of rope (25–50 feet)
- Snare wire
- Wire saw
- Someone responsible who knows where you are going. You can't fit this in your kit, but make it part of your emergency plan!

Snare wire? Wire saw? Fishing kit? Yes, these items sound a bit extreme, and no, you're not likely ever to need them. Should you carry them anyway? That's a hard question to answer, because the line between dayhiking and adventuring is hard to define. We think you'll know when you've pushed the limits far enough to cross the line. Meanwhile, no matter where you set your limits, stay safe. It's a prerequisite for having fun.

KNOW YOUR LIMITS

Medical emergencies can happen anywhere but are particularly serious when they occur far from the roadhead. So the first rule for staying safe is to avoid taking unnecessary chances. Understand that chance is entirely relative to your own fitness and experience, and that *fitness* and *experience* are two different terms. For instance, if you've never been out of Dodge and are breaking in your first pair of hiking shoes, forget charging down a thirty-degree scree field just because you saw Homer do it. Homer is probably an experienced mountaineer with thousands of trail miles under his boots. Or maybe he's just a fool. Though normal dayhikes should never require technical work, you may wander onto precarious ground. In most national parks, lives are lost every year when hikers seeking a more challenging route hazard onto the steep and fall into the next world.

If you're young and fit, the tendency is to charge pell-mell into anything that looks exciting, to take the steeper, more treacher-

Bob Gaines, *Four Mile Trail, Yosemite National Park*

ous route when it presents itself. Nothing wrong with going for the gusto, provided you know the consequences; but these are difficult if not impossible to determine if you're new to the outdoors. So go easy until you understand the hazards.

The difference between experience and fitness is underscored by the large number of experts who are injured every year while hiking, scrambling, and climbing. The trouble is just this: People with years of outdoor experience but who are out of shape try to do the same things they did when they were in top form; then they blow out a knee or break an ankle. Granted, the majority of dayhikes do not feature log crossings and scrambling, and you can't very well hurt yourself strolling through a forest or across a desert that's flat as a billiard table. But once the terrain gets a little tricky, go only as hard as your body can easily handle.

That much said, people still get hurt in the backcountry. Being prepared is the key to limiting the consequences.

4

Desert Travel

In time, I learned to let my feet make the decisions,

and they were usually right.

—In Southern Light: Trekking through Brazil and Africa, *Alex Shoumatoff*

Chris Townsend

Desert comes from a Latin word, meaning

"abandoned," though the dictionary defines it as a dry, barren region that will support no man. But desert is a term of many tempers and magnitudes, from the vacancy of the middle Gobi to the bullet-proof weald ringing an Australian billabong. Excepting wastelands, which are smitten by sameness, most deserts are distinctive in a million eccentric ways. And yet there are constants: Where there is sand, grit, and gravel instead of soil, where the earth fans out into austere lines and magnificent distances, where the sun fills half the sky and the hot wind blows, we have desert. And wherever the water flows, if only barely, we have life.

We cannot compare life in the desert with life in the forest, in the mountains, along the coast, or anywhere else on earth, for only the desert contains such solitude. This solitude has always brought nourishment, wonder, and fear to those who have lived with it. Man looked out over the loneliest land ever to come out of God's hands, and awestruck, turned inward as naturally as the flowers on a saguaro cactus fold in on themselves in the morning light. Stunned by our own desertness, emptier than the landscape around us, our minds reached out for the unseen. That we could never grasp the desert's infinity has never kept us from trying, or more important, from believing that if not in this life, then in the next, infinity might be ours.

In antique times this ideal blossomed

in the desert and found expression in stone, which is time in mineral form: the pyramids of Khufu and Khafre; Ramses II's towering twin statues at Luxor; the massive and chiseled columns of Amon's temple at Karnak; and the Sphinx, who for nearly five thousand years has gazed upon the ocean of sand, heard the wisdom of Solomon, seen Jesus walk across the dunes, and who understands that a desert is the land not only of gods and mysteries, but of wasted beings crawling after mirages, of vultures circling overhead.

The desert will have your respect—or it will bleach your bones.

Since my earliest memory the desert has bewitched me. Perhaps it's because I was born in the basement of Southern California, in the blazing Coachella Valley. Then maybe it's because ancestors on my father's side were Comanche Indians, and a taste for heat and open spaces runs in my veins. More likely it's because, on most every winter weekend from my late teens through my twenties, I drove out to Joshua Tree National Monument, in the high desert, to go rock climbing. During that decade I acquired not so much a love as a need to be there, much as a person develops a craving for harsh liquors. And as with all things harsh, you take the desert on its own terms, or you live to regret it.

The desert has the power of the elements, will tolerate you at best and ruin you at worst. To the person whose water runs out far from the well, for the soul who stumbles under the midday sun with no hat, and for the sorry hiker in gym shorts and T-shirt, blasted by furnace winds—there is no help. But for every austerity, the desert has a dozen compensations. Most evident are its striking contrasts.

I remember one breathless May afternoon at Joshua Tree, when Jim Haley and I were kicking along the bottom of a scorched arroyo, our tongues nearly dragging in the gravel beneath our feet. The whole earth seemed to cry out for rain, and nothing could have seemed more unlikely. For half an hour we'd moped along looking for something interesting to climb on the outcrops that reared up out of the flat nothingness like huge walnut shells—tanned, cracked, and wrinkled by eons of sun and wind.

Presently the arroyo deepened and bottlenecked into a keyhole passage scarcely twenty feet across. All ideas about climbing were tanked as we searched for shade from the overhead sun, and found none. Even the steep sides of the bottleneck were on fire. We'd already chugged through our gallon canteen of water and could only hunker beneath a crippled yucca, panting like dogs. To the east, rags of clouds gathering above sad gray hills. The wind gusted. The clouds darkened and growled. We hadn't been beneath the yucca five minutes when a scalding thundershower drilled down. Water gushed down wrinkles in the crags, quickly swelling into waterfalls. Within minutes, the floor of the arroyo churned ankle-deep.

Up on the gray hills, brown sluices coursed down erosion fissures, collecting in the lower flanks, converging at the mouth of the arroyo, and, swollen by spontaneous side creeks pumping in from surrounding mesas, fashioned an angry river in the bottom of the gulch. Through the narrow breach in the keyhole we saw, perhaps a quarter mile distant, the flash flood uprooting century-old palm and Joshua trees and tracts of brambles, cacti, and anything else blocking its surge.

We lit off through shin-deep soup toward a low-angled outcrop as behind us the bottleneck choked with boulders and debris conveyed there by the river. The gathering flood spewed thirty-foot brown geysers through rifts in the jetsam dam grinding in the keyhole, the pressure so great that the trunks of huge palms were twisting like corkscrews and snapping with the concussion of cannon fire.

We groped onto a slanting stone bench, swirling and knee-deep streams of dark slosh pouring off stone awnings. We kept clawing up the streaming little crag until our hands were mottled with blood blisters and our ankles twisted and knees raw from barking the rock. But we'd scrambled to the top of the crag, commanding a view of the bottleneck and the dam of trees that finally let go, disgorging a seething muddy wave down the arroyo, sloshing far up the outcrops and grainy ramparts that contained it. The huge brown breaker tore around a corner and, just as suddenly, the swirling lagoon settled and sank as though someone had pulled a giant plug from the bottom of the arroyo. Water from the hills drained quickly and brought with it more trees and brush, which flowed straight into the bottleneck and clogged the slot, and the lagoon started backing up again. Jim, peering out through a mask of brown slop, yelled, "Hombre, that's as close as it gets."

Would the brown wave have charged with such gusto had Jim and I not been there? How did the land feel about sacrificing hundreds of elder trees, of having its hide scoured and scarred? Odd to consider such things, but that's the power of the desert, where the mood swings are violent and the contrasts beyond imagining.

Vegetation provides the sharpest contrast—literally. In spring, white daisies, yellow eriophyllum, purple namba, and desert dandelions shoot from the inhospitable dust in profusion. The barrel and hedgehog cactus bear blossoms fine as any garden, but these plants are no one's friend, and charm only at a distance. Most things in the desert sting, stab, stink, or stick. Much of the flora bristles with quills, ranging in treachery from the saber-tipped flutes of the yucca to the villainous prickly pear, whose paddle-shaped joints are peppered with wartlike yellow clusters of spines so silky that no modern tweezers are sufficiently fine to remove them from your skin. It's no more use trying to scratch them off than it is to try to keep from scratching. In a month they will fester their way out of your life. During the seasons I spent climbing and ranging around the high desert, maybe once a year someone with a little too much liquor on board would head out for a nighttime trek. A distant howl meant he or she had done the dance with a "barrel bummer" (barrel cactus) or an "oughttakillya" (ocotillo). A cautious traveler is not inevitable prey to every thorny thing in the desert, but spend enough time in the desert and you'll feel a barb or two as surely as the beachcomber feels the barnacles. Thorns are one of a thousand aspects of the sand that foster the heightened alertness the desert conjures in all who pass through it. And if the thorns don't persuade you, something else, often unforeseen, is bound to snap you awake.

During late-night filming in Arches National Park, just outside Moab, Utah,

Bob Gaines, Joshua Tree National Monument

several of us were wandering through the contours of an eerie canyon. The air had a tang of frost in it, and the silence was so deep I could hear the blood in my ears. Suddenly a snarl from far overhead. The air grew charged and the hair stood up on our arms. Then from nowhere, a sizzling shaft of yellow lightning drilled the earth barely a quarter mile to our left, the concussion blasting us off our feet and rupturing the eardrum of one cameraman. Nonetheless the same cameraman was back out there the following night, for night hiking in the desert is superb.

Everything exists in a sharpened state of calm and clarity. We see the coyote for the shifty scoundrel he is, advancing only when our backs are turned. The desert turtle plods along with its secret itinerary, while the diamondback rattler coils in the swelter. Rodents creep from holes, gnaw through your pack, and devour your victuals. Ants tote pebbles twice their size. And if you're lucky, someday you might see a bighorn sheep bounding over the rocks, its ripcorded muscles rippling with each thrust from its haunches. The bighorn is too autonomous to strike a pose. It is all concentrated essence that, like the land, carries no fat on its bones.

When the sun goes down the desert's majesty is felt low in your gut and high in your head. If the skyline holds a few wisps of high clouds, the sun will explode in a cataclysm of colors. Then through the pure air, constellations crowd the night

Five Paths to Hotness

Heat is a funny thing. Worshipped by some, it's cursed by others. One time it's a beach lover's fantasy, another it's a desert walker's nightmare. Ask bedouins about desert heat and you probably won't get much of an answer. For them heat is a fact of life, neither good nor bad. If you're a bedouin, heat just is, and you learn to adapt to it. Here are five ways people can get hot under the collar, and suggestions to help you adapt to the heat of the moment, wherever that might be:

- *Air Temperature:* As the air approaches and exceeds body temperature, it will act like a conventional oven, cooking you slowly. There's not much you can do about it other than seek pockets of cooler air in sheltered nooks among the rocks, in caves, or near water.
- *Conduction:* Anyone who has walked barefoot knows that on a sunny day the ground can be like a hot stove—much hotter than the air. Anything directly exposed to the sun absorbs its radiated heat, regardless of air temperature. To cool down, avoid ground that's been exposed to the sun for a long time, or dig underneath the surface.
- *Radiation:* When the sun shines directly onto your skin, it is actively heating you up, no matter the air temperature—it's like standing in a microwave oven. Just step into the shade or wear a broad-brimmed hat and loose-fitting, light-colored clothing to stay cooler. In the high Andes you can broil in the sun or shiver in shade just inches away.
- *Convection:* A breeze normally cools you because it evaporates your sweat more quickly. If the wind is strong enough, however, it can turn a basic scorcher into a blast furnace, dramatically accelerating moisture loss. Clothing can help reduce the effects of wind.
- *Metabolism:* As your body functions, it generates heat as a by-product. The more work you make your body do, the more heat it puts forth. Want to cool down? Slow down! It's worse if the outside temperature is hotter than you are used to. Go easy until your body acclimatizes—about one week or so.

sky, so brazen we could reach out and snatch a handful of diamonds if only our arms were a little longer. The moon stuns the eyes, and when its light grasps the profile of a Joshua tree, arms crooked into gestures of torment, the terrain becomes fearful and we sleep. And sleep in the desert is deep as your mind.

Tiring of such sights and experiences is like tiring of air or water—impossibilities, since these are requirements. But needs are a matter of degree, and it's a fascinating study to know those who require the desert as the rest of us need money.

I recall one freeze-dried codger who for years we'd see kicking around the most forsaken tracks of sage. As usual, we'd be scouting for something to climb. God only knew—or cared—what "The Ten-Thousand-Year-Old Man" was looking for. That's what we called him and that's what he answered to, for his face was rucked and seamed as the floor of the Dead Sea. People said he ate only the sweet knobs of the candy cactus. He was thin as a broomstraw, and beneath his leathern skin we could see the working of his bones. He always wore a small pack, said to be full of ingots, but we never knew for sure since he'd only mumble a clipped reply to our greetings, then shuffle on.

This creature was a metaphor for all

Water-Related Facts

Just because you are dripping in sweat doesn't mean you are okay. When you are coated in sweat, your body is not being effectively cooled by evaporation and you become susceptible to overheating.

- How long can you survive without water? According to Dr. William Forgey, author of *Wilderness Medicine:* At 120°F, you will live 2 days; at 90°F, you can expect to live 5 to 7 days; and at 60°F, 8 to 10 days.
- Cut out caffeine (tough for caffeine heads used to hanging out in coffee bars sipping lattes) and alcohol. Both are diuretics that remove valuable water from your system.
- Allergies or not, don't take antihistamines, which can block the

nerves that stimulate sweating. If you don't sweat, your body is unable to cool itself, and that can lead to overheating and collapse—even if you are drinking plenty of water.

- Peek at your pee. That's right. The backcountry is not the place to be bashful. Check the color of your urine regularly, and note the frequency of nature's calling. If your body is producing relatively clear urine five times a day, your fluid intake is fine. Cloudy or dark urine and an urge to purge fewer than five times per day mean you need more fluid.
- Experts suggest that on average, a hiker will consume approximately 2 gallons of water per day when the temperature sits around 100°F—

and up to 3½ gallons as the mercury climbs.

- In an emergency, when all looks hopeless, you can create enough water to stay alive with only a clear plastic bag and a few leaves. Chances are you have a clear, plastic baggie (the larger the better) in your pack. Place a handful of crushed or cut leaves into the bag, then blow into it to fill it with air, and then seal it using the zip-top closure, twist tie, or string. Place the bag on an incline in direct sunlight with the vegetation uphill. Moisture will evaporate from the leaves and condense on the bag. You won't generate enough water to quench a raging thirst, but in a pinch it will keep you alive.

the desert rats in the world, and he seemed as integral to the landscape as a thread-plant or a scorpion. Few of his kind are ever born there. They come for one reason or another, or maybe none at all. Though they all have plans to leave, none of them ever does. In every desert, distances can trick you; so can the passage of time. You go for a day and stay a week. Though time stands still as a monzonite butte, a week—or a lifetime—flashes past quick as a jackrabbit.

My Uncle Leonard left a Blackfoot reservation in his late teens, stopped over in Indio, California (where I was born), and never left. For thirty years he grew grapes on one hundred blistering acres of Coachella desert, and his features settled into the semblance of those tawny sands. He looked and smelled like the desert. Even his voice carried the low whisper of a desert breeze. When he died, they scat-tered his ashes over the sand that had styled him. Anything else was an unthink-able sacrilege.

For all its harshness, the desert refuses no guest. The booming thunder of winter storms and the delicate song of spring winds do not discriminate between King Tut and the horned toad, and you only need listen and move your feet to discover that the tune is sufficient. The desert is not for everyone. Some find its trappings too severe, its silence inhuman, and its climates bleak. But for others, the desert is a place of seductions.

The question for most first-time desert rats is—What do I *do* once I'm there? Many desert travelers discover their expe-rience is rarely lessened, and often enlarged, by doing little or nothing at all. That is, the classic agenda of most hik-ers—starting at A, slogging to B, and

Seeking Out Water

Finding water in the jungle is relatively easy—just wring out your shirt for starters. But in the desert, when mile after mile of sand and rock stretches in a shimmering sea before your eyes, the search for water can become somewhat tenuous. Here are a few ways to "divine" water from the earth:

- Reflections can mean a mirage, or they can mean a possible water source. Evaluate the distance to be traveled and then head toward the potential water only if you are reasonably sure that it actually *is* water and you will be able to travel that far.
- Dry streambeds are possible sources of water. Just below the surface, you can sometimes find damp soil and even water, which will pool in an excavated hole. Don't waste your time, however, if the hole you're dig-ging looks unpromising. Move on and try elsewhere.
- Any sign of wildlife, especially birds sitting in a tree, may mean nearby water, as all ani-mals require a water source. A word of caution if your water-ing hole happens to be on the African savanna: You could be viewed as just another com-petitor for a limited resource. In Rudyard Kipling's books the water hole was a place of truce among animals, but don't assume a lioness has read the same books you have.
- If you see a storm coming, find catchment basins or lay out a tarp to trap as much rain as possible. Fill every available water-holding device as quickly as you can, for the shower might be brief.
- Sometimes you'll find small pockets of dew in the wee hours of morning. Lap up as much as you can.

Don't Drink the Water

Yes, you must treat your water in the desert because even here, *Giardia* raises its ugly mug. If the water you are eyeing is full of silt, which is the case with most desert streams, ponds, and rivers, you won't want to drink too much without first letting the silt settle—a must anyway if you plan to filter your water (see also pages 90–92).

Ingesting large quantities of silt with your water can lead to a bad case of the squirts (projectile diarrhea every bit as unpleasant as it sounds)—something just about every participant in the 1995 Eco-Challenge Adventure Race across the high desert of Utah suffered from. The high mineral content of the water coupled with the copious quantities of iodine tablets we dropped into the water to ensure purity threw our digestive systems into disharmony. Having the squirts in the desert is not only unpleasant, it's dangerous because your body loses fluid at an alarming rate but you don't want to eat or drink. Only by consuming pure, filtered water over a 24-hour period and flushing out our systems did we recover.

Of course, you can't just filter the water, either, because the silt will clog just about any filter within minutes. The solution? Carry a collapsible plastic or nylon bucket that you can use to scoop up a gallon or so of heavily silted water. Let the silt settle to the bottom— this takes about 30 minutes—and then carefully filter the top 3 quarts, being certain not to stir up the silt or pump any of the sediment through the filter cartridge.

Don't Forage

Think you can survive by eating cactus and nuts in the desert? Forget it, says Dave Ganci, desert survival expert and author of *The Basic Essentials of Desert Survival*. According to Ganci, there are too many variables contributing to edibility—what part of the plant is edible, how much you can eat before it becomes toxic, and at what time of the year it is edible—to make "grazing" even thinkable. He recalls lecturing students in his Arizona Outdoor Institute while mindlessly popping jojoba nuts into his mouth; he ended up vomiting suddenly in front of his class. A perfect illustration, he says, of the dangers of foraging in the desert.

Dress for Success

No matter where you encounter heat—jungle, desert, or mass transit—you'll be most comfortable if you dress in loose-fitting garments made of lightweight, natural fibers that allow air to circulate while body moisture evaporates (see also pages 61–62). In dry areas, when drinking water is in short supply, you're better off with long clothes that cover your arms and legs, thus protecting you from direct exposure to the elements and keeping a zone of light humidity (from perspiration) next to your skin. Keep in mind that the lighter the clothing's color, the more sun is reflected and the cooler you will be—black is the color of death, literally. Carry warm clothing if you plan to hike into the night. Nighttime temperatures in the desert, except possibly in summer, can get downright frosty. Since the desert terrain is filled with loose and unstable footing and sharp, spiny objects, supportive and well-made footwear, such as that found in a quality approach shoe, is a plus.

Add a cotton hat to top off your ensemble and shade your noggin from the sun's heating rays.

returning to A by whatever route—is of less relevance in the desert than it is, say, in the mountains. Most popular desert areas have attractions worth seeing: old mines, ruins, petroglyphs, overlooks, natural bridges, gulches, even cactus gardens. But setting out on an ambitious cross-country trek often gives fewer rewards than slowly wandering around, scouting for turtles, making garlands from wild-flowers, relishing the skyscape, perhaps eventually gaining a hot springs or the abandoned shack of an old hermit. Handcuff yourself to a rigid itinerary and miss the magic of simply being there, for the desert is as much a state of mind as anything else. Shuffle the backdrop for the sake of the eye, but the desert mood derives from an atmosphere that exceeds individual features.

COPING WITH THE HEAT

Temperatures and conditions vary dramatically in given areas, and as always, conditions determine what gear is appropriate. For summer swelter, loose-fitting, light-colored clothing will reflect the heat. Cotton absorbs sweat from your skin, and will cool you as it evaporates. As a kid I remember thumbing through old *National Geographic*s featuring stories on bedouins and other desert folk, always wondering why in such blinding heat they were so covered up by muslin

robes and scarves and turbans that I could barely see their eyes. Leave it to those who live there to have figured out the best way. The bedouins wear loose, breathable garments, first, to produce the aforementioned cooling effect and, second, to avoid direct sunlight. Desert UV rays are intense, and can fry you alive when the temperatures are hot or cold. Lather exposed skin with sweat-proof sunscreen. And always wear a hat—the wider the brim, the better. Desert glare is manageable with sunglasses, which most travelers consider required equipment. Stiff-soled boots belong in the desert like arrowheads belong on the moon. Of all the Indians who ever lived in the desert, none wore anything on their feet more substantial than moccasins. A lug-soled approach shoe is adequate for virtually all desert terrain.

Dehydration and heat prostration are the principal villains in all hot climates, particularly in arid deserts. It is virtually

Night Hiking in the Desert

One of my favorite times to hike in the desert is at sunset and then on into the night, especially when the moon is full. Night hiking is not without hazards, however. Scorpions and rattlesnakes are most active during the nocturnal hours, giving the hiker good reason to pause before placing hands, feet, or seat anywhere the eyes cannot clearly see. Too, the possibility of walking into cactus is increased with the lengthening of shadows and reduction of visibility.

impossible to drink too much water, and easy not to drink enough. Again, a conscious effort to keep your belly full of liquids is required. The credo says: If you wait till you're thirsty, you've waited way too long. Drink ample water, sweat buckets, and stay cool. Dunk your head in any available clean pool or river, and soak that bandanna as well. Everyone responds differently to heat, and if you're not accustomed to it, discover your limitations slowly. There is a three-hour window of intensity at midday, when the sun is at or near its zenith; in summer heat, it's best to avoid too much activity or direct sunlight during this stretch.

During cool months, layer clothes as needed, remembering that the sun can torch your skin just as grievously at thirty degrees Fahrenheit as when it's one hundred in the shade. Winter months usually bring wind, and the untreated face is subject to wicked windburns and chaffing. Lip balm and, again, sunscreen

Desert Travel Tips

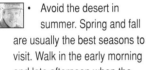

- Avoid the desert in summer. Spring and fall are usually the best seasons to visit. Walk in the early morning and late afternoon when the sun is not as intense as at midday. Hit the trail early, then take a long siesta in a shady place until the temperatures drop.
- Know the water conditions and where you might be able to find water. Don't count on finding it, however; a spring that is listed as running and of good quality may have dried up since the last field check. Carry 2 to 3 gallons of water per person per day, more if you anticipate a completely dry trail.
- Keep a weather eye skyward. Thunderstorms in the distance may mean flash flooding in a canyon through which you intended to hike. If there are thunderclouds anywhere nearby, stay out of washes and gullies!
- Biting insects can be bothersome. Carry a good insect repellent of 30 percent DEET (use products with less than 10 percent DEET on kids).
- The sun is usually intense. Wear a hat with a visor and light, loose, long-sleeved shirts and long pants. Sunscreen all skin, exposed and unexposed. Remember to reapply sunscreen periodically, especially to bare legs after a stream crossing.
- Okay, so it may look altogether funky, but if you are more concerned with staying cool than with looking cool, consider the British desert explorers who traveled the hot sands of the world under a "brolly" or umbrella. There's a lot to be said for always walking in the shade.
- Carry a multitool (such as by Leatherman or Sog) with you at all times. Should you suffer the misfortune of direct contact with a yucca plant or other desert cactus and have to resort to a bit of "spine plucking," you'll be grateful for the gripping and pulling power of a needlenose pliers.
- Hydration systems that rely on one large bladder of water stored inside a pack or other portable container are all the rage these days, and I must admit, they are convenient. Most have a drinking nozzle so that all you have to do is walk and sip, sip and walk. There is one minor risk with such a system, however, that could turn into a full-blown nightmare— what if the container develops a leak? While I do rely on a bladder system myself, I back it up with two or more "hard" bottles, such as the wide-mouth 1-quart Nalgene variety. If I do spring a leak, I at least have reserves to keep me alive while I work my way out of the pinch.

Shanks Mare
on the Pony Express Trail

September 2, 1994, found 53-year-old Joe Nardone safely in San Francisco following a 2,000-mile journey along the Pony Express trail, much of it crossing high desert, that began 153 days earlier on April 3. Nardone walked the entire route to draw attention to the trail and prove that despite what many historians assert, the trail really ended in San Francisco, not Sacramento. The first person ever to walk the entire trail, a journey that required around 4.5 billion footsteps and caused 15 blisters, Nardone found time to put up monuments to the Pony Express at six station sites and give 28 lectures. What will Nardone do next? Sit down and complete a wall map and book on the Pony Express trail, of course.

are essential in avoiding a "ten-thousand-year-old face."

Food is a problem for several reasons. In rugged heat, many people lose their appetite. Understand that to keep cool, you must sweat, and your metabolism works overtime to do so. This requires calories, without which you may worsen any queasiness from the heat or from insufficient fluid intake. The question is: What foods go down easy—or at all—in dire heat, and at the same time don't spoil in an hour? Tastes differ, but many find that food with either a lot of liquid (fruit) or no liquid at all (dried fruit) work best. Experiment to discover what most agrees with your taste and system, but you can pretty much rule out heavy meats and breads for daytime con-

Staying on Course

Navigating in the desert can be challenging, especially in the deserts of the American Southwest. In the flats, vegetation can obscure what few distant landmarks there are. Where there are dunes, the sand can undulate forever, making sighting and maintaining a course next to impossible. Most challenging of all, however, are the hidden canyons and deep washes (arroyos) that can impede your progress along a route you thought would be easy cruising. It is not uncommon to hike 10 to 20 miles out of your way around an impassable canyon.

Before you head out from your car or base camp, heed the following suggestions:

- Seek out landmarks that stand out vividly from the surrounding landscape.
- Most deserts are crisscrossed by an often confusing network of "roads"—more vehicle tracks than developed routes. When following one of these tracks, many of which appear on detailed land maps and many of which don't, take careful stock of every turn, intersection, fork, and direction change. Your observations may prove the only way to determine where you have gotten to—signs don't exist in most cases.
- Distances are deceptive! The distinct landmark that seems so near may be 30 miles distant. In the dry desert air, everything appears much closer than it is. The rule of thumb for estimating distance and time of travel is to multiply your most conservative estimate by three.
- Since features and man-made objects change so often in the harsh environment of the desert, trust only the most recently updated topographic maps.
- Before you head out, inquire with the local land management agency about the best routes of travel and the current land, road, trail, water, and weather conditions.

sumption. And avoid condiments (like mayo) that quickly go rank in the heat. You might have to cajole yourself into eating when the urge is not there, just as you must drink water when you're not thirsty. In temperatures above eighty degrees or so, most everything spoils in a matter of hours. Most desert day trips start and finish at a vehicle, where an ice chest is a valuable commodity for both grub and fluids.

INSECTS AND OTHER DENIZENS OF THE DESERT

Bugs vary in cruelty from place to place and season to season. Deerflies, mosquitoes, chiggers, and fulsome ants (to mention a few) are rife in many deserts. Diverse insect sprays, balms, and potions are commonly used, though even the best cannot keep a determined bug from behaving shamelessly. The best defense is to cover up with loose-fitting clothes, thus offering insects diminished access to dining.

Attack from rattlers, scorpions, and other perfidious fauna are rare, but unwanted nonetheless. Since humans first stepped into shoes, standard practice in the desert is, before gearing up, to shake all empty shoes and check all open pockets for anything that might have found lodging there.

Rattlers usually give fair warning via their tails, though it is possible to surprise them when scrambling over rocks, as they will often sun themselves in light, open spaces that reflect or conduct heat. Stay alert and lessen the slim chance of surprising a serpent. One time at Granite Mountain, just outside Amboy, California, I pulled over a rounded ledge and came face to face with a rattler. I don't know who was more alarmed—me, who damned near jumped off the cliffside, or him, who shook his tail like castanets. I retreated for a moment and the rattler slithered into a crack.

Keeping a Wild Eye

If you want to view wildlife on your desert jaunt, plan your trek for after the sun begins to set. The majority of desert animals confine their movements to the cool desert night. When the sun is beating down, the desert appears lifeless because most creatures are tucked in the shade of vegetation and rocks or burrowed under the sand's surface, where even a few inches down the temperature can be as much as 15 degrees cooler. Keep a sharp eye out for animals that may stray underfoot as you wander at night . . . stepping on the tail of a kangaroo rat won't generate much more than a mild adrenaline rush (for you and the rat), but treading on any part of a rattler is another matter. If you want to see wildlife, find a quiet point overlooking an oasis and then settle in for a wild night of nocturnal observation. A strong, lightweight flashlight with a red lens is a must for nocturnal viewing—red because it won't scare off wildlife or destroy your night vision as a white beam would. If you want to be treated to a spectacular show and see the "eyes" of a tarantula or scorpion glowing back at you, you absolutely need a portable black light, which is fairly expensive.

Good-quality binoculars let you view distant geological structures, as well as identify smaller birds flitting among vegetation, and observe, without disturbing, the fascinating behavior of other desert inhabitants. I carry a small hand lens with a magnification power of 10 so I can admire the patterns inside small flowers and the world that exists between tiny grains of sand (see also pages 140–141).

Trail Food: Making Fruit Leather

 Although drying fruit and other foods works much better if you own a dehydrator, an ordinary oven will serve as a makeshift dehydrator, capable of churning out dried trail foods adequately enough. When I am trekking in the desert, I love to nibble on a good fruit leather: it tastes great, won't spoil, and doesn't sap the water supply by making you feel far thirstier than you should—stay away from jerky.

To make fruit leather, coat a large cookie sheet with vegetable spray or grease lightly with vegetable oil and preset the oven to 140°F. (Use an internal oven thermometer if your oven has only a "warm" setting for this temperature.) Puree fresh fruit (I am partial to peach, apricot, nectarine, and/or apple) in a blender until smooth—no lumps, wayward seeds, or other items to spoil the consistency. If the fruit puree is not sweet enough, add white corn syrup to taste; if you prefer a natural sweetener, add honey instead. Do not use sugar—it will make the leather grainy and brittle. Add a few drops of lemon juice to enhance the flavor. Pour the puree onto the greased cookie sheet so that the mixture is an even ¼ inch thick, and place the cookie sheet in the oven. Using a pot lid or something nonflammable, prop open the oven door about 6 inches so moisture will escape from the drying puree. The fruit leather is dried to the correct consistency when it is pliable, but not sticky. (Cooking times will vary depending on moisture content of fruit.) Gently peel it off the cookie sheet to form one large roll. Cut the giant roll into 4- to 5-inch-long sections. Seal each section in plastic wrap and keep it cool until you are ready to hit the trail. Yummy!

DESERT NAVIGATION

The majority of deserts feature open, arid spaces that most travelers avoid. Desert destinations generally gain regard by dint of interesting topography, like the fantastic natural bridges in Arches National Park or the labyrinthine slot canyons throughout Colorado Plateau country. As always, the more convoluted the terrain, the greater route-finding skills are required to stay "found." Virtually all heavily traveled routes are either well marked or rendered self-evident by the passing of many boots. Less traveled but fashionable junkets, like the tangled canyons in Zion, Utah, are anything but straightforward, however, and the novice is wise to seek a guide rather than risk getting lost—a dire proposition in any desert, where exposure and lack of provisions can kill you in a matter of days, sometimes less. And in slot canyons, say, it's possible for so-called experts to get lost. I know, because I did.

Richard Teague and I were fresh off Longs Peak, in Rocky Mountain National Park, and we detoured through canyon country on our return to California. We figured there was small adventure in probing one of the known slots, and instead headed into one completely unexplored (so far as the guidebook said), marking our way with little chalk arrows—the standard method for spelunkers—drawn on the vertical flanks of the narrow, twining slot. For those unfamiliar with slots, they typically consist of circuitous passages (at times so slender you must turn sideways, exhale, and squeeze through) between sheer rock walls sometimes rearing hundreds of feet. Anyway, we hadn't been in the slot an hour when it started to rain, and our critical chalk arrows were no more. Richard—who had a stubborn flip in his hair that spelled trouble—was certain he could retrace our way, but only managed to get us hopelessly lost. In brief, we wandered around for hours till we finally found a wide crack on one of the walls and managed, barely, to climb out onto a ridge and scramble to open ground. I mention this not to daunt the casual desert traveler, who would no more head into an unknown slot than marry her uncle, but rather to underscore the fact that most frequented desert areas feature more than dune walking. On the other hand, it is almost impossible to stray on common excursions. And if these don't do the job, consider kicking back in the sand and watching dust devils whir across the horizon and up into the pale sky.

5

Mountain Walking

Yesterday, after dragging my weary bones to a mountain slope,

where nature achieves such a magnificent effect with the simplest

props, white rock, red fields of Alpine roses, a patch of snow, a

waterfall, and lots of green, I hardly knew myself.

—Freud the Man and the Cause, *Ronald Clark (quoting Sigmund Freud)*

Bob Gaines

"Designed and executed in fury," wrote

Englishman John Dennis in 1688, gazing on the tortured crags and precipices of the French Alps. Poet William Wordsworth, admiring a painting of the identical range, thought it a testament to the "Creator's faculty and grace." Other observers have, in so many words, called the mountains the beginning and the end of all natural scenery, a legacy in ice and stone to our insignificance, and an emblem to the glory of existence. Tagore maintained that mountains were the earth's gesture of despair for the unreachable. On a mundane level, I'm certain Sir Edmund Hillary felt otherwise when he and Tenzing Norgay clawed to the summit of Everest.

Basic geography aside, when mountains suggest such different things to different people, who is to say what the spirit of the peaks is all about? Every hiker with a pair of lug-soled boots, it would seem, for this question has been asked and partially answered since the first person climbed the first mountain ages ago. While the whole business may puzzle us, the mountains are not confused. The peak remains oblivious to our labels. All designations reflect the fears and dreams that *we* pack there with us, opinions that are typically challenged by the mountains themselves.

In an article I read, a native of Mississippi compared the swelter in his high school classroom to the inside of a kiln. From this hot seat, deep in level Mississippi, the author's "mystic obsession" for cold peaks aroused in him a regard for snow and mountains much like that of natives who worship volcanoes in the adventure/horror flicks on late-night cable. He compared his romantic concept of mountain life with that of nineteenth-century English poets, who obsessed about the mountains while ambling up and down hills in the Lake District. He writes:

"It was everything the Swiss farmers hated about the mountains (and they did) that made them irresistible to those of us who grew up in ordered, predictable flatlands, be it Mississippi in the late '50s, or England in the early 1800s."

The author left Mississippi for college in Colorado. At a freshman retreat, he finagled a svelte Denver girl into ditching the volleyball game to march up a nearby 13,000-foot peak. Altitude sickness gripped him at the first switchback and he saw his romantic ideal done to death in a fit of vomiting. The girl excused herself, joined two matrons, both in their seventies, and hiked to the summit. Mississippi never looked so good. Within a year, the same author found his alpine legs, and has lived in the mountains ever since.

We may love the mountains, and must for a time—or always—live among them for life to make sense to us. This may seem extravagant to the offhand mountain walker, but it's dogma to the moun-

taineer; and it's instructive to glance at the attitudes that spring from mountain climbing, because those who spend their life and passion in a given area possess insights denied the rest of us.

Every climber who has spent adequate time "on the steep" has mixed emotions. Climb enough and the mountains become one's identity, sustaining goals and giving direction to youthful energy, a condition that can grow into mania. Then an avalanche might carry away a couple of friends, or perhaps a rockfall bashes a partner into the next world, and the mountaineer is sickened that his chosen domain could show such indifference to its champions.

The mountain hiker will probably face none of these scenarios, but they point up a standing rule with all mountain travel: The bigger, steeper, colder, and more remote a mountain range is, the harsher a mentor it will be. Every mountain range throws down a gauntlet, daring the willful to challenge its heights—be it forging straight up an ice-shrouded face or slogging along a trail up the backside. And as mentioned earlier, there is often a backdoor trail that leads to the top of the mightiest alpine mountain. Here, the line between climber and hiker becomes fluid, for the summit is the same no matter how you attain it.

Ranges vary, and the wise mountaineer matches competence with realistic objectives. Mountain travel is qualitatively different from all other modes of wilderness travel. In fact, the hiker is not exempt from encountering on the most pedestrian trail at least some of the hardships that face the climber. Most people find that, given a suitable trail, favorable conditions, and challenging but not withering exertion, mountain walking is a balm. But there are significant differences between hiking *near* the mountains and hiking *in* the mountains—namely, elevation and terrain.

By global standards, most so-called mountains in the continental United States are trifling. But you still might feel as though you're sucking down half the sky with each breath as you plod up that draw, a point that was driven home to me during college, when I worked weekends as a climbing instructor at Tahquitz and Suicide rocks, just above the mountain hamlet of Idyllwild, in Southern California. The town rests at about 5,000 feet, and the summit of Tahquitz tops out at nearly 9,000. When rock climbing caught on in the late seventies, scores of people, young and fit,

A Cold Hike through Hell

High magazine, the official publication of the British Mountaineering Council, dubbed the Chilkoot Trail in northwest Canada the "Worst Trail This Side of Hell." Recommended by *High* as a "challenging trip," the Chilkoot received this somewhat dubious honor for its deep snow, ice, −40°F temperatures, blizzards, avalanches, and treacherous terrain. Once the traditional trail for those seeking gold in the north country and made famous by Jack London, the Chilkoot no longer annually claims thousands of lives as it once did. Still, it's no mere walk in the park.

streamed up to Idyllwild to try climbing. Classes started on Saturday morning, and students usually got going at dawn and

A Deadly Pace

Perhaps you've heard the phrase "He hiked us to death." While the implication is usually figurative, it is possible to die of hypothermia just because you don't know how to walk—especially when trekking among the throne rooms of the mountain gods. The key to healthy hiking is choosing a mountaineer's pace—a slow, methodical, inexorable, and relatively rhythmical step—that can be maintained all day long without sweating. When taking a break, and you should do so for 5 to 10 minutes each hour, seek out sunny and wind-protected locations. Put on extra insulation and sit on a foam pad, not directly on cold ground, which can suck the heat and life right out of you.

Timing Is Everything

The best time to cross a mountain stream is early in the morning. The flow is lowest then because the snowpack doesn't melt as fast at night as during the day. Keep in mind, however, that if you must return the way you came, the same stream that flowed tamely in the morning may be a roaring torrent of snowmelt in the afternoon. The best place to cross, no matter what time of day, is at the widest part of the stream. Look for a section that has flattened out, usually around a large bend. Look also for a gravel bottom rather than slippery rocks for your crossing site. Remember to unfasten your pack's waist belt and sternum strap so you can easily jettison it if you falter. A trekking pole or ski pole is indispensable for any deep-water stream crossing—a third point of balance offers a tripod effect that is stable even in a very swift current. Angle it up- or downstream, whichever feels more secure.

drove up from sea level to join the group. Once we began the sheer, half-hour trudge up to the crags, more than one triathlete or crack runner upchucked a solid shaft of quiche and orange juice onto my boots—not for lack of fitness but from exertion and the sudden change in altitude. The birds chirped and the trees nearly touched the clouds, but the romance was *gone*.

Acclimatizing to altitude—anything over 5,000 feet can be considered altitude—hinges on factors other than base fitness. I've seen fat, chain-smoking duf-fers whistling at 12,000 feet, and I've seen professional basketball players get light-headed at 5,000 feet. Full-blown mountain sickness—flu-like symptoms with a splitting headache—is bad news, so ease into the mountains, particularly if you're driving up from low altitudes and immediately hitting the trail.

Most people are not bothered by altitudes below 7,500 feet; it is the strenuous nature of some mountain hiking that tends to be a more common problem. But there are infinite opportunities for a day-

A Rocky Experience

Hike in the mountains long enough and you will end up crossing a boulder field (talus slope) or two. Never walk across the middle of a talus slope—there is no way of telling whether the next rock you step on will trigger a rock slide, sending you on a downward journey that would ruin your day. Step carefully; each boulder within a boulder field is often delicately balanced, even if the boulders are the size of small houses. Cross a talus slope only on a diagonal route and only one person at a time. If a boulder begins to move, keep moving forward to get out of harm's way as quickly as possible.

Chris Townsend

Take short steps and keep your weight over your feet when descending talus slopes.

hiker to roam in the vicinity of mountains, in alpine surroundings. And this is what most people consider mountain walking—trekking through the shadows of the big peaks in the High Sierra, Sequoia, Tetons, Wind River Range, and so forth. It is a different proposition once you start tackling mountainous terrain, which need not be technical to sap you. Let's first look at alpine walking.

Altitude Sickness

Altitude sickness doesn't discriminate—it can affect anyone regardless of age, sex, or physical condition. In fact, some of the best and most well-conditioned athletes suffer altitude sickness. Altitude sickness can occur despite a history of not being susceptible. Edmund Hillary, world-renowned mountaineer, experienced altitude sickness years after he had summited Everest. Hiking too high too fast appears to be a major cause. Altitude sickness occurs most commonly at elevations above 8,000 feet but can set in beginning at 6,000 feet. Dehydration and overexertion are major contributing factors.

The following are precautions that minimize the likelihood of becoming altitude sick:

- Climb high and sleep low is one tried-and-true technique employed by mountaineers, but this is not practical when your cabin or campground is at 8,000 feet and you are hiking at 9,000 feet.
- Keep your ascent moderate by not climbing more than 1,000 feet per day above 7,500 feet.
- Jumping into the car at sea level and leaping out at 9,000 feet to hike hard will blow any acclimatization plan clean out of the water and open the door for altitude sickness. Dr. Paul Auerbach of Stanford University hospital suggests spending some time with your feet up in a cabin or campground before heading up or down any trails. If that means adding a day to your weekend in the name of health, so be it.
- Dehydration is a causative and a worsening factor, so stay well hydrated. You should urinate frequently and your urine should be clear or light colored. Avoid coffee and tea; both are diuretics that cause fluid loss. Liquor is not only a diuretic, it also clouds judgment, and the symptoms of a hangover mimic those of altitude sickness, confusing diagnosis.
- Acetazolamide (Diamox) is a prescription drug that appears to enhance a person's ability to acclimate to altitude. It also reduces the effects of altitude sickness. Like any drug, it has side effects; seek the advice of your physician before using it. It is a sulfa derivative, so persons allergic to sulfa drugs should not take it; it is also a mild diuretic, so regular fluid intake is essential. Medical experts recommend a dose of 62.5 or double that, 125 mg, twice per day just prior to ascent to altitude and continuing for a day after the highest altitude has been reached.

How do you know if you have altitude sickness? An early-morning headache that doesn't go away is one fairly sure sign. Low energy, insomnia, shortness of breath, nausea, and loss of appetite are all symptoms, either alone or in combination, of altitude sickness. Descending and reducing your level of activity are the standard remedies once you feel altitude sick. Do not push it! While mild symptoms are more a nuisance than a health threat, they are a definite warning to acclimatize.

Altitude sickness can progress to moderate and then severe, resulting in hospitalization or even death in extreme cases. Confusion, vomiting, difficulty walking a straight line, and severe shortness of breath are signs of impending severe altitude sickness. The victim should immediately descend to a lower altitude and receive oxygen treatments as quickly as possible.

ALPINE WALKING

Loosely defined, alpine walking involves following trails set in the mountains. Though draws and passes are standard fare, most alpine tours follow valleys or work along the flanks of mountains. This is frequently spectacular going, an odyssey that can appease our irritations and transport us. So many things happen in a person's life, and we forget much more than we remember. But who forgets their first time in the mountains?

Perhaps it's a blinding strip of blue between two storm clouds, or a dwarf pine, its crooked roots gripping the naked rock like eagle's claws, that first grabs you; but once your eyes are opened, you're drawn along by unseen hands.

A wild colt may become a sober horse, but when you're young, and need to roam, the mountains are especially brilliant. As years pass and your vista broadens, so goes your wonder. I remember, at age nine, when I first saw Half Dome, veiled in ancient shade, its massive cleft face streaked with black lines said to be the tears of the Indian maiden Tis-sa-ack, who mourned the loss of her lover before hurling herself off the summit. And I remember walking in the mile-long shadow of Mount

(text continues on page 130)

Wired Up or Wireless?

The wilderness as we used to know it will never be the same . . . technology has seen to that. With a flick of a lighter we can cook up a space-age meal on a gas stove and then tuck ourselves into the relative security of a nylon shell stretched over an ultralight aluminum frame. We wander across snow on futuristic materials and climb rock and ice with lifelines of synthetic fibers and manufactured metal alloys. It is of little consequence that we're adding phones, global positioning system (GPS) units, watches that tell direction and altitude, radios, portable satellite dishes, and even portable hyperbaric chambers to the list— these are just more examples of technology designed to assist.

Draped in a security blanket created by technological advancement, the wilderness becomes less a foe and more a friend. With the press of a button on a GPS, users can find out instantly where they are on a map. A toy in good weather conditions perhaps, but what about the group of skiers who found themselves lost in a snowstorm near Aspen, Colorado, a few years ago? Had they carried a GPS unit, they would have quickly determined where they were in the whiteout and found the nearby cabin, eliminating the need for the massive rescue effort that was launched to save their lives.

Mountaineers on Denali and other worldly peaks routinely stay in touch with their base camp for directions, weather updates, and, in case of emergency, potentially life-saving rescue. Is there a real difference between the highly technical climbing gear mountaineers use and the electronic features of a GPS unit, a radio, or a satellite dish?

Some will argue against electronic devices on the grounds that the wilderness should remain free from the "intrusion" of mechanical devices, yet what would you call a stove or a compass or even a backpack manufactured from special layups and foam-injection technology?

Tim Casey, a real estate agent and wilderness lover from Breckenridge, Colorado, carries a cellular phone with him on backcountry trips and mountain bike excursions as a safety precaution— no different than carrying a first aid kit or a simpler signaling device. Casey still carries all the requisite safety gear and repair supplies with him and points out that the phone stays off unless he really has to use it. He wishes he'd had the phone a

Bob Gaines, Zion National Park

number of years ago when he partially collapsed a lung in a nasty biking accident. An arduous and potentially life-threatening self-rescue followed, which would have been eased by a phone.

Some backcountry physicians use cellular phones to stay in touch with hospital staff and rescue personnel, saving time and lives. Rescue rangers can stay in touch with victims to calm them and can often eliminate a costly search. GPS units have also saved time in finding lost hikers or gear in the wilds.

Like any tool, electronic devices can be used irresponsibly. The climbers who, while clinging to a rock face, called Dave Baker, owner of the Summit Hut in Tucson, Arizona, just to find out how to get back onto a climbing route Baker had put up are a perfect example.

But then, so is the yahoo who starts a forest fire with a high-tech stove or the beginning climber who uses fancy climbing gear to ascend to a point of no-return from which he or she must be rescued.

It comes down to choice and

responsibility: Use the tools technology offers as an appropriate form of preparedness and self-reliance and a suitable addition to your arsenal of well-established backwoods skills (see also page 167).

Chris Townsend

A global positioning satellite receiver.

Fastpacking

Fastpacking, in all its blossoming glory is, according to runner Jim Knight, "kind of like backpacking (or hiking), but much faster. More fluid. Neat. Almost surgical. Get in. Get out." Call it wilderness running or backcountry power walking, but whatever you do, don't call it boring! Fastpacking is, as more and more trail runners-cum-backpackers are discovering, visually fresh, mentally stimulating, and an excellent way to see a lot of beautiful country in a relatively short time—something mountain bikers have been crooning about for years.

Not too long ago, the Loma Prieta, California, chapter of the Sierra Club unofficially endorsed the sport as one of the most environmentally responsible ways to travel through the mountains. Why? Because fastpackers move lightly, quickly, and efficiently, thereby minimizing trail and campsite impacts. The attraction of fastpacking lies in the opportunity to access remote areas in less time with not more than 15 to 20 pounds on your back. In fact, experienced and well-conditioned fastpackers travel between 20 and 35 miles each day—oftentimes much more.

Fastpacking appears to be growing as a direct result of an increased interest in trail running, which, by all indications, is experiencing a relative boomlet of its own.

At least two surveys I know of suggest that trail running and fastpacking have a potentially strong future and may be stepping beyond the elitist and cult moniker some have placed on their participants. A 1994 *Backpacker* magazine reader survey suggests that 35 percent of their 200,000 subscribers consider themselves runners, and the NPD Group Inc., a customer and syndicated research group, reported that 82 percent of all backpackers consider themselves runners.

I can attest to the thrill of clipping off large chunks of real estate in short order. I enjoyed a 30-mile exploration of the Ohlone Wilderness Trail in early May 1995 while the wildflowers were in peak bloom. Friends and I—all backpackers, not serious runners—ran, walked, and jogged the route in just under seven hours—still smiling and looking ahead to the next adventure.

Still, fastpacking has its limitations. The longer the trip without the possibility of resupply, the more food weight is added to your pack, making it harder to run, jog, and/or power-walk with pleasure. Experts recommend you carry not more than 10 percent of your body weight when fastpacking.

Easy resupply and scenic beauty have made the 211-mile-long John Muir Trail in California especially attractive to both initiate and experienced fastpackers. When traveling from north to south, beginning in Yosemite, there are a number of campground or mini-store/restaurant resupply points at designated intervals, minimizing the food and fuel that has to be carried. The 8-to-10-day journey crosses ever higher passes and culminates in an exhilarating finish high atop Mount Whitney, at 14,494 feet the tallest peak in the continental United States.

There is a saying I've heard from a number of sources and no one seems to know whom to credit, but the philosophy is sound and seems to be the creed of the fastpacker: "to bring less is to have more." Perhaps we should all take a closer look.

EQUIPMENT CHECKLIST

Dana Miller of Ultimate Direction carried the following items on a two-day, 100-mile trans-Uinta adventure run in 1990. Weight is as crucial as bulk—don't carry more than 20 pounds or 10 percent of your body weight in your pack.

Toiletries

Toothpaste
Toothbrush
Dental floss
Washcloth/bandanna
Sunscreen
Lip balm
Toilet paper
Ibuprofen

Sleeping Gear

Flashlight/headlight
Sleeping bag
Ground cloth/poncho
Closed-cell foam pad
Rain fly shelter/tarp
Parachute cord

Clothing

1 pair of Lycra tights
1 pair of running shorts
1 pair of Capilene bottoms
Capilene top
long-sleeved shirt
short-sleeved shirt
2 pairs of socks
Sweatband/headband
Wool gloves
Running shoes

Food

2 freeze-dried dinners
2 packages of noodle soup
6 packages of instant hot cereal
6 packages of hot cocoa mix
Drink additive (such as Exceed,
   CytoMax)
Trail mix
10 energy bars

Miscellaneous

Camera/film
Emergency radio
Propane/butane backpacking
   stove and fuel
Pocketknife
Spoon
Water filter
Pot and lid
Matches/lighter
Blister kit
First aid kit
Topo maps
Compass
Lightweight, narrow-profile pack
   with built-in hydration system
   (such as Ultimate Direction's
   Escape pack)

Kenny Souza churns up a San Francisco Bay–area hill—the Avia Scramble.

Thor, in the Canadian arctic, wondering if Eskimos a thousand years before had looked up at the monolith and felt the power of stone ten million years old.

On the other hand, I remember tromping twenty miles into Sequoia to climb a big rock face called Angel's Wing. We camped in Bear Paw Meadow, and thought nothing of the name till that night, when a band of black bears razed the camp, demolished our packs, and filched our grub. That meant a forty-mile trudge to get resupplied, and by the time we'd returned a storm had moved in and we were done for. It is said that a big range can create its own weather. True enough. Violent storms can move in fast and close down an area for days. Sometimes the bugs are so vile you fear insanity. And just after cresting what you're certain is the last rise, you see in the distance a dozen more, most of them worse than those you've left behind. The trail sign says seven miles, but it feels like fifty. You'll ask yourself what the hell you're doing there, and you probably won't know till you get back home and stare at the walls, wondering why the thrill is gone.

The mountains present too many variables to know what will happen, and that, I think, is the beauty of the thing. On the other hand, preparation is that much more crucial. You can control which boots and clothes you wear, what you eat, and where you go, but you can't control the weather or the chance that you may sprain your ankle in a chuckhole, or the fact that Fatima said the trail was layer cake and it feels like the Bataan Death March. You should expect these things, because you'll most likely experience at least some of them.

The mountains are possibly the most popular venue for dayhikers, and there's hardly an accessible range anywhere in the United States that is not crisscrossed with trails. Popular routes within national and state parks are commonly

Trail Food: The Taste of Jerky

A specially designed dehydrator dries jerky and other foods best, but an ordinary oven can turn out tasty trail foods adequately enough. Homemade beef or turkey jerky is superior in quality and flavor to most commercial brands and it's easy to make. I wonder why more hikers don't make their own.

My favorite cut of meat for jerky is flank steak. Figure on 3 pounds of meat for approximately 1 pound of jerky. Before you begin slicing, firm up the meat in the freezer—slicing will be more even.

First remove any excess fat, then slice the meat across the grain to a thickness of between $\frac{1}{8}$ and $\frac{1}{4}$ inch. Marinate the sliced meat overnight in a tightly sealed container in the refrigerator. I prefer teriyaki marinade, which you can make easily enough by combining 1 cup of soy sauce, $\frac{1}{2}$ cup of dark brown sugar, 2 teaspoons of ginger, 4 to 6 cloves of crushed garlic, and $\frac{1}{2}$ teaspoon of freshly ground black pepper.

Preheat your oven to 140°F. You'll need an internal oven thermometer if your oven doesn't have a 140°F setting—the ideal temperature for drying meat. Coat your oven racks with nonstick vegetable spray and then spread the strips of meat across the racks. Be sure to place a sheet of aluminum foil at the bottom of the oven to catch the drippings. Prop open the oven door about 6 inches with a pot lid or something else nonflammable so that the moisture can escape from the drying meat. Your jerky should be ready—dry, but not brittle—in approximately 8 hours.

maintained by rangers who keep the paths clear of debris. Such trails are normally well marked and so well trod you'd have to be drunk to lose your way. Established trails are featured on topographic maps, or larger-scale maps available at park headquarters. Less frequented trails are sometimes not indicated on maps, and if not maintained, sections may be impassable due to fallen trees, rainouts, rock slides, etc. (more on this later).

If you're new to the mountains, consider joining a local outing club. Virtually every backpacking/outdoor store offers such excursions, usually led by someone fluent in alpine ways. If this tactic is impossible or undesired, and you must forge out on your own, no problem. Simply go with well-established paths for your first few efforts. There's no big mystery to walking in the mountains, but there's no sense in committing to a grueler till you know if you like the work. Each area has favorite dayhikes that are engineered either to cover choice ground or to reach an enchanting destination, such as a spectacular overlook or the rim of a cordillera. Go during the weekend and almost certainly you'll share the common path with others. Head out during the week and have it all to yourself.

Because popular alpine trails are often in good repair, it is routine to cover considerable distance despite steep stretches up switchbacks followed by leg-pumping descents—common barriers in the mountains. Generally, you cover many more miles during an alpine hike than when hiking in the woodlands, desert, and other areas. For this reason it's essential that your gear is squared away, especially your boots. The farther from the trailhead, the longer you'll have to deal with any changes in weather. In other areas you can often get by with no specialized gear at all, faking it with whatever you have. Plenty of people do the same in the mountains, they just suffer

You've Got to Be Kidding!

The Appalachian Trail has had its share of crazy individuals stepping a lively beat down its path, but perhaps none so "out there" as one Robie Hensley. He chose to ignore the traditional approach trail to the summit of Springer Mountain, Georgia, the southern terminus of the AT, and parachute onto the peak. Hensley promptly shed his chute and began hiking. According to the Appalachian Trail Club, Hensley is also the only known AT hiker (and perhaps any trail hiker) to have pizza delivered, by helicopter, while backpacking—makes you wonder if it was delivered in 30 minutes or less, doesn't it?

more when it rains and they have only a sweatshirt and a two-dollar poncho. A few layers of high-tech clothes and a good rain jacket are boons in the mountains. But nothing matters as much as what you have on your feet.

Fit is 90 percent of a good boot, especially in the mountains, when you're covering serious miles. Many people find that an approach shoe is sufficient—provided the area is dry. Just as many prefer the support of a lightweight hiking boot. You have to be crazy and ignorant to favor a serious mountaineering boot for alpine walking. They're too heavy and too stiff, and the rowdy lug soles chew up the trail. Whatever boot you choose, make sure it's broken in and comfortable before heading out for the Long March.

Mountain air alone is enough to fashion a robust appetite, but the chief factor is exertion. You walk half the day and you're hungry enough to eat naugahyde. Snack at regular intervals. I suppose it's possible to pack excessive grub, but all the days I've spent on the trail, whatever food anyone brought along always got eaten.

Trusting stream water is a judgment call. It's ludicrous to say all streams are polluted, especially once you put some miles between yourself and the roadhead. But if you're there, someone else is likely to be there as well—or has been recently. And if that someone was crass enough to defecate or urinate in the stream, or if an animal did likewise, you'll pay horribly if the waste gets into your system. Scientific tests of popular areas have shown that many streams, even remote ones, have some degree of pollution. Play it safe and pack your own water.

MOUNTAINOUS TREKKING

Mountainous trekking begins when you encounter steeper terrain than that found on switchbacks, or when the trail ends and you head cross-country. Scree and moraine fields, rock slabs, and boulder fields are common obstacles. Proper climbing is not and should never be considered an option for the dayhiker.

Dress for Success

For summer mountain hiking, I usually wear shorts and pack a pair of lightweight wind/rain pants just in case. Loose-fitting, sturdy nylon shorts have always been my preferred trail duds, particularly those that have nylon underwear stitched right in. Loose nylon doesn't bind or get clammy like cotton or canvas, and for dayhikes that's important. My favorite short and long pants are Ex Officio's Amphi Short and Amphi Pant, respectively. I prefer a loose-fitting long-sleeved shirt so I can roll down the sleeves for added sun protection. The Baja Plus Shirt by Ex Officio is soft, comfortable, loose, well ventilated, and dries quickly. If you anticipate hiking through muck, loose dirt, gravel, water, snow, and other debris that always seems to find its way into your boot, try ankle-high gaiters. Certainly not a fashion statement, but if your feet are happy, who cares? Weather changes are a given in the mountains, so pack along a warm sweater and a rain parka with a generous hood. I carry a wool cap (a beret, actually), wool mittens, and an extra pair of long underwear—just in case. On several occasions, I overestimated my traveling speed and underestimated the difficulty of the terrain, and was forced to spend a night under the stars—made comfortable only by the extra clothing I religiously pack.

Hiking is done on your feet. Climbing requires both hands *and* feet. The inviolate rule is: Never tackle any sustained piece of terrain that requires your hands for support. Grabbing a root or branch is common practice for brief stretches, but never commit to something requiring continued arm power to see you through, whether it's hand-walking up vines to scale a gulch or grappling up naked rock. Many people are killed every year when they scramble onto technical terrain. The majority of accidents don't result from the scrambling/climbing itself; they happen when the passage dead-ends and you must try to reverse your way. Climbing down is invariably harder than climbing up, so avoid terrain that you cannot easily descend *without using your hands*. If there's any doubt, back off. On terrain as low-angled as thirty degrees, once you start tumbling it's nearly impossible to stop—and if and when you can, bones will probably be showing. The issues are gravity and terrain.

Climbers always avoid poor-quality rock, and never—unless forced into it— hazard onto grainy, vegetated slopes stacked with teetering blocks. And this is precisely the kind of cliffs where most "climbing" accidents occur (i.e., hikers scrambling onto dangerous heights). Take a climbing course before tackling anything requiring your hands for upward movement. More than a century of trial and error has gone into refining the safety system for technical climbing, and experts are killed every year even when the system is properly used. If you are unfamiliar with technical climbing but still clamber onto the steep with no safety system—your days are numbered. If you want to go climbing, take that course. Enough said.

There are countless shades of difficulty between hammering up the face of El Capitan and ambling along an alpine path as flat as a sidewalk. We limit the spectrum by staying with the no-hands policy. What is left? Plenty . . .

A common practice is to work up the lower flanks of mountains or rocks to get at the base. Oftentimes this involves negotiating rock slabs or scree and boulder fields. The key is vigilance. Watch where you step and where you're going. Common dangers on rock slabs are loose blocks, gravel, moisture, and slime, any of which can send you tumbling. If the slab is relatively smooth, usually there are boulders lying about. Don't let their size fool you into thinking they are solidly placed. The slightest pressure can set ten-ton blocks in motion, and once they get moving the destruction is awesome. A good policy on slabs is not to hike in single file; rather, spread out laterally—if only slightly—so if

someone dislodges a rock or stump or whatever, there's no one directly below.

Another hazard is gravel and slime on otherwise hard rock. On even gently angled rock, a veneer of grit or patch of muck can send you sprawling. Watch your step. Wet rock doesn't compromise your footing much, provided the angle is low and your boots are flexible. But add a little dirt and slime and you're suddenly on a greased treadmill. And remember, it's always easier going up than coming down.

Broken terrain—especially with intermittent sections of dirt, hummocks, gravel, scree, and rock—should be negotiated with caution. Treading over mush and grass that grows over hard dirt or rock is like walking on ballbearings. And if you go ass over teakettle on a slick surface, you'll probably slide a ways before stopping.

Chris Townsend

A trail switchbacks up a steep mountainside.

After a few outings you develop an instinct for where to tread and what to avoid, so take it slow until you develop the knack.

Avoid steep dirt of any kind—even brief sections. Plants don't help much. They'll often come out in your hands if you're foolish or desperate enough to try to hang on. Remember: No hands. Dirt footholds should not be trusted to support your weight, because they won't.

Scree fields, commonly found on the banks of steep hills, consist of a thick covering of loose gravel and rocks, rarely larger than footballs. Working up them is murderous—one step up and two steps back. But plowing down them (scree-skiing) can be sensational. And dangerous. Take it easy till you learn the little balance tricks that make the practice doable.

A last consideration is stream crossings. Trails are rarely designed to go through a stream, but sudden storms and a host of other factors can make a stream crossing desirable if not essential.

The first rule is never to try to cross a flowing stream with a rope lashed round your waist. If the current is strong, it will pull you under, and the person on the other end of the rope will not be able to pull you out again. This happened to friends of mine who had just climbed the Leaning Tower in Yosemite. Seeking a shortcut after spending two blistering days on the climb, they decided to ford the stream that feeds Bridalveil Falls. In short, my friend roped up, waded in, went under, and drowned. I never understood why the person holding the rope didn't release it when things got desperate. Perhaps it all happened too fast. Either way, this episode confirms that crossing a river while tied to a rope can be lethal.

Another common mistake is to take off your boots and cross in bare feet, hoping to keep your boots dry. Obviously, a slow-moving, shallow little creek with a sandy bottom is easy work. Anything else requires boots. Bracing against the current puts great pressure on your feet, and if the river bottom is rocky or jagged, as it often is, bare feet are no good. Just what you can and cannot cross is a judgment call. If you have doubts, hike along the river and look for calmer water, and turn back if you can't find any.

Last, always unclip the waist strap on your pack before trying to cross a river. If you go under and you can't ditch your load, you've got that much more between you and the air above (see also page 181).

6

Woodlands/ Forest

A good walk requires . . . endurance, plain clothes, old shoes, an eye for nature, good humor, vast curiosity, good speech, good silence, and nothing too much.

—*Ralph Waldo Emerson*

Michael Hodgson

In the mythology of many nations, the

forest is the Mother, and the life cycle of trees—from seed to seedling to full glory to dead-standing—is presented as a metaphor of life. As mulch nourishes the trees, the green shade and silences in the woody corridors restore us. When the pilgrims lived in the forest, they called it the poor man's overcoat. Many rich people have since discovered something fine there, a mood or feeling that took them back to when they too were on speaking terms with wood and wind. If trees are the earth's endless effort to speak with the stars, as Rilke maintained, it must be true that trees can talk to us. What do they say? Nothing in words. And the message comes home at a level too simple ever to be known secondhand. A couple of hours in a forest is usually enough for anyone to appreciate its grace, and to understand the notion that those who plant trees love others besides themselves. Who planted the forest? It's a foolish question only to those who would benefit most from a couple of days wandering through the trees.

To enter a forest is to begin a personal journey as rich in memories as the musk of ripe cedar. The first smell of great trees is enough to transport me back to my uncle's pine hunting shed in Idaho, where I passed several summers during my early teens. Free as a hawk I would roam, idly as I pleased. Hiking along the timberline, it seemed the entire place belonged to me and me to it, that immense tract of forest

my own private Arcadia. Often it was quiet. Only the sound of the wind. Always the wind.

The hours passed quickly. The summer flashed by in a moment. Everything seemed so curious and new. From the hut, a narrow glade ran to the top of a butte overlook whose brink plunged two thousand feet to a lower valley. The vista—boundless sky and a luxuriant green carpet formed by the treetops far below—seemed a billion years old. Miles in the distance ran a great river. The wind roared over and off the butte and carried with it the frank scent of bark and leaves. A snow-covered mountain, far on the horizon, glinted blue. Many days I spent there with my uncle's dog, a mongrel shepherd named Horny, who loved to ravage perfumed lapdogs. Horny and I would wander out to the shack to be alone. I would go and dangle my legs off the brink of the overlook and coax Horny near the lip, but he'd only bark and fret and paw the rock, far back from the edge. I'd laugh and stand up and look around, feeling like God. What was there to it? A lone wolf baying a valley away, a pinecone falling to the ground? The sound of water on the rocks? Yes, that more than anything. The butte was dark and streaked and wet with water running over it, trickling and dripping in summer or fall and always with the same little sound. That sound was part of the great vista and part of the feeling of the place. I used to wonder about

When You Can't See the Forest for the Trees

When navigating by map and compass, keeping on the right course depends a lot on your being able to sight off distinctive landmarks and then keep them in view. When nature blocks your view with a few thousand trees that all look relatively the same, what's the solution? If you are hiking with a partner, send that person ahead, keeping him or her in sight and on course using hand signals. Your partner should stop just before disappearing from view and serve as a "human landmark," a point of reference for you to hike directly to. Use this technique until you reach a point from which you can again identify the natural landmark you originally took a bearing from. If you don't have a hiking partner, sight off trees and other recognizable landmarks at intervals of 100 yards or less, using the same leapfrog method mentioned above. (See "Basic Navigation," page 74, for more detail.)

Knife Sharpening 101

Numerous guidebooks, articles, and how-to instruction manuals address the importance of knives as tools for outdoorspeople, yet few address knife sharpening. A knife blade grows dull and less efficient with use, so you should have a sharpening tool such as a simple Arkansas Stone or ceramic sharpener, or better yet, a sharpening system like the ones mentioned below.

Contrary to myth, the angle of a blade's cutting edge has nothing to do with sharpness—large- and smaller-angled cutting edges are equally sharp. The angle at which you sharpen a blade and consequently the angle the cutting edge is ground to, affects the durability and drag of the cutting edge. In other words, the smaller the angle, the less the drag but the more delicate the cutting edge. A larger angle means more blade drag but more durability, and thus less frequent sharpening.

Knife experts recommend the following sharpening angles:

- *11 to 15 degrees:* X-Acto blades, woodcarving tools, and specialty blades. Frequent sharpening will be required for this highly delicate edge.
- *15 to 17 degrees:* Intended for fillet, boning, and other thin specialty blades. Frequent sharpening will be required.
- *17 to 20 degrees:* Common angle selected for kitchen knives.
- *20 to 25 degrees:* Wider bevel

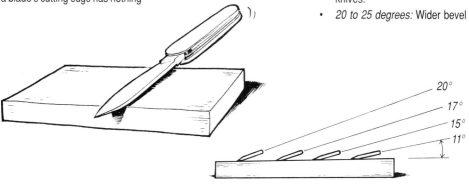

Which angle you choose for sharpening your blade has a lot to do with how delicate the edge is and how frequently you will need to resharpen it.

the endless little song of water dripping and falling, with nobody to hear it and nobody to wonder about it but me. Yet when I was gone it kept dripping, always dripping. My youth, the water's little song—it seemed they always had been and neither could ever change.

Sometimes after a downpour, a rainbow would arc above the butte overlook, or a peregrine falcon would loft on the updraft above the lip, just beyond Horny's yelping jaws. And once a great shard of rock calved away from the butte and

rushed down through the forest below, leaving a trail of stumps and dust. Horny turned his nose to the wind and sniffed the flinty smell of pulverized granite, barking at what he could not see. Then I yelled and my echo cracked down over the valley and kept cracking forever. Why the echo? I asked Horny, who sniffed the ground and dashed after a wildcat.

I was spellbound by the solitude, the rush of darkness, the pale moon, and the memory of the hulking black bear Horny and I once ran into. Horny had chased a

and more durable edge intended for pocketknives, folding hunting knives, fixed-blade field knives, and serrated knife blades. Durable and long-lasting cutting edge.

- *25 to 30 degrees:* widest bevel and longest-lasting edge. Intended only for heavy-duty use such as with utility knives for cutting cardboard, carpet, wire, or linoleum.

Is it possible to maintain an exact angle with just a sharpening stone? Yes, but only with lots of practice. A far better solution is to outfit yourself with a knife-sharpening system. With a specially engineered clamp and angle guide, anyone, even a youngster, can sharpen a knife blade to a desired angle. Gatco and Lansky Sharpeners are two of a number of companies offering specialty knife-sharpening systems, ranging from $19 to $50.

On stones intended for hand sharpening, oil or water will keep metal shavings and bits of stone in suspension so they don't clog the sharpening stone and affect its honing efficiency. On power sharpeners, water is used to cool the stone so that the knife's blade does not overheat and become damaged.

When is a sharpening stone all used up? A stone should be flat for effective sharpening. Over time, the grinding process will wear a noticeable belly or curvature in the stone. You can tune your stones from time to time by rubbing them back and forth on 100-grit silicone carbide sandpaper placed on an absolutely flat surface. If, after performing stone first aid, you still notice a curvature, it's time to toss the stone and buy a new one.

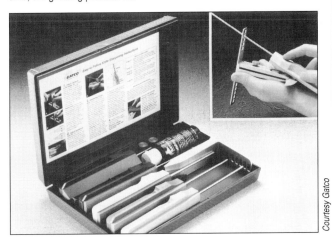

Courtesy Gatco

A good knife-sharpening system takes the work out of knife care.

whirlwind into a box canyon choked with cottonwoods and flushing aspens. I followed through the leaf storm and into a clearing—and straight into the bear, who reared up on its haunches and roared through its slavering muzzle. Its head was big as a stop sign. Then Horny went and bit the bear square on the balls and we set off at speed, winding through the close weald. The raging bear stampeded over the slender aspens and we escaped only by

climbing a big boulder that the great bear could not scale—though he tried, his fearsome claws raking off great clumps of lichen and moss on the sheer rock. For many hours, well into the cold night, the bear roared and circled the boulder, and by about midnight we had to start jogging in place to keep from freezing. When at last we made it back to the shed, I lit the kerosene lantern and fed every stick of kindling into the potbellied stove. Finally

Choosing Good Binoculars

 Binoculars are an important addition to the equipment list for any outdoor adventure if you want to see more than the toes of your boots. They bring the distant world close, allowing you to visually leapfrog up a mountain, capture the intricate detail of a hawk's feathers overhead, or scan the surface of a lake—all without taking a step.

A natural metamorphosis from the early telescopes fashioned in the 1600s, today's binoculars offer increased magnification power, wider view, and improved brightness. Choosing the right binoculars, however, can be confusing—there are hundreds of models, ranging from $10 cereal-box sport glasses to $700 (or more) autofocus binoculars that have the latest in microchip technology.

Before you shop, do some homework. Make a list of your needs. Will you use your binoculars primarily for viewing wildlife, sports, stars, or a combination thereof? Will you use them in normal lighting or the shadows of late evening or

deep forest? Will they be routinely exposed to elements, or relatively protected? Is durability a factor?

How much are you willing to spend? If you know you'll use your binoculars once or twice a year, you can probably make due with a lower-priced model. Don't settle for the cheapest pair you can find, however. You will regret it. Generally, the higher the price the better the optical quality and the more durable the housing—to a point. Beyond $250 to $300, you probably won't notice a difference.

Once you have established relatively firm shopping criteria, head to the store. It is helpful when comparing various models and manufacturers to focus on a few basic specifications.

Power, or *magnification,* determines how much an object is enlarged. With 7 x 35 binoculars, the object is magnified seven times; it appears seven times closer than it is. You will find some binoculars with a 10x magnification, but unless you plan to use a

tripod, stay away from these models. Movement causes degradation of the image that offsets any gain in magnification.

Objective size is the diameter of the front, or objective, lenses. The objective lens of 7 x 35 binoculars measures 35 millimeters across. Larger objective lenses allow more light through and are better in low-light settings.

The *exit pupil* is a measurement of the amount of light that reaches the eye. The larger the exit pupil, the more light is transmitted. The exit pupil of 7 x 35 binoculars is 5 mm (35 divided by 7; always divide the higher number by the lower number). A 3 to 5 mm exit pupil is generally adequate for normal viewing. An exit pupil of 7 mm is best for low-light use.

Field of view is the width of the area you can see through the binoculars at 1,000 yards. The field of view for 7x binoculars is typically 7 degrees, or 369 feet. This information is always printed on the instruction sheet, if not on

thawed, I stoked one of my uncle's Havana cigars, stretched out on the elk hide, and listened to the dead-soughing of the trees. "What do you think?" I asked Horny, who shook out his long stout body, rattled his collar, and yawned. "Answer me, dummy," I begged, smacking him. "Answer me." Horny pawed the floor and barked louder and louder still and I kept yelling "Answer me," our laughing and barking the only sounds in the dark forest.

And I'd fallen asleep just as I lay, fully clothed, and did not wake till the birds came calling. Looking out the open door I could see the distant blue mountain, and I lay there for a while longer, Horny and I, deep into Idaho.

Now, twenty years later, the sight of the forest draws me back to that pine shed, to the wonder of drifting through the tall grove. The magic of the memory isn't so much in the sudden smell of sap or the view

the binoculars. A pair of binoculars with a 9-degree or higher field of view is a *wide-field* model. A wider field of view is helpful for observing wildlife.

Prisms are the little gizmos that bend the light entering the binoculars, allowing you to see an upright image with increased magnification and brightness. *Porro prism* binoculars are somewhat bulky and heavy but offer accurate depth of field. *Roof prisms* have less accurate depth of field but are lighter, more compact, and therefore more expensive than porro prism models.

Focusing is either fixed, center, or individual. Fixed is convenient but loses in overall image quality and versatility. Center focusing adjusts both eyepieces at once and is usually the preferred option. Individual focusing is a pain!

Finally, opt for a waterproof housing (be aware that it won't handle prolonged submersion) if you anticipate using your binoculars in dusty or moist environments. Lens coatings help with contrast, light reflection, and color saturation—multicoated is best—but are no substitute for an adequate exit-pupil rating.

TLC TIPS

- Never touch binocular lenses with your fingers. Instead, remove grit and grime with a few puffs of a blower brush (available in most photo stores) and then brush away any remaining particles. Remove haze and fingerprints by gently wiping with a lens tissue dampened with a drop of lens cleaner.
- Don't leave your binocs in the hot sun, the trunk of your car, or where heat may warp the casing.
- Store your binoculars in a padded nylon or leather case. Add a packet of silica gel to help absorb any moisture.
- Clean the exterior of your binoculars only with a lint-free cotton cloth or a silicon impregnated cloth. Some manufacturers supply these with your purchase.

USAGE CHART

- Binoculars fill virtually any indoor and outdoor need, from opera to football to wilderness exploration. However, no binocular will meet every need. The following list recommends applications for a sampling of magnification powers.
- 6 x 30: stadium sports, indoor sports, theater, bird watching at a home feeder
7 x 25: hiking, bike touring, nature observation, stadium sports
7 x 35: general purpose, bird watching, boating, stadium sports, wildlife observation
7 x 50: general purpose, stargazing, boating, hunting, bird watching
8 x 40: wildlife observation, stargazing, long-distance bird watching

from the high outcrop. Rather, the memory of an unfettered life that would never end, magical and totally my own. That's what the forest has always affirmed in me—promised me, really. And every time I go back it makes good on the promise.

There are many kinds of forests, and trying to say what they are "like" is as slippery as attempting to describe your spouse. The forest is a place of great contrasts, of profound tranquillity and ear-shattering racket. One time in Borneo, Jim

The Bear Truths and Other Wildlife Tips

Snuffle, snuffle, slurp is a nocturnal sound that when heard outside your tent flap means one of two things—either your camping partner has developed a case of the sniffles while trying to gorge secretly on your highly prized personal stash of sweets, or *Ursus americanus* is rototilling its way through your pack in search of anything remotely edible.

Before going hiking or camping, you will want to know which animals frequent the area you intend to trek in. From kangaroo rats to bears, animals are an inquisitive lot that are likely to take advantage of every opportunity for free food. A kangaroo rat gnawing through a pack to reach some nuts inside is not an immediate threat to nearby humans, but the damage to the pack could create real problems.

A bear, on the other hand, rummaging through camp and smelling food in or around a tent will be very surprised when it encounters humans as well as chocolate or fish. The surprise and resulting screaming and growling can, and has, led to unfortunate consequences, and in a conflict between bears and unarmed humans, bears usually cause the

most damage. This is not to say that bears should invoke panic whenever they are nearby, just that they should be respected and that proper precautions should be taken to protect them and us.

The first step in avoiding unpleasant encounters is to bearproof yourself. Hang all food well away from camp; leave no food

Chris Townsend

Bear bagging is one way to prevent bears from ruining your hike by devouring your food and raiding your camp.

Bridwell and I were camped between the flutes of a towering ramin tree, in the middle of ancient rain forest. We were just knocking off when we heard the crack of forked lightning, followed by the sound of a three-hundred-foot tree falling, snapping the girthy limbs of neighboring trees and finally, the WHUMP! of the giant slamming into the ground. The earth shook and we bolted from our berth faster than Lazarus bolted from his cave. Weeks passed as we worked our way through

in packs; and never take food or clothing that smells of food into your tent. If you keep your camp clean, you should not experience any serious bear problems. A bear may still attempt to wander through just because you are on its selected route for the evening. If a bear should approach you in camp, yell, wave your arms, bang pots—anything to alert the bear to your presence, which should encourage it to retreat. If it chooses not to retreat (and this technique is the one to use if you encounter a bear on the trail), *you* should! Move away from the

bear slowly and methodically with your eyes to the ground, making no aggressive gestures. Speak to the bear in calm but firm tones to help it recognize that you are human and not a threat. If the bear attacks, don't run! Ball up, protect your vitals, and lie still.

When traveling through bear country, your best defense is to stay alert. Some people have taken to wearing bells or clapping hands or whatnot to alert bears to their presence. In theory, this seems like a good idea. If the bear knows you are there, you are less

likely to surprise it and it is more likely to move out of the way. On the other hand, some of our wilderness areas are beginning to sound like a bad rendition of "Jingle Bells," and evidence suggests that bears are interpreting bells and other human noises like clapping as an invitation to dinner. Not exactly the approach we want.

A better alternative is to travel quietly and to learn to recognize bear country. Look for sign. Listen frequently for noises. Try to see a bear before it sees you. If you are traveling in bear country, each district has its own rules and guidelines. Be sure to find out what they are and follow them.

If there is no bear hazard and you choose not to hang your food, be aware that an eager rodent would just as soon gnaw through fabric to get to food, but it will usually take the easy route if an invitation is left via an open zipper or flap. Leave pack pockets open anytime you leave your pack for a period of time. To ensure you receive no unwanted visitors in your tent, leave all food outside your sleeping area.

Michael Hodgson

A black bear wandered near Michael in the Marble Mountains of California.

one of the planet's exceptional rain forests, and we learned that falling trees were an everyday happening. For decades, even centuries, these giants stood mute, stretching higher and higher; then, in one cataclysmic gesture, they'd come thundering to the ground, their bodies replenishing the soil that once had spawned them.

I've been in aspen forests where no trunk was bigger than a baseball bat, and I've driven a Volkswagen van through the huge redwoods in Sequoia. Some forests are quiet as a church. But at night, the rain forest is a cacophony of screeching, clicking insects.

What are the general rules for hiking in the forest? There is only one that I know of: When the forest is thick, when you can't see far ahead, don't wander out of eyeshot of the trail. In truly dense rain forest, little is more frightening than realizing you are lost. Because there are frequently no bearings, no mountains or other markers, a sense of direction is almost impossible to maintain. This is especially true when the trees are tall and bunched overhead like trellis mesh, and even the sun cannot be used as a directional guide. During the failed colonization of Papua New Guinea, directly following the Second World War, Australian kiops (bush rangers) would drag a line behind them when penetrating the thickest forest; without it they would never have found their way out. Even a compass is of limited use. It will give you the direction, but it can't find the trail.

The forest is a place of wonder, where the mind settles and feelings stretch out to things firmly rooted and alive. Perhaps no one has ever enjoyed the forest more than John Muir. I'm reminded of the time while he was exploring a tributary of the Yuba River in the Sierras that he climbed to the top of a one-hundred-foot-tall Douglas spruce and hung on for his life as a windstorm blasted the forest with force enough to sway the treetops in twenty-foot arcs. Wrote Muir:

> *We all travel the milky way together, trees and men; but it never occurred to me until this stormday, while swinging in the wind, that trees are travelers, in the ordinary sense. They make many journeys. Not extensive ones, it is true; but our own little journeys, away and back again, are little more than tree-wavings— many of them not so much.*

This priceless passage affirms for me the notion that no matter how far we hike in the forest, away from our cars and back again, our treks are little more than tree-wavings. The fortune of the forest is not measured in miles covered. The magic is simply in being there. Trees and men.

A Better Canteen

Wide-mouth plastic bottles are super for carrying water as long as you have a pouch or pack pocket to carry them in. But without the pocket, bottles can become a nuisance. With a little duct tape and a 3- to 4-foot section of webbing, you can add a serviceable carrying strap, turning your bottle into an easy-to-carry canteen.

Using tubular or flat webbing (color and style are up to you), create a loop by tying an overhand bend or a ring bend knot (see illustration). Put the bottle inside the loop so that the webbing runs completely down each side and supports the bottom of the bottle, then use the duct tape to secure the loop to the bottle. The knot should be positioned just above the lid so that the bottle will not rest on your shoulder when you are carrying it.

A length of webbing, a few wraps of duct tape, and presto!—a simple 1-quart Nalgene bottle becomes a serviceable canteen.

Capturing the Moment in Freeze-Frame

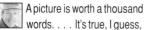 A picture is worth a thousand words. . . . It's true, I guess, provided you take good pictures. Your choice of a camera depends on your budget and how much gear you are willing to schlep along. Much of the time, I am perfectly happy with my compact point-and-shoot 35 mm Pentax. If the mood strikes me, however, and it frequently does, I'll carry along my Nikon with two lenses—a 28 mm to 75 mm telephoto and a 75 mm to 300 mm zoom. I prefer 100 ASA film, but if the light is going to be low, as it often is in the woods, I will turn to 200 ASA or, rarely, 400 ASA (this film tends to produce much grainier images). I always shoot slide film.

No camera will do you much good if you can't get to it. It's not uncommon for a well-intentioned photographer to hike an entire day and not burn a single shot because the camera was secured inside a pack. Make sure your camera is accessible. SunDog, LowePro, Tamrac, and PhotoFlex are some of the better-known manufacturers of padded camera cases that can be carried as a chest pouch or attached to a waist belt. I prefer a chest pouch, although it does limit visibility at your feet—a drawback to negotiating difficult terrain. Some hikers prefer an ordinary fanny pack, which they spin around to carry in front. I can't fault the ease of access, but it's hell on steep climbs—the fanny pack gets in the way of your thighs and knees.

The following tips can add more "art" to your shots or ensure that they will be worth showing to friends.

- Silhouette shots aren't hard to capture. Backlight or sidelight your subject, but be careful not to look directly into the sun's glare if they move. Unless it is early morning or evening, underexpose by one f-stop.
- Bracket your shots if you are in doubt about the exposure or your light meter's accuracy. Shoot one stop, according to your light meter's suggestion, then shoot twice more—one f-stop lower and one f-stop higher than the light meter suggests.
- Rainbows are beautiful to the eye, but they won't look like much on film unless you underexpose by one f-stop.
- Looking to capture a full moon? Use a tripod and shoot directly at the moon at f/8 for 1/250 second with a film ASA of 100. I suggest bracketing here for certain.
- When shooting in the woods, overexpose by one to two f-stops and use a flash if available.
- Pictures of a small waterfall or a babbling brook can be dramatic if the water is carefully blurred. To blur moving water, use a tripod and shoot at 1/30 second.
- Shooting in the fog is very dramatic. For best results, increase the exposure by one to two f-stops above the meter's suggestion.
- Looking to capture an animal or a hiking companion running by? Pre-focus, preset the meter, fix the lens on a specific object, and shoot when your subject passes the object you are focused on.
- Centered subjects look stiff and posed, and the photo downright amateur. Place the subject off to one side and let the light or surrounding landscape add to the story.
- Remember to create a sense of scale in your photos. A giant Sequoia or a distant mountain will appear as nothing more than a tiny image in a photo or slide, unless you place an object of known size in the picture. For macro photography, I often slip a penny next to tiny flowers to show just how small they are.
- A flare across your favorite shot can be prevented if you use a lens hood or learn to cup your hand just above or to the side of the lens to block out stray light.
- The essence of most amateur wildlife photography is animal butts—way off in the distance. Learn to anticipate a shot, move in front of the action, and then set up the photograph so your image fills as much of the frame as possible. You will be best served by a 300 mm lens.

Sometimes drainage bars can become clogged with debris. Clearing the uphill side of the bar enables drainage to resume.

Over time, a berm will build up alongside a trail, causing water to form a puddle.

You can often smooth the berm and improve drainage by scraping some soil onto the trail, creating a slight downhill slope.

Caring for the Trail

In these days of diminished public lands funding, you are more apt to discover trails that are in dire need of maintenance, especially in the woods. Without carrying a pickax and shovel with you everywhere you trek, there are some simple things you can do to improve a trail's condition.

- After the winter season or following a heavy rain, it is not uncommon to come across drainage areas, known as drainage bars, that are blocked by debris. Without damaging the bar (dam) that extends across the trail, clear the uphill side of the bar for a distance of 3 to 4 feet off the trail. Add any cleared dirt to the downhill side of the bar to help prevent damage from hooves, tires, or boots.

- Over time, a berm will build up alongside a trail, preventing water from running off the treadway. In most cases, you can simply use your boot to scrape soil off the berm and onto the trail, smoothing it so that there is a slight downward slope to the downhill side—that way water will drain off readily. If additional maintenance is called for, it is best to notify the local land management agency and leave the work to experts.

- The most common trail damage is created when hikers blaze a new trail to negotiate around deadfall or other debris that has dropped onto a trail. If you can, move the deadfall off the trail to the downhill side and then cover up the "new" trail with vegetation so that hikers return to the intended route.

Outdoor Myths That Drive You Crazy

It took me a while—almost three years of Boy Scouts and two years of summer camp—but eventually I learned that flexing your arm muscles while a mosquito is biting you will not cause the mosquito to explode. No doubt the few who sought to repeatedly convince me otherwise found tremendous hilarity in my "poor technique."

"Jeeze Mike," my best friend would say with mock concern, "you must not be doing it right. Try it again, only this time, really flex your arm muscles tight. I just can't believe you haven't popped one yet."

Why it never seemed a little suspicious that I was flexing while they were slapping is beyond me. Three-hundred-odd mosquito bites later, I learned that it is far better to swat and smile than lie in wait for the satisfaction of magically exploding an insect on my arm.

Each year outdoor myths are propagated by seemingly sage and compassionate outdoorsmen and -women—namely counselors, guides, and close friends. These seemingly innocent myths are apt to cause physical and emotional damage to the numerous youths and adults who fall victim to them.

Some of the more common myths are:

- "You can keep all manner of wild animals away from your camp by carefully urinating around its boundary. Be especially careful to soak the area around your food cache and tent." While this may have worked for Mowat in the movie *Never Cry Wolf,* and has been tried for centuries by woodsmen to ward off wolves, it really isn't practical. It will, however, ward off all manner of friends who may have thought about camping with you, and it is sure to attract an amazing amount of interest if tried in a park campground.

- "Smoke always follows the most handsome or beautiful camper around the fire." This is just the kind of advice any choking and teary-eyed camper is looking for and is sure to make the recipient feel much better—provided there is a tank of oxygen nearby after he or she passes out. Smoke is actually attracted to a vacuum of sorts, usually created by the tallest or largest object

nearest the fire. If you are standing and the rest of the group is sitting, the smoke will usually drift toward you. If you build a small rock wall behind one part of the fire ring and then all sit beside the fire on the opposite side of the wall, the smoke will rise in the wall's direction and not into your eyes—does that mean it's a beautiful wall?

- "You know, if you place a small pebble in your mouth, you won't need as much water because the stone will draw water into your mouth." Brilliant! And just where is the water coming from? Your body, of course. This myth has found its way into practice from desert and tropical warfare when the pebble-in-the-mouth trick helped minimize suffering but did nothing to solve the need for water. Two quarts of fluid per day per person is the absolute minimum; 3 to 4 quarts is best. After that, you can suck on all the rocks you want.

- "The fastest-moving water is always the purest." Actually, faster moving water is more likely to be loaded with *Giardia lamblia* than slower water. This is because fast water keeps *Giardia* in suspension and slow water allows the little critters to settle. Of course, you should be filtering or treating all your water anyway, no matter where the source is.

- "If it's biodegradable, you can bury it because it will return valuable minerals to the soil." Actually, it will create an unsightly mess for the next traveler to enjoy upon arriving at the picnic or camp site, as bears, coyotes, skunks, and other animals will eagerly dig up and scatter the trashy feast. If you pack it in, you pack it out—no exceptions.

- "Male fish are able to detect human female scent on a lure, and so they become more aroused into striking." A buddy of mine, Tom Stienstra, shared this gem with me not long ago after his girlfriend caught more fish than he had for the third or fourth fishing trip in a row. I don't know if there is any truth to it, but then again, if my girlfriend ever catches more fish than I do, I'll know why.

Trail Food: Apple/Apricot Fruit Chew

When wandering through the woods, there is nothing quite as good as a flavorful fruit and nut treat followed by a cool water chaser. Making your own fruit treat is easy if you follow the recipe shared with me by a client when I was guiding backpacking trips in Southern California many years ago. Mix together 2 cups of finely chopped and dried apples, 2 cups of finely chopped and dried apricots, and ½ cup of instant dried milk (nonfat is okay). Add 4 tablespoons of frozen fruit juice concentrate (I prefer apple or orange), 2 teaspoons of cinnamon, 4 tablespoons of honey, and 4 tablespoons of light corn syrup. Roll the mixture into one long fruit log about 1 to 1½ inches in diameter. If you wish, roll the entire log in 1 to 2 cups of chopped walnuts and then in powdered sugar.

An ordinary oven will serve as a capable makeshift dehydrator if you don't own a dehydrator. Preheat the oven to 140°F (use an interior oven thermometer if your oven doesn't have this setting), then prop open the oven door about 6 inches so that the moisture from the drying fruit roll can escape. When the log is firm, take it out of the oven, allow it to cool, and then slice it into 1-inch-thick sections. Wrap each section in plastic and hit the trail.

7

Stepping Out
ON
Snow and Ice

Life was the sound of crampons scrunching the snow,

the lights of the refuge coming up, and Life was the power

and the glory of all the mountains I had ever climbed—as I walked

along the frontier in the moonlight.

—Space Below My Feet, *Gwen Moffat, the first British woman to become a mountain guide*

Chris Townsend

The Eskimos—properly called Inuits—use

dozens of different words for snow, each term referring to some particular quality: corn snow, hardpack, slush, and so forth. The varieties are many, but every one is cold; and in snowy climes, the first concern has always been protection against the cold. We all will reach for a coat when the snow falls, but the capacity to withstand cold differs remarkably from person to person. Take the first time I visited Kalimantan, Indonesia. The island (third largest in the world) rests on the equator, and the coastal air was so humid it left me stunned and breathless. Even a sun bum like myself stumbled around in a sweat-soaked daze, astonished to see locals saunter about in turbans, long-sleeved shirts, even leather coats. A coastal native had joined us when, three weeks later, we were two hundred miles into cool, jungled highlands, all of us snorkeling around a shady lagoon trying to spear snapping turtles. After two weeks inside a barbecue, the crisp water felt like the fountain of youth—to us. But after ten minutes, the coastal native staggered from the lagoon and curled up in a ball, his teeth chattering in his head faster than a pair of those wind-up dentures you buy in joke stores. Accustomed to coastal swelter, the man was left mildly hypothermic by a plunge into the pool.

Another time, while waiting out a storm on Ellesmere Island, the northern-most landmass in the world, I went ice fishing with a pilot who shuttled millionaires up to the North Pole. The pilot, born in the Canadian Arctic, had wintered in Ellesmere, and his fishing garb consisted of tennis shoes, Levi's, and a flimsy bomber jacket that he wore unzipped. It was five below zero. I had on so many pairs of pants I waddled like a duck, and what for the six sweaters and three parkas, my arms stuck straight out, scarecrow style.

Staying warm in cold environs is a special study, and so is walking over snow and ice. This is not a book about climbing techniques, or the business of traveling over anything but relatively harmless terrain, the kind of ground normally found on trails. If you want to tackle steeper ground, where crampons, ice axes, and ropes are required, seek instruction. Casual dayhikes should never require technical gear; if you ever get to where such gear is necessary, turn back.

For my money, dayhikes in the snow feature the best of both worlds. You get to enjoy moving through a wild, inhospitable environment without the hassles of trying to camp in it. Unlike myself, many people raised in snowy climes cherish the chance to spend long periods in the snow. It's all up to the individual. But whatever your tastes, your gear must be squared away or you'll pay dearly.

I still remember my first experience with snow. Pop and I piled into the station wagon and drove up the winding road to Mount Baldy. My father, it seemed, knew less about the cold wet stuff than I did, and in our tennis

Layering for Cold Weather

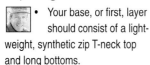

- Your base, or first, layer should consist of a lightweight, synthetic zip T-neck top and long bottoms.
- Add an expedition-weight top for a second upper layer.
- Achieve necessary extra insulation by adding, as needed, a lightweight fleece jacket, fleece pants, and a down jacket large enough to accommodate the fleece underneath.
- Cover the clothing ensemble with a waterproof/breathable mountain parka shell that is large enough to fit over all the layers. Add a long pair of waterproof/breathable shell pants with full side zips to aid in ventilation and putting them on and taking them off.
- A pair of gaiters is essential to keep the snow out of your boots.
- Other essentials include a fleece balaclava, a warm fleece hat, thin liner gloves, insulated fleece mittens with a waterproof outer shell, and warm socks.
- Cotton kills. It's been stated so many times that the words are almost cliché, but still folks continue to head outdoors wearing cotton and wonder why they're cold. It is a useless winter fabric since it absorbs sweat so readily, and once wet, it doesn't dry, leaving the body to chill and opening the door for hypothermia.

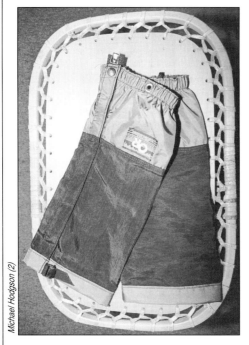

Michael Hodgson (2)

Gaiters help to keep snow and debris out of your boots.

It's not hard to stay warm in the snow if you know how to dress.

shoes and Levi's, we suffered. But my worst experience came years after I knew the hazards of traveling through the snow in something less than good boots.

Richard Harrison and I had been climbing about two years and reckoned we were up to repeating a big wilderness route in the then-remote Red Rocks outside Las Vegas, Nevada. The approach involved a six-mile trudge across glum desert just to gain the cliff. We had no idea how to get off the top of the cliff and back to the road, and figured we'd just wing it once we got there. Though the temperature was around fifty-five when we set off, the mercury steadily dropped as we climbed higher on the wall. About a thousand feet up, with perhaps three hundred feet to go, a storm moved in and we barely made the top before snow flurries roared into a full-blown whiteout. We holed up in a cave for an hour, then headed out when conditions didn't improve. Our only guide as to where the hell we were heading were truck horns on the highway, miles away. We'd hiked to the cliff in tennis shoes, and would hike back in the same. Five hours later we were on the

Warmer Winter Wandering

Heading out by ski, snowshoe, or foot into a winter wonderland is a mystical and, to some, ultimately satisfying outdoor experience. Only when a region is heavily within winter's chilling grasp can one enjoy a stillness that is impossible to find during the warmer months that bring with them insects, crowds, and a host of disturbances. Heading out into the snow, however, requires a little more forethought and a different attitude to remain safe, comfortable, and happy. The following are a few tips and suggestions to consider:

- Unless you are using Lithium batteries, keep your flashlight, camera, and other items that use batteries warm. If the batteries appear dead, try warming them next to your skin before tossing them. What may appear to be dead batteries might only be cold ones—alkaline batteries are bad, but rechargeable are the worst.

- If you are traveling all day, keep your water bottles stored upside down in your pack or pack pockets. Why? Because water freezes from the top down; by storing your bottles upside down you will still have drinkable water near the cap. Forget this tip and you will have to resort to licking ice, assuming you can even remove your bottle top.

- Always travel with the following items readily accessible and on your person, not in a pack pocket: knife, waterproof matches, sunscreen, map and compass, candy, and energy snacks.

- Looking like you are trying to make a Ninja fashion statement is wise. Black clothing absorbs solar radiation most efficiently, keeping you warmer and helping your clothing to dry more quickly should it get damp.

- Get in the habit of tucking your mittens/gloves into your coat if you take them off at a rest break. More pairs of mittens and gloves lose their owners at rest stops than you can even imagine. Having bare fingers in freezing air is not only uncomfortable, it could mean frozen flesh and even a loss of body parts you once considered essential.

- Generously coat yourself in sunscreen, even under your earlobes and just inside your nostrils. The sun reflects unmercifully from snow and can manage to toast some mighty strange places you never thought could tan, let alone burn.

highway and managed to hitch a ride to the dirt road that led to the trailer where we were staying. The snow was shin-high, and it took us three hours to tromp the two miles to the trailer. Our friends were gone and the door was locked. We kicked in a window and spent the rest of the night soaking our feet in the bathtub. The only fortunate thing was that we both were wearing wool socks, which retain some warmth when wet. My feet tingled for weeks, and I couldn't put on a pair of climbing shoes for a month.

You have no chance at anything but all-out torture if you don't have waterproof, lug-soled boots. The lugs provide purchase in all but the hardest ice. Anything else and you'll spend half your time slipping around. A perfect-fitting boot is crucial. A tight-fitting boot is almost worse than no boot at all. Even if your boots are waterproof, and you're wearing the newest high-tech socks, your feet will get cold the second you stop walking. Tight boots drastically reduce circulation in your feet, and though it's improbable that you'd get bona fide frostbite, frost nip is common and can result in numb toes that will stay numb for up to a year.

Special Health Concerns

 • *Snow blindness* is actually more sunburn than blindness, but since you can't see worth a damn, the name has stuck. Symptoms can take from 8 to 10 hours to manifest. It is important to understand that your eyes can burn just as your skin can. That's why eyewear with side shields and lenses that effectively block UV is essential. The first sign that you have succumbed to snow blindness is a dry and irritated feeling, rather like your eye socket has dust ground into it. Snow blindness is not permanent, and your eyes will heal in a darkened environment. Cold compresses may help alleviate the pain.

• *Immersion foot* (trench foot) is not something a dayhiker should experience, although it is possible if you head out for repeated hikes from a cabin over a period of several days. It occurs when your feet stay wet and cold, which leaves the skin white and mottled with interesting shades of blue and red mingled in. The condition is painful, and the skin can crack, which may then lead to infection. Your best bet is to keep your feet warm and dry at all times.

• *Frozen lung* awaits you if you push the pace too fast on a very cold day, say below 0°F. No, the lungs don't actually freeze, but the resulting irritation of the bronchial tubes will lead to a burning pain and spasms in your airway—no fun, believe me. The solution is to wear a face mask, a balaclava, or a scarf wrapped around your face. If you find yourself with frozen lung, the prescription is up to two weeks of rest and relaxation, breathing humidified air and tanking down lots of water.

• *Frostbite.* Frostbite can be prevented by ensuring that all skin is loosely covered—allow for circulation under the layers. This is especially important for hands and feet. With mild frostbite, the skin becomes pale and numb but is not hard to the touch. Apply body heat directly to the affected part; do not rub it or place it next to a hot source of heat—permanent damage could result. Seek medical attention quickly. With severe frostbite, the skin becomes pale, numb, and hard to the touch. Keep the area frozen, bundle it with loose clothing to protect the tissue, and seek immediate medical attention.

ICE

Beyond gear considerations, the chief question is: How do we make our way through snow and ice? So far as ice goes, we don't set out to traverse a slab of glare ice. Even if the terrain is dead flat, working across ice is hazardous without crampons (a frame of spikes you lash to your boots). And the use of crampons, snowshoes, and the like is not the province of this book. But the question remains: What do we do when we run into a patch of ice?

First, it's rare to encounter ground as slick and smooth as a hockey rink. Most ice is dusted with snow or grit, and you can walk over it with caution. Walking across naked, gleaming ice (or trying to) is always dicey. There's no particular hazard to falling onto your duff when your feet skate out from under you, as they often do on ice. If the ice is even slightly angled, however, stay clear. Once you slip and start sliding, it's a Nantucket sleigh ride with no stopping till either the ice ends or you crash headlong into a tree or boulder. And it's shocking the speed you can pick up in a matter of twenty feet.

Years ago I was just getting interested in ice climbing (something I quickly became disinterested in) and decided to hike to the top of a certain frozen waterfall to get a look at things. The top was a flat, benchlike floe of black ice, smooth as Carrara marble. I took a few steps out onto the ice bench and stopped. But I didn't stop. I noticed myself skidding almost imperceptibly toward the lip of the frozen waterfall at about a half inch a second. I tried walking away, but my boots paddled on the ice and I

Trail Wisdom

Thinking of turning your winter jaunt into an overnight? Could be a lot of fun, if you know how to stay warm. Use the following tips as your guide to nocturnal heat generation and retention (and see page 98 for more information on hypothermia):

- If it looks as if the temperature will drop below freezing, bring your boots and water bottle into the tent to keep them from freezing. In extreme cold, sleep with your boots and bottle.
- Before turning in for the night, nibble something with high calories. Your body has to burn this fuel, which will help it stay warmer during the night. Old-

timers used to mix a teaspoon or two of butter or fat with a cup of cocoa or stronger libation before hitting the hay. Same purpose, different method—the choice is yours.

- Fluff your sleeping bag before crawling inside. Fluffing creates more air space between the fibers or feathers—air space easily warmed by your body.
- You can boost the efficiency of a sleeping bag in several ways: by wearing long underwear to bed (a fresh, dry pair), by doubling up sleeping bags, by using a sleeping bag liner, by sleeping in a parka, and

by sleeping in a tent.

- Sleeping on a thick and comfortable sleeping pad will also add warmth. Your body loses more heat to the ground than to the air—try lying on an unheated waterbed to get the idea. Closed-cell foam or a foam-filled inflatable is much better than an air mattress.
- When the temperature drops unexpectedly and you find yourself shivering in your sleeping bag, put on your rain gear (pants and jacket) to act as a vapor barrier and to hold in your body's warmth.

started skidding faster now, maybe six inches a second. The bench was angled toward the lip of the falls at about three degrees. Desperate, I dropped to my knees but kept inching toward the lip. There was nothing I could do, and the agonizing slowness of the business gave me ample time to picture myself sliding over the brink and plunging two hundred feet to the boulder-strewn base. Finally, I lay down and starting flopping like a gaffed tarpon, just managing to roll to some bushes on the margin of the ice bench, only a few yards from the lip of the falls. Most hikers won't be daft enough to repeat this foray of mine, but it illustrates the fact that once you get moving on ice, it's all but impossible to stop.

Hiking over ice without crampons is like driving over ice with no chains. Don't expect to get far. A little ice is to be expected, however, so go slowly, and stay clear of any inclines.

Snow

Traveling over snowy terrain can involve hazards—rarely on the trail, though frequently off it. Many hazards are unseen; some are predictable. There are differences between hiking over ground that is covered with snow, and working over permanent or semipermanent snowpack.

Winter Eyewear: A Sight to See

It's hard to really enjoy the winter wonderland if you can't see it properly, and yet more often than not, sunglasses and goggles are just an afterthought. The excuses are as numerous and varied as the snowflakes swirling through the cabin eves: I'll just get a pair at the resort; Too expensive; I'll just lose 'em; They make me look like Darth Vader!; They always fog; I break every pair, so just give me something cheap. . . . Whoa, Nellie. Proper eye protection is as important if not more so than the ski package, ski racks, fashion clothing, and other accessories people routinely buy.

The higher you get above sea level, the less screening of radiation there is. Due to the reflective nature of snow, up to 85 percent of the UV radiation may be reflected upward, even more reason to use goggles (or mountaineering-style sunglasses) in sunny and also slightly overcast conditions.

If you want to cut through the mumbo jumbo of harmful and not-so-harmful rays, it is important to understand the basics. Long-term exposure to UV radiation has been linked to serious eye disease such as cataracts, and short-term exposure to temporary afflictions such as snow blindness. There are three types of UV radiation: UVC, which never reaches the eye and is not harmful; UVB (known as tanning rays), which creates painful but usually temporary damage to the cornea and which can repair itself; and UVA, which is absorbed by the lens of the eye and results in damage that is difficult to repair and, in the case of retinal damage, most often permanent.

At the very least, the goggles or sunglasses you select should remove 100 percent of the UV radiation. A number of companies, such as Suunto for Cébé, are also touting the importance of infrared radiation (IR) or radiant energy protection, even though IR has yet to be established as harmful under normal viewing conditions. Still, in high mountain environments, under an intense sun, conditions are far from normal.

Where goggles depart from sunglasses to service the needs of the skier and winter recreationist is in their design. Wrap-around goggles protect the wearer from both direct and indirect (reflected) radiation and help to deflect snow, debris, and wind away from the eyes.

Snowshoeing is an ideal way to enjoy the winter landscape without slipping and sliding.

All goggles are sealed around the face with a soft hypoallergenic foam and secured with an elastic strapping. The better (pricier) goggles are designed with double lenses, which act as a thermal barrier. Air is sealed between the two surfaces so that the inside and outside temperatures are equalized, thereby reducing the potential for fogging. You need to be careful not to handle these goggles too roughly. If the seal is broken, moisture could get between the glass layers, and that leads to fogging every time.

Another anti-fogging tactic is a coating applied by the factory to the surface of the lens. These fog coatings create a surface that absorbs moisture and dissipates it quickly.

Vents provide yet another defense against fogging in goggles. Some are downright novel, such as Scott's venturi design, which creates a chamber of low pressure when the wearer is moving, forcing air through the top of the goggle and back out the bottom. Since ventilation can irritate eyes, especially those of contact wearers, Smith goggles feature a regulator that allows airflow to be adjusted for varying conditions.

Wearing glasses adds a challenge because it puts another lens into the goggles, which doubles the opportunity for fogging and can affect fit. Always make sure you are purchasing goggles designed to fit over glasses—most manufacturers have special models for this purpose. Wear only glasses with nylon frames and polycarbonate lenses, as these will minimize fogging. Also, pick up some anti-fog solution for your glasses; most likely your glasses will fog before the goggles.

How much should you care about fit? In general, the foam padding should create a uniform seal around the face without tightening the band to skull-compression tension. No goggle is 100 percent fog-free, but unless you plan to be aggressive on your snowshoes or skis, I recommend models with more room (less streamlined) because the increased air space means less likelihood of fogging. Sure, you'll look like a giant bug, but if you can see, who cares—it's function that matters, and that translates into protection from the sun and snow, wind deflection, and minimal fogging. After all, you want to be able to *see* all the fun you're going to be having, don't you?

Once you have your gear squared away, there is not all that much to add as to the particulars of trudging up a snowy trail. Even in the dead of winter, popular trails are typically beaten down by boots, and the going is straightforward. Move off the trail, however, and you're in for some hard work at the least.

Three typical modes for moving cross-country over snow are slogging, postholing, and fording, drills that range in pleasure from grim to hateful. *Slogging* is self-explanatory, and happens when the snow is roughly boot-deep. *Postholing* is required when the snow is about knee-

deep and the temperatures are too high for the snow to firm up to where you can walk on top of it. Instead, you literally fall through with each step and have to extricate your leg from the "posthole" you have punched. This is grievous work, full of hidden surprises. In windy areas, heavy snowfall tends to fill in the bumps and hollows in the terrain, offering a rather uniform surface that belies the broken ground below. You can take one step and punch through to mid-shin, take another step and plunge in to your waist. I find this work about as enjoyable as sitting on a hot stove, but there are times

Trail Food: Winter's Day Picnic

 Whether you are outdoors enjoying a brisk winter's hike through local woods or gliding among snow-laden mountain pines on skis, steaming hot soup, a chunk of sourdough bread topped with cheese, and a hot drink will go far in chasing the chill away. Pack along the hot liquids in a thermos or have them awaiting your return to the car. Remember always to pack additional water. Hot drinks and soup are no substitute for liquids needed to prevent dehydration. The following are two of my favorite recipes, given to me by a friend, David Strumsky, when I guided for a company in Southern California.

BROCCOLI FOREST SOUP
2 heads of broccoli
2 tablespoons of butter or vegetable oil
1 yellow onion, diced
4 cups of cashew milk (Soak
  2 cups of roasted, no-salt
  cashews in 4 cups of water for
  15 minutes. Puree in blender
  until liquefied. The sweet, nutty
  flavor blends outstandingly well
  with the broccoli.)
2 tablespoons of soy sauce
1 bay leaf
2 tablespoons of cornstarch mixed
  thoroughly with 2 tablespoons
  of cold water (optional)
Cut the broccoli into small florets and steam until tender (don't over-cook). Set aside. Sauté the onion in the butter in a large soup pot over low heat until the onion is clear and tender. Add the cashew puree and the soy sauce. Measure 2 cups of liquid and puree it in a blender with half of the broccoli. Dice the remaining broccoli. Combine the puree, bay leaf, and diced broccoli with the liquid in the large soup pot. Warm to serving temperature—do not boil. Add cornstarch mixed with cold water to thicken if desired.

GINGER TEA
2, 1-inch cubes of fresh ginger
3 or more tablespoons of honey
4 cups of water
Peel the ginger and grate it. Place all the ingredients in a pot and bring to a boil. Cover and simmer for approximately 25 minutes. Uncover and cook on medium-low heat for 15 minutes. Strain and serve. An instant version of this is available at many health and Asian markets in a box of individual packets.

If ginger tea is not to your liking, try adding one drop of extract (almond, vanilla, peppermint, orange, etc.) to a cup of coffee, hot chocolate, or tea.

when postholing is required—to get to an overlook, for example. Trying to cover any real distance using this method is a poor choice, however. Freezing feet and soaked legs are inevitable.

Fording is done when temperatures are relatively high and when the snow has a lot of air in it. This resembles plowing

My Goggles Are Fogging . . . What's the Deal?

Fogging is a winter trekker's number two problem after staying warm. Here are some tips for preventing fog (the kind in goggles, not around the Golden Gate Bridge):

- Do not overdress. Be warm, but not too warm. Snowshoeing and other strenuous activities generate heat, and if beads of sweat are forming on your forehead, your goggles will be fogging. Peel off a few layers until you are comfortable.
- If it is snowing and your goggles begin to fog, check to see if the snow has clogged the vents. If the top vent is covered, the heat cannot escape, and your goggles will fog. Remove the snow.
- Neck gaiters will direct warm air directly up and into your goggles through the bottom vent, especially if you pull the neck gaiter over your nose. Don't snowshoe (or engage in other prolonged aerobic activity) with a neck gaiter.
- If your goggles do fog, never wipe them clean. To do so reduces their effectiveness. Anti-fog-treated lenses will heal themselves given time.
- Never clean your goggles with glass cleaner, since that removes the anti-fog coating, and use only commercial anti-fog sprays or liquids on your goggles when the factory anti-fog coating has worn off or been removed.
- Glasses wearers, try putting on the goggles before leaving the lodge. This will prevent the glasses from getting cold.
- If you take a tumble (and who doesn't), shake the snow from your goggles but do not wipe them. Blot the water droplets dry with a soft cloth. Wear them dry, or remove them and place them foam side down on your thigh so the moisture-laden air can dissipate and the no-fog coating can absorb the remaining moisture.

Thanks to Kim Hix, of Bollé (a goggles marketer), for these tips.

Goggle Lens Color for the Conditions

- Amber or yellow colors are intended for use in flat to hazy light and offer the high contrast necessary in high-speed, high-altitude sports such as skiing by filtering out blue light, which otherwise makes focusing difficult.
- Vermilion (pink) actually helps absorb light in foggy or gray conditions, increasing contrast and depth perception, a must for high-speed sports in winter.
- Brown lenses offer the true-color-perception characteristics of a gray or smoke lens, but also retain some of the blue-light-removing/contrast-increasing characteristics of a light amber lens.
- Clear. Why? Because if you're snowshoeing at night, it's the only lens color that will allow your eyes to see anything at all.
- Gray or smoke-colored lenses are best suited for driving or general use, when depth perception is not as important as true color perception.
- Blue and purple lenses are not recommended, because they actually increase the contrast-destroying characteristics of blue light.

through wet, waist-deep cement and is perhaps the best reason to stay on the trail. Fording is best imagined by visualizing the old movies where an intrepid mountaineer is leaning into a ferocious head wind and breaking trail through chest-deep fluff.

Snowshoes and cross-country skis were invented to accommodate travel over terrain that you'd otherwise have to post-hole or ford. It's bleak performing the latter two practices, though they are bear-able modes for distances too short to warrant lugging the snowshoes or skis. But even for brief stretches, a hiker is well advised to bring along a walking stick ("third leg") or, better yet, a couple of ski poles to maintain balance.

Especially on firm snow (or what appears firm), streams and melt water often undermine the surface layer, resulting in hidden pits below. This was brought home to me

Snowshoeing

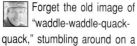 Forget the old image of "waddle-waddle-quack-quack," stumbling around on a pair of creations that resemble elongated garbage can lids.

Winter wanderers are finding that snowshoes open up a world of possibility. Even a beginning snowshoer can often travel over more territory with less effort than an experienced cross-country skier. Why? Because snowshoes are stable and offer superior flotation and grip in even the worst snow conditions.

I can still remember my father, a number of years ago, returning a trial pair of cross-country skis politely to my shop and pointing curiously to a pair of snowshoes on the wall. I gave them to him, and didn't see him again until just before sunset, when he reappeared with a huge grin on his face.

Snowshoes are simple to use. With what is known in the industry as a "modified-H" style of binding, your shoe or boot is held securely to the snowshoe using a combination of toe holster and heel strap—relatively easy to get on and off, even with gloved fingers.

Looking for something more aerobic than a trudge in the woods? No problem. The narrower profiles and lighter weight of today's metal snowshoes allow the user to walk or even run normally. Even snowboarders are turning to snowshoes as a means of heading up into untracked snow for that all-important "virgin" run. Whether for running, cross-training, mountaineering, walking, or working in deep snow on fence or traplines, plan on spending around $200 to $250 for a snowshoe and binding package. Some shoes come with bindings, such as the Atlas, while others, such as the Sherpa brand, require an add-on purchase. For a few dollars here and there, it is possible to add accoutrements such as insulated bindings (for those really cold days) and heel cleats (for days when even a surefooted snowshoe wants to act like a runaway train).

In general, the old school of thought was that the longer and broader the shoe, the more buoyancy provided and therefore the more weight it could support. With that in mind, fitting wooden and laced snowshoes was done by comparing snow conditions with the size and weight of the individual and the gear being carried. More weight and softer snow meant longer, wider snowshoes. High-performance demands and recreational usage have changed the picture somewhat. The most important considerations are the snow conditions and whether a person is hiking solo or in a group. A solo hiker will need a shoe in the range of 9 x 30 inches or 10 x 36 inches for breaking trail. When hiking in a group, however, trail breaking is shared, making flotation less important, so a shoe in the size range of 8 x 25 inches is appropriate. If you plan to run and use snowshoeing as a form of cross-training for aerobic benefits, you will want to purchase the

when Leroy Hurt and I hiked up to Suicide Rock one spring, hoping to get in some climbing. It was a long, knee-deep slog up to the cliffside. Once there, we were thrilled to find that a steep snow cone lay against the base of the cliff, completely covering the first thirty feet of the climbs. Since those first thirty feet were the steepest and hardest of all the climbs, by scampering up the hard snow cone we could skip the crux lower section of routes that then, as begin-ners, we would otherwise never have been able to climb. That was the idea, anyway, when Leroy started up the cone; but the second he gained the rock, the lip of the cone snapped off, and Leroy disappeared. Shortly, screams echoed from deep inside the cone. I belly-crawled up to the rock and peered into the hole where Leroy had vanished, and there, twenty feet below, knee-deep in a freezing lagoon of slush, was my climbing partner. For half an hour Leroy

smallest, lightest shoe possible.

If you are at all uncertain about how you will use the snow-shoes or what size is best for you, don't buy for a while—demo them. An increasing number of retail stores offer demo rentals, as do many ski resorts.

Once you have your snow-shoes, no other gear is required. Standard hiking boots, or even running shoes if you are seeking a workout, are all the footwear required. Dress in layers as you would for skiing, but be prepared to peel down to the minimum since snowshoeing can work up quite a glow. If balance seems to be a problem, or you just want an additional security blanket to keep from falling in the white stuff, opt for ski poles; one in each hand will offer four-point stability in awkward conditions.

A few basic techniques can make your initial foray a little easier:

- Always switch off the lead when breaking trail, as it can be both tiring and awkward.
- When climbing, keep your weight over the balls of your feet.
- Traversing a slope is more difficult but can be accomplished by either "sawing" or "kicking" the uphill edges of your snow-shoes into the snow.
- Heading downhill, keep your weight over the balls of your feet and be conscious of digging the heel cleats into the snow. Lean back and you will "butt-slide" all the way down for sure.
- As for level terrain, there isn't much more to it than one foot in front of the other.
- If you are of the snowshoe persuasion, let me gently remind you that ski trails are for skiers only. Foot and snowshoe traffic should be kept off to the side of any established ski trail so as not to ruin the trail for those sure to glide along later.

Be sure your snowshoes have adequate flotation, a good steel claw underfoot for traction, and a simple-to-use but secure binding system.

tried clawing out of the pit, but managed only to freeze his hands so badly that for a month afterward he could take a leak only by using his thumbs—or so he claimed. I finally rigged a line and hauled him out.

Anytime hard-packed snow is angled and abuts a big rock or a tree or any substantial obstacle, beware. The lip may be undercut, setting a trap for the unaware.

Any lip should be considered suspect.

During spring, snow goes through a daily cycle. What is frozen at night often turns to slush after a couple of hours of sunlight. Conditions vary, but hardpack is much more suitable for hiking than muddy slop is, so when the season is thawing out, plan on covering ground in the early hours, when the snow is firmed

Keeping Digits Toasty and Boots Dry

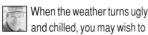 When the weather turns ugly and chilled, you may wish to turn to chemicals and electrical devices to ward off ill effects to your feet. No, I'm not suggesting kinky footwear. A number of battery-operated and chemically based products can help ensure dry, warm, and happy feet.

Among the chemical alternatives are Heat Factory's Insole Boot Warming System and Grabber's Toe Heaters. The Grabber's system is quite simple: two adhesive-backed disposable packets that stick to the outside of a sock above the toes. They heat to approximately 100°F and last 5 hours once exposed to air.

Although the chemical process in the Heat Factory product is the same, the method of application is different. Its boot-warming system is an orthopedically shaped insole, which comes in six sizes, with a cavity in the toe area to accommodate the foot warmer. The Heat Factory design replaces the boot's standard insole.

If chemical packets aren't your thing, perhaps electrical

warming devices are. Lectra Socks concentrates the heat in the toe area, where it is needed most. The socks are a combination wool/acrylic/stretch nylon in gray with red trim. According to the manufacturer, the connections are positioned to minimize chaffing or rubbing. The battery pack attaches either to the boots or to your leg with an adjustable strap.

Foot Furnace by Hotronics is a compact battery-powered foot-warming system. A microprocesser signals a microchip inside the heating element and delivers up to 8 hours of warmth in your choice of four temperature settings. The insole can be trimmed to fit into shoes or boots and plugs into the battery pack. The lightweight battery pack clips easily to your boots or shoes, or attaches to your leg with an adjustable safety strap. The batteries are rechargeable and work up to 8,000 hours.

Keeping shoes dry lengthens their life and minimizes bacteria growth (and, thereby, shoe and foot odor). Beyond the old standby method of stuffing a boot full of

newspapers, you have two alternatives—one high-tech, the other passive.

The Footwear Dryer by Dry Comfort uses an ordinary hair dryer to dry shoes, boots, and, yes, hip waders effectively and rapidly. Although decidedly funky (and, some feel, provocative—one woman at a consumer show I attended seemed shocked and wondered aloud, "That isn't what I think it is . . . is it?"), be assured that it does work, and well. Still, unless you are going to be near an electrical outlet whenever you have wet boots, it has limited application.

Stuffitts, manufactured by Rochester Shoe Tree Company, are cedar-stuffed, nylon-cased shoe accessories designed in the shape of a foot. Each pair is connected by a nylon strap. After a workout, you stuff the Stuffitts into any athletic shoe and they go to work absorbing excess moisture and "descenting" the shoe with the aroma of cedar. They come in three different sizes for men's, women's, or children's footwear.

Avalanches are a danger when the mountains are snow covered.

up. I've been caught in conditions requiring something between mud wrestling and ice swimming. No good. . . .

Avalanches

Avalanches present one of the few inherently lethal hazards of backcountry winter travel. A knowledgeable hiker can recognize avalanche conditions, but trying to predict when a big one will cut loose is always a crapshoot. We can only touch on the subject here. Anyone planning to do much travel through snowy, mountainous areas is encouraged to take an avalanche seminar. Local search-and-rescue teams normally give such classes a couple of times a year, and the fine points can be understood in a matter of hours.

To appreciate the dangers avalanches present, know that 10 percent of all those caught in an avalanche die. A person completely buried has only a 33 percent chance of surviving, and a person buried deeper than seven feet is always

lost. A quick search is essential. After six hours, a hiker buried by an avalanche has only one chance in forty of being found alive. These are sobering statistics—all the more reason to familiarize yourself with the subject.

Briefly, avalanches normally sweep slopes between twenty-five and forty degrees that are prone to snow buildup and are subject to winds. Snow does not adhere well to steep walls, which continually slough off the buildup; lower-angled slopes usually lack the gravity for a slide to pick up momentum. But not always. In the case of steep walls (which you may be walking beneath), high cornices and/or berms can and do cut loose and will sweep a seventy-five-degree mountain clean. The devastation is mind-boggling. And once a "white monster" gains a head of steam, the runout can extend thousands of meters onto the flats below. Nothing short of a dense forest can slow it down. And even here, the fringe of the woodland is often flattened for a remarkable distance, huge pines and redwoods snapped off at the roots like toothpicks, gigantic boulders tossed far below. While statistics are kept about avalanches, such numbers group small snowslides along with white monsters. Fact is, when a biggy lets loose, whoever is in its path is almost certainly a goner. For our purposes it's good to know that trails are virtually never forged where avalanches are a consistent threat.

Avalanches most often occur on east-

Winter Footwear—The Ageless Mukluk

The mukluk has been around for eons. In fact, a prehistoric man was recently discovered frozen in glacial ice wearing, you guessed it, mukluks—boots made of skins and stuffed with mosses and grass for insulation. By design, a true mukluk is light and flexible, allowing the foot maximum freedom of movement and consequently maximum opportunity to stay warm.

Traditionally, mukluks worn by Inuits were made of thick hide and then insulated with dry vegetation—grasses, reeds, moss, straw, etc. If the insulation got wet, which it frequently did, keeping the feet warm was a simple matter of pulling out the old insulation and restuffing with dry. Fine as long as there was dry insulation within easy reach, but a serious problem if no insulation was available and the feet remained wet.

Still, in most instances, the mukluk design was a sound one that has kept hunters' and explorers' feet warm for centuries. Mukluks, however, weren't really practical for everyday wear, since the soles were made of skin—wear a leather moccasin on the trail for a few days if you need convincing.

For that reason pac boots, with their waterproof rubber and plastic soles and waterproof leather uppers, became the standard "cold-weather footwear of choice." But technology has once again made mukluks worth considering. The primary drawback of traditional mukluks was their lack of a sole. With the advent of a flexible sole, the modern mukluk has become street- and trail-worthy.

Just as with a traditional mukluk, warmth in the Steger brand of moosehide mukluk is increased by adding more insulation—the more insulation you desire, the larger and wider mukluk you need. The major difference, besides the high-grade rubber sole, is that Steger uses boot liners of wool felt, fleece, or Polar Plus instead of reeds and grasses.

Traditional mukluks aren't made to be waterproof because they don't have to be—they are intended for wear in cold environments when the snow is dry and the conditions aren't wet. The moosehide of Steger's mukluks can be waterproofed with Sno-Seal or Biwell, but waterproofing cuts down on the breathability, which affects the function and warmth.

A good mukluk is designed to breathe, keeping the foot dry as well as warm. Waterproof boots and pacs certainly keep the moisture out, but they also seal the moisture in, resulting in cold, sweaty feet.

Another manufacturer, Yeti, makes mukluk-style boots of nothing more than Polartec, foam, and felt that they claim will keep feet warm even at −80°F. They are warm even when wet because air is constantly circulating throughout the boot, keeping the foot warm while the foot's heat dries out the boot. I've worn these boots hiking at 10°F in a heavy snowstorm. I intentionally walked through a stream, soaking the mukluk, and then wandered around for several more hours. Miracle of miracles, my feet did stay warm.

Despite the variations, all mukluk-style boots share one consistent characteristic—breathability. Traditional thinking holds that rubber, leather, and felt (i.e., a pac boot) make the warmest boots, but mukluk manufacturers dispute that. Even the traditional pac boot manufacturer Sorel offers a breathable-upper mukluk boot that they advertise as "setting a new standard in cold-weather performance."

facing slopes that are scoured by winds. Gullies and bowls are prone to accumulate massive snow buildup, particularly after storms (when most avalanches happen), so give such areas a wide berth.

Avalanches are triggered by many things: the weight of a hiker, the melting and collapse of weak layers in the snowpack, falling cornices that disrupt the top layer of a precariously balanced load of snow. Learn to understand the danger signs, and stay clear.

Iditarod champion Rick Swenson concurs that breathability is key. "In cold temperatures the by-product of your body's own heating mechanism—sweat—becomes your worst enemy. When the temperatures are extremely cold, your own sweat could freeze your toes off."

True mukluks, and to a certain extent pac boots based on mukluk technology, feature flexibility and foot comfort, both of which help a foot stay warm. What do you do when your hands get cold? You move them around, wiggling the fingers and flexing the muscles. The combination of freedom of movement and air space provided by a good mukluk design allows a foot to stay warm even under harsh weather conditions.

A pac boot made of stiff leather and hard rubber retains and, to a certain extent, conducts cold. Mukluks will keep you warmer because your feet can move and breath. They are also much lighter. Tromping around all day with pac boots is not fun; a light mukluk allows the user to walk and even run with comfort—a main reason that world-famous explorer Will Steger uses mukluks on his expeditions.

I've worn mukluks and they do live up to their claims, but don't expect to see them becoming the winter footwear of choice anytime soon. The mukluk does not excel in slush and mush, major components of urban and parking lot living. The 32°F slush puddles of this world still belong to pac boots—they're cheaper and they keep moisture out.

Lost!

A dayhiker can never afford to get lost, but especially so in snowy climes. You won't have the necessary gear to camp and to stay warm and protected through the night, so if you wander astray, you're left to try to survive with what you have on. Even the best cold-weather garb cannot create heat. It can only help to contain what heat your body generates. Once you slow down, or stop, your body produces far less heat than when you were exerting yourself. And once you start getting hungry, your metabolism slows that much more, and shortly you're into the danger zone. As mentioned earlier, hypothermia can kill. And seeing someone who is truly chilled to the bone is a sight you'll never forget. Like the time Bob Gaines and I were in Yosemite taking photos for some reason or another. Winter was approach-

Measuring Up

What the heck is a clinometer and why do I need one? A clinometer measures vertical angles or the slopes of hills or other objects and is especially useful if you plan to do any serious snowshoeing, backcountry skiing, or winter mountaineering where avalanches might be a concern. With a clinometer built into your compass, you will be able to estimate the steepness of terrain accurately and determine the risk of avalanche danger. Other than in winter, however, a clinometer doesn't offer much for the recreational user except a way to determine slope angle, and it enables you to say, "We hiked up a forty-five-degree slope—wahooo!"

Chris Townsend, the Sierra Nevada

ing, and during our first night a storm blew in and soaked the valley. The next morning, puddles were frozen on the sidewalk. Several hours later we were up at Vernal Falls and ran into two hikers who had gotten lost and had to bivouac out in the open. Both were blue, beyond shivering, and once they got to where people were, they both collapsed (still several miles from the roadhead). Bob remarked, "The last time I saw something that cold, it had fudge on it."

Altimeters and GPS Receivers

Altimeters are useful additions to your navigational system, especially when you are attempting to navigate in a world of snow and possible whiteouts. A pocket altimeter measures barometric pressure and then converts it into an altitude reading, even if it is dark or you are completely fogged in. By constantly registering present elevation, an altimeter can be useful in determining when you have reached a given elevation and, consequently, a contour line on a topographic map, which can then guide you to your eventual destination—minimizing energy-wasting up-and-down searching for the "camp I know is here somewhere!"

The best altimeters are temperature-compensated so that temperature fluctuations do not affect the reading much. To be really useful, an altimeter must have increments of no more than 50 feet, or even less, and be accurate to within 100 feet. If you think that you will be rough on your altimeter, an electronic one may be best suited to your needs. They are also easier to read and use. For greatest accuracy, however, a mechanical altimeter with geared movement is the choice. Mechanical altimeters have one other distinct advantage over electronic ones: There are no batteries to fail, making them the best choice for extended cold-weather use.

One last word of advice. Since an altimeter registers barometric changes, it will "adjust" altitude readings as the barometric pressure rises and falls, even though the altimeter remains at a constant altitude. You will be wise to learn to recalibrate the altimeter on a regular basis, using known points of elevation as you pass over them.

Of course, as the prices for global positioning system (GPS) receivers continue to drop, it makes more sense to own one, since they not only tell you your altitude but also plot your location, even when you can't see your hand in front of your face. The GPS is a network of 24 satellites that orbit the earth twice a day, transmitting precise time and position information. With a hand-held GPS receiver, you can determine your location anywhere on earth.

A GPS receiver picks up a satellite's signal and, by measuring the interval between transmission and reception of the signal, calculates the distance from the satellite to the receiver. Using the measurements of at least three satellites and some fancy math footwork known as algorithms, the GPS microprocessor triangulates an accurate position fix. Three satellites must be acquired for the GPS to display longitude and latitude accurately, and four satellites must be acquired to add elevation to the mix.

Most GPS receivers will allow you to display information in longitude/latitude, Universal Transverse Mercator (UTM grids are used on many Bureau of Land Management and other survey maps), or military grid. Some, such as the Trimble, display actual map quadrant names and then give inch measurements to aid in locating your position on the listed map.

Basic GPS receivers offer simple features and the minimum circuitry necessary to acquire position fixes, which is all most of us need or want. Any good GPS should be able to be turned on cold and establish a position fix without your assistance. The more pricey a GPS becomes, the more bells and whistles it offers, up to a complete personal computer interface for uploading and downloading navigational information.

8

Coastal Wandering

But look! Here come more crowds pacing straight for the water,

and seemingly bound for a dive. Strange! Nothing will content

them but the extremest limit of the land.

—Moby Dick, *Herman Melville*

Bob Gaines

I have a little beach house in San Juan de los

Callos, Venezuela, a sleepy village with cinder-block dwellings scattered along the edge of the sea. The beachside cabanas, roofed with fronds; the pushcarts selling cane juice and shaved ice along the waterfront; the old men stretched out on the sand and playing dominoes, an ebbing bottle nearby; even the old church standing vigil on the hillside, shuttered against the glassy heat—these things are found in all beach towns, which are exactly the same throughout the country . . ., even down to considering themselves different.

Most of the townspeople were born in the homes they live in, and you can't imagine—nor can they—that they would ever leave. Their lives move with the wind and waves, and their eyes never stray far from the mountainous atmospheres of sky and sea. The shore and the land belong to each other in turn, according to the tide; the people and the place are each other's by birthright.

An ancient cemetery, with granite headstones and rusty iron crosses, rests between my beach house and the ocean. On a starry night, perhaps an hour before dawn, I'll sometimes walk through the graveyard and down to the beach. I've always had problems rising early, but never in San Juan de los Callos, maybe because the sea has always been a conspirator in human restlessness. Standing on the sand, with ocean before me and the departed behind, eternity feels to press in on me from both sides. Walking along and looking out to sea on a clear, moonlit night, the world speaks of its great age.

The edge of the sea is a strange, stunning place, where peace and unrest have always been partners. Lashed by the elements, the shore is ever changing. But beyond in the silvered distance lies a seemingly changeless universe, existing long before we were around to ponder it. I sometimes wonder about the first person who ever experienced this view, and what she thought when looking up at the stars arcing over the ocean. And the souls in the graveyard? Do they think the stars are cold and distant, and bitterly compare the stars' desolation to their own? Or do they see beauty, contentment, and rest? Maybe the old tombstones are only totems for those who have gone beyond the horizon, and are looking back at us. The thought is reassuring, and soothes the loneliness of the seashore at night. There is no need to drive away the darkness with lanterns. It is enough to walk quietly along where the water meets the sand, and wait for the fireball to climb over the edge of the world.

Close on the flush of sunrise come coveys of birds, driving ahead, splitting off, and gathering again. There is a bird in Venezuela whose back and sides are white but whose stomach is red. Sometimes when a constellation of these birds wings along the beach, all at once and by some mysterious agency they veer out to sea and the chevron turns from white to red, and then back to white again.

Below, arriving unannounced and from nowhere, sandpipers scamper along, their feet stamping crisscrossed patterns into the wet sand, now dotted with crackling pinholes into which the pipers thrust their beaks. Then they're off again, hot-footing away from dissolving breakers. How can anything move its feet so quickly? And how can its head bob back and forth like that? I asked my five-year-old daughter about this business with the bobbing head, wondering how it was possible, and she said the piper has a hinge in its neck, like a door.

Beach-Tested Wisdom

 • Beach trekking requires you to prepare for wind, moisture, and unstable walking conditions. Even if the weather feels hot and dry a mile or so inland, it may be moist and cool at the beach, or quickly turn that way. Anticipate rapid changes of conditions and dress accordingly, with layers that can handle and dissipate moisture. I always pack along a rain parka, wool cap, polar fleece sweater, and warm pair of pants even when I believe I'll be hiking in shorts and a T-shirt much of the day. Since you will likely be hiking across sand, rocks, rubble, driftwood, mudflats, and other surfaces over the course of a day, your footwear must be versatile yet supportive. See "Putting the Best Foot Forward" on page 172.

• We coastal wanderers have a tendency to gaze seaward much of the time. This is why we're there, after all, and it's a good way to spot rogue waves that might otherwise sneak up on us, but it also means that we're unaware of what is immediately underfoot or overhead.

Underfoot hazards can include rattlesnakes in dry driftwood, slippery rocks, and even mud that can suck us under (if it looks too wet to walk on, it probably is). Overhead we need to be aware of falling rocks and the debris that commonly tumble from unstable cliff edges. Speaking of cliff edges, if you are walking along them, and we would advise against it, you risk becoming one of those falling items that tumble on unsuspecting hikers below.

• Always be aware of the tides. I don't go hiking on any coastline without first getting my hands on a local tide table. Why? Foolish is the hiker who is caught unaware by a high tide and gets cut off from any means of escape along the beach. He or she may end up clinging uncomfortably to a cliff face for several hours at best, or getting pounded and then swept out to sea by the incoming surf at worst.

• Never turn your back on the sea. I've heard of, though never experienced, huge rogue waves that come sweeping in

out of nowhere to dump tons of debris, driftwood, and turbulent water on an otherwise tranquil beach scene. If you happen to be on the beach and not watching the incoming water, you might get caught up in a "wash and rinse cycle" you won't soon forget.

• If you ever do get swept off your feet and out to sea, stay calm (easy to say, harder to do). Don't fight the current; it is much stronger than you. Swim along the shoreline until you feel the pull of the undertow weaken, which it usually will, and then begin to work yourself toward terra firma.

• While the intertidal zone, that area between the high and low tides, is perhaps the most durable of all surfaces and virtually impervious to impacts from a passing hiker, the dune or backshore region above the intertidal zone is most fragile. Try to limit your impact and footprints to the intertidal zone. If you must move above the high water mark, do so carefully and only on established routes of travel if possible.

As the sun climbs the sky, it cooks kelp beds floating close on shore, a vast supper club for fish. Every few minutes a bird drops from the sky and dive-bombs into the kelp at speed, surfacing ten yards away with something writhing in its beak. My daughter asked me where these birds sleep, but I've never been able to answer her. She doesn't mind that I don't know, as long as we go search out some pebbly spit and collect sea stones. The most ordinary pebble is wet and luminous on the seashore, but loses its brilliance when you take it back home. I often feel the same way.

At the edge of the sea there is restlessness in the calmest moments, a nervousness that drives the pageant of combers and rustles the reeds on the dune tops.

Trail Food: On the Trail of Mix

For the best trail mix, head directly to a health food or specialty food store. Typically, these stores have large bins full of delectable trail mixes alongside other bins of dried fruits, nuts, seeds, and more. Begin with a basic mix, such as a tropical blend of nuts, papaya, coconut, raisins, and more, then add other ingredients to your heart's content. I never pass up an opportunity to add butterscotch chips to my mix. As for estimating how much you will need, I have found that a half pound of trail mix per person per 8-hour hiking day does the trick nicely. If you want to try something truly exotic, then taste-test the following:

Mix 2 cups of cereal (containing flakes, bits of fruit, and nuts), 1 cup of chopped walnuts, 1 cup of sunflower seeds, 1 cup of golden raisins, and 2 cups of bittersweet chocolate chips (I prefer Giardelli's brand)—you can also substitute butterscotch or peanut butter chips. Heat over a stove or in a microwave until the chips are melted. Stir the ingredients until they are all well coated with melted chips. Spread the mixture onto a well-greased cookie sheet to form an even layer that is about 2 inches thick. Chill the sheet and then cut it into squares; wrap in plastic for your hike.

Bob Gaines, Playa del Solmar, Mexico

Along the shore all things know that the sea holds a prodigious might that on occasion must assert itself. This power normally moves with uniform precision, ebbing and flowing with the tide, much as a caged tiger paces to and fro. And when the tiger lunges, or when the waterspout twists across the water and the hurricane bends the cocoa palms in half, we're given a new idea about power.

Eight years ago I spent several months on the North Shore of Hawaii. I went there to shoot the opening of a movie called *Farewell to the King,* which begins with two soldiers in a rowboat, trying to get ashore through pounding surf. The director and writer, an ex-surfer, decided to film the scene at Waimea Bay, sanctum sanctorum of big-wave riders. I'd grown up in Southern California, and names like Waimea Bay, Pipeline, and Sunset—all situated along a dozen miles of beach—always sparked memories of grainy old films featuring men riding mountains on surfboards. I would almost have gone for

Putting the Best Foot Forward

Walking over terrain that more often than not is wet, unstable, and perhaps slippery has implications for your footwear. While lightweight hiking boots work just fine, I favor sandal shoes (especially when I'm tide pooling) or multisport shoes (when I'm more concerned with getting from point A to point B and my trip will be mostly dry). The following will help you select beach footgear.

MULTISPORT SHOES

Think multisport and you immediately think Nike, the company that more or less created the category a number of years ago as an outdoor spin-off from their popular cross-trainer shoes. Described by some as an "athletic shoe on hormones," the multisport shoe is designed to be instantly comfortable, moderately supportive, and relatively durable. Keep in mind, however, that while these shoes are suitable for many activities,

they are not the ideal choice for any one. The folks at Nike, One Sport, Adidas, Hi-Tec, and Merrell all agree that if you want to specialize in backpacking, mountain biking, or trail running, you should buy specialized footwear.

But multisport shoes excel for the generalist—those among us who like to do a lot of things just a little bit and only want one shoe.

This shoe is also ideal for the vacationer with limited luggage space, heading to a destination such as Moab for mountain biking in the morning, trail running in the afternoon, and rock scrambling in the evening—one shoe, many activities. It's also perfect for beach wandering because it offers enough support to protect your foot, isn't so expensive that you will worry about

A multisport shoe is an athletic shoe on hormones.

free, because it was December and the giant waves were just forming.

I have never seen this famous stretch of beach in the summertime, but I'm told that Waimea Bay is a millpond, and the other sites are much the same. But in midwinter, storms periodically brew in the Aleutians, thousands of miles away, and through some wonder of the deep, the ocean's wrath expresses itself most forcefully along this twelve miles of North Shore beach. I wasn't there a week when the first big surf hit land. Boomers had started rolling in the previous night, and we drove from Waikiki up to the North Shore early the next morning.

Waimea Bay describes a horseshoe a half-mile deep and one mile across. The waves roll in along the right-hand edge of the bay, where the shoreline cuts abruptly inland and is girded by enormous, mottled stones. We scrambled out onto these and watched the titanic breakers course by. When a thirty-foot wall of water curled over and broke, the earth shook and spume shot fifty feet in the air. Once the

getting it soaked in salt water, and is comfortable enough to keep pace with your scrambling all day long.

SANDAL SHOES

Not quite shoes, certainly not sandals, they can best be described as "shoes with sandal attitudes." Adidas may have created this shoe category a number of years back with their Adventure Sandal.

Not happy with the support offered by a sandal, yet feeling that a lightweight hiker was too much, Adidas created a hybrid. Because they offer more support, sandal shoes are a better alternative than "reef shoes," the lightweight slip-ons made of neoprene and mesh that are more slippers than shoes.

Sandal shoes are intended for adventurers who will be spending as much of their day in the water as out of it. The support, minimal, is designed to be comfortable, keeping the shoe light and extremely flexible. The uppers are breathable and generally include mesh or some other provision for drainage—ideal when you are portaging a boat, scrambling over rocks or around tide pools, or wandering in and out of streams. Closed toes protect from possible abuse from submerged obstacles or trail debris. To aid in wet or dry traction, the tread and sole are designed to be low-impact yet suitable for use both on the trail and in the water. Unless you enjoy the grinding of sand on your feet, you will want to wear socks with your sandal shoes. If you want to keep your feet warm in cold water, opt for a thin neoprene sock—just be sure your sandal shoes fit with the added thickness of neoprene. And how should a "sandal shoe" fit? Like a shoe, of course.

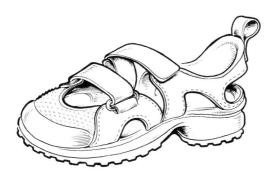

tsunami passed, the ocean would convulse with eddies and riptides, swirling with sand churned up from the floor of the sea. It seemed mad that any human would challenge such force, but there they were, a group of perhaps a dozen, slashing down the vertical face of these mountains of water. Paddling over the top or dropping down the face of these rollers, the surfers would howl. But when the mouse laughs at the cat, there is always a hole nearby; and so it was with these crazy watermen, as just left of the breaker's path lay a little draw, calm in comparison, where after a wipeout or when paddling out, a surfer could grab a minute's rest before stroking into the action.

For an hour we stood there, drenched to the bone. Everything looked so exaggerated it felt like the landscape of a dream. With that dizzy mixture of fear and excitement, I wondered if these waves and these surfers were made for each other, and found completion together.

I was working with a correspondent for *Surfer* magazine, who was anxious to see the action on the other beaches nearby, for each beach has particular features—hidden reefs, shallow coral bottoms, and so forth—that cause the waves to break in different ways. On this day the waves were a solitary drama of the sea, without the supporting cast of high winds and driving rain. Given such perfect weather, rather than drive to the next site, we hiked along the beach so as not to miss a single foot of this spectacle.

At the next break, the waves were a third as high as those at Waimea, though twice as fast. Rather than a dozen master watermen, as we'd seen at Waimea, hundreds of surfers were ripping up the faces of these ten-foot breakers. For one of the few times in my life I wished I'd gotten involved in another sport other than climbing.

Then we met Mel and Sharon, a cou-

ple from St. Paul, Minnesota. Both doctors and avid hikers, they'd spent their previous vacations kicking around the Great Lakes and in the Canadian woodlands. This time, for the novelty of it, they'd opted for a normal vacation and had booked into the Hilton at Waikiki. But after three days of slumming around luaus, they were tiring of the ukulele and the barbecued swine and had set off in their rental car that morning, looking for diversion. They'd pulled over at Waimea and, like us, had hiked on, entranced by the giant waves. We four continued along the waterfront, and after half a mile stumbled on one of the queerest phenomena I've ever seen in nature.

A small creek emptied into the ocean from the lush shrubbery girding the beach. Though now only a trickle, apparently when the rains fell hard, the trickle swelled into a proper river, judging by the channel it had carved through the sand—a culvert of sorts, maybe twenty feet across and ten feet deep. When a wave slammed into the beach, a terrific shaft of water, a sort of liquid locomotive, would blast up the culvert and eventually peter out another hundred feet inland. The attraction was not the sudden flood, however, but the several dozen people who were howling and cocking around in the bottom of the culvert. The mix included several naked boys; a truck driver in overalls, whose rig was visible on the road nearby; a bronzed elder with the face and demeanor of King Kamehameha, who went at about 450 pounds; and a small black dog, to mention a few. Every time the swell would roar up the culvert, the crowd would dash seaward and dive straight into the teeth of it. About ten seconds later they'd surface far up the trench, a writhing mesh of twisted limbs, bonked heads, and skinned elbows, wheezing, water streaming out their noses, completely mud-covered, every orifice packed with silt. King Kamehameha always ended up in a seated position, like a victim of Pompeii; after a few moments of stunned silence, his white teeth would shine behind a mask of slop and he'd start in with a high-pitched, spasmodic giggle that betrayed his royal girth.

Sharon was the first of us to join the others. The business looked like a perfectly good way to break your neck, but after we three men saw the hundred-pound neurologist take several journeys and surface in one piece, we jumped in as well. It was early afternoon before we left. I lost a shoe, and Mel feared cracked ribs when he came to rest beneath the king, but we didn't care.

Another couple of miles down the coast and we began to hear the pounding of distant mortar fire, or carpet bombing. Leonard (the *Surfer* magazine correspondent) started jogging. We wound through a copse of palms and ran directly into a crowd of several hundred spectators, all gazing out at one of the great contests between man and nature: The Banzai Pipeline.

I had read articles and seen films of this break, but I had to see it firsthand to appreciate or even believe the violence involved. The waves were huge and steep as doom; unlike other North Shore breaks, Pipeline waves build and crash so close to shore that the concussion shudders through the sand and up your legs. Leonard said he'd never seen "Pipe" bigger—and people still trying to ride it.

The four of us elbowed our way to the waterline and stared out at a wave rearing up about fifty yards out. Half a dozen surfers paddled hard and dropped down the twenty-foot face. Jostling for position, they carved bottom-turns, then shot right across the green wall. As the breaker arched over it formed a hollow pipe, inside of which the surfers would

Tide Pooling

Tide pooling, especially with a young child or an adult who is young at heart, is an absolute hoot. Poking and peering into pools searching for crabs, sea urchins, seashells, sea cucumbers, octopuses, starfish, and the like can keep the explorer occupied and entertained for hours—I've whiled away many an afternoon wandering from pool to pool, or along Northwestern beaches at a low drain tide, searching out what was previously untouchable. To make the trip more enjoyable, I recommend packing a viewing "eye." I use an old diving mask; when pressed up against my face and then placed into the water, it enables me to enter the world below visually and clearly. You can make your own quite easily by cutting the end off an empty #10 coffee can and then covering it tightly with clear plastic wrap and securing the wrap in place with a rubber band. When you get to a deep tide pool that you want to look into, just place the can into the water, plastic end down, and look through the can like a viewing window—you'll be amazed at how clearly you can see. Sometimes you may wish to turn over a rock or log to see what lives under it. Do so carefully and gently, taking care not to crush what lives underneath. Replace the rock with equal care when you are finished looking. Again, never, ever turn your back on the ocean, or you risk getting drenched by a sneaky wave. Please don't collect anything from the beach that is living. In most cases, doing so is illegal—besides, marine animals are much better cared for in a wild environment. Finally, remember as you wander that most beachfronts are considered public property right along the waterline, but once you head up the beach, above the high-tide limit, you enter a zone that may be private. It is your responsibility to know whether you are treading on public or private beachfront. If in doubt, ask at the public access point before venturing out.

Bob Gaines, Playa del Solmar, Mexico

crouch, screaming along and totally out of view. This is precise business since the gap between the crashing curl and the end of the tube is the length of several surf-boards, at most. It's a little like trying to outrun chain lightning. And the hazard isn't so much the pounding you'll get if the pipe guzzles you (which ace watermen can normally survive), rather that the water is only six to eight feet deep, and the floor of the sea is a heartless coral reef.

Courage cannot answer for atten-dance inside that ferocious barrel. Only a rare kind of madness can—madness, tim-ing, and the skill to maintain speed and escape the pipe before it collapses on itself. On that first wave, four of the six surfers were crushed; two emerged cleanly on the wave's shoulder, waving their arms above them. Then the wave closed out altogether and belched a cannon blast of spume out the end of the tube that blew the two riders clean off their boards.

Many times during my climbing days I felt the fist of fear close on me; but the only other time I'd felt it by *watching* something was the first time I saw the

bull-riding world championships, in Las Vegas. Like bull-riders, the surfers at Pipeline were confronting what it all comes down to in the end, the irreducible brute element. Charging down its face was a direct deed more real than fire. A colossal wave and a coral reef. Two tons of bucking, snorting chuck roast from hell. These things had the clarity to snap me fully awake. And that's the first and last reason people seek adventure—to feel alive, which is its own reward.

Twenty feet in front of us, waist-deep in foam, ten surfers stood shoulder to shoulder, waiting for a lull. Shortly they jumped onto their boards and stroked for the safety beyond the "break zone." Once there, perhaps a hundred yards out to sea, the building waves would pass under a surfer without taking him or her with them. Lulls are short, so timing is critical. Several surfers lagged behind the main pack; the leaders were already cresting the first wave of the new set, catching air off its back side. A second later and the last of the pack paddled up the towering face, their arms moving like bee's wings. Everyone cleared—but one. Caught dead-center in the thunderous break zone, he rolled over with his board in the vain hope that the monster would pass over him. I felt the worm turn inside me as his dark profile was drawn up inside the torrent and then torpedoed over the falls and onto the reef. Splinters of his shattered board shot into the air and bobbed atop the spume. Minutes seemed to pass before he surfaced fifty feet out. When several others dragged him ashore, he looked like someone who had fallen off a motorcycle on the freeway. Mel spent ten minutes huddled over his limp form. Water streamed from his nose and he sucked air in wheezing, reedy gasps. Then the paramedics came, strapped him on a gurney, and carried him off. Mel figured he had two punctured lungs; he knew he had a concussion and a broken arm.

Gidget and weenie roasts belonged here as much as arrowheads belong on the moon. On a big day, Pipeline is war, and the war is for keeps. Death rides with every wave. I could hear it roll across the water, could taste it in the mist, could read it on the face of everyone who paddled in after surviving a big set at the Banzai Pipeline.

Several hours later the sea flattened out and the four of us hiked on, past Sunset Beach, another famous spot, and finally stopped at a calm section of coast dotted with tide pools. We found one with a sandy bottom, carpeted with green and orange sponge, and we slipped in and sat down, four talking heads rising from the water.

Over the previous twelve hours we'd walked maybe ten miles, among the most memorable miles of our lives. Between the four of us we'd trekked through many of the world's varied terrain, and floating there in the tide pool we all agreed that the forest and the jungle and the mountains had nothing over the edge of the sea. I only wished that we could have carried on, but just ahead, the shoreline was a no-

go grid of tiny deltas, lagoons, and cliffs.

Such obstacles are typical along the waterfront, and can make foot travel difficult to impossible. For instance, about five miles south of my place in San Juan de los Callos, the shoreline is fringed with a dense copse of palm trees that run for forty miles. Why the saltwater does not kill these trees I do not know, but trying to get through them is hopeless. At high tide the grove is flooded and choked with barbed fronds and malicious insects. At low tide a space opens between the palms and the sea, but the break is carpeted with a black, clayey muck. One step into this and you sink to your waist, and keep sinking unless someone hauls you out. Farther down the coast the sea dashes straight into a cliffside, and farther south still is a white dune/shoreline running twenty miles, with not so much as a twig in the way of cover. The sand is so blistering and the heat, reflected off the white sand, is so acute that the stretch is known as Dead Man's Beach.

Coastal walking can involve circuitous, inhospitable terrain requiring many of the skills needed in other terrain. Such barriers are rarely mentioned on maps, and even if they are, the edge of the sea transforms itself with every storm.

Every shoreline bears reminders of the past—the graveyard on the shore and the driftwood strewn about the sand; likewise, the seashore speaks of the endless flow of time, as the pipers' footprints are erased by withdrawing waves. Here, where the water meets the sand, the drama of life played its first scene, and every evening, as the sun explodes on the horizon and slips into night, the ending is rehearsed. Meanwhile, all of us caught in the net of life walk the coast together. We can never know where the land ends and the sea begins, for the two are as inseparable as the place and the people of San Juan de los Callos.

9

Canyons

AND

Waterways

Tread softly, because you tread on my dreams . . .

—W. B. Yeats

Chris Townsend

For my fifteenth birthday, my mother

bought me passage on a raft trip down the Salmon River in Idaho. From the second the boats hit water I was begging Henry Felany—head boatman and owner of White Water River Expeditions—for a job. A month later I signed on as a slave laborer for Henry's ten-day float trips through the Grand Canyon. I took a Greyhound to Turlock, California (Henry's headquarters), then rode with two tons of gear all the way to Lees Ferry, Arizona. Most of the three-day junket I spent suffering in the back of the semi, in brutal July heat. The moment we gained the river it was all sixteen-hour days rigging boats and organizing food and equipment. By week's end I was so bushed that the only thing keeping me going was a look downstream, where the river curved into shadows and the low canyon walls echoed the roar of distant rapids.

I didn't know the meaning of work until my first day in Lees Ferry; I'd learn about adventure the moment we hit the first cataract. Thundering along, three-quarters of a mile in the depths of the earth; drifting through continents of smooth water; letting my mind drift up mysterious side canyons, purple, orange, ten million years old—these things changed me. By the time our flotilla drifted onto Lake Powell a lifetime later, everything that needed to happen had happened. I didn't know what and I didn't know how,

but if I was ever going to do anything with my life I knew adventure of some kind would be my starting point. It may be the only thing I've ever known for sure.

Over the next twenty years I never took up river running as a special pursuit, though rivers were usually nearby, and I often trekked along them and sometimes took to the water for conveyance or sport. The fact that I never became an expert boatman or kayaker translated to big fun and periodic terror, for by accident or stupidity I sometimes found myself in world-class whitewater. After my trips down the Grand, and with the exception of my traverse of Borneo, I never ran a river with an expert. (In Borneo, we brought Jim Slade along, unquestionably the most experienced riverman in the United States.) But rivers have always shown me more than treacherous water.

So-called primitive cultures often live along the riverside, usually in open spaces friendly to rice and spud farming with room enough for sprawling communal structures. Move upstream and the river becomes the only realm in nature that can attract and fashion people as unique as the terrain itself. Deserts rate a close second, but the most memorable folk I've ever met have been on rivers. Thoreau, in observing the frontiersmen who had battled out a life along the upper reaches of the Concord River, considered these men "greater than Homer or Chaucer or Shakespeare, only they never took the time to say so. You look at their lives and imagine what they might write, if ever they should put pen to paper."

When I first read this statement I thought one or the other of us was a fool—most likely Thoreau. What could he mean by these words? He did a job sprucing the frontiersmen's milieu with maples full of glee and sap and the august flight of ospreys. And he painted a heroic portrait of the rivermen themselves, "men fuller of talk and rare adventure in the sun and wind and rain, than a chestnut is of meat." But the bit about "greater than Homer" seemed ludicrous nevertheless, and would continue to for ten more years—till I was plodding up the banks of an Amazonian tributary, some ways above the infamous Macunaima mine in Brazil, an open-pit tropical Klondike from which miners had already scraped out over a billion dollars in gold.

Indians had hiked this trail for eons, and though the going was slow and thorny, the way was evident, always snaking along the riverbank. In an hour, we passed the last boat scouring the riverbed for gold. Another hour and we were beyond the last panner and into primordial terrain. The forest reared higher, the river narrowed, and the current quickened.

We marched through curtains of green light slanting down from the closing trees. The caboclos (the indigenous, half-Indian locals) called it *la salon verde,* "the green room." Gnarled fuzzy ropes coiled down from the canopy, flecked with wildflowers and strangler figs. Several uprooted trees floated past, and now and then we passed islets of rushes in river shallows. Bullfrogs croaked from small muddy creeks dribbling into the river, and twice we had to get in the water and swim past coves of mangrove through whose riotous roots blared the

---

A Plague of Mosquitoes

- During insect season, seek higher ground away from streams and bodies of water, even if it means you will have to hike an extra few hundred yards. Higher ground means stronger breezes, which will help keep the squadrons of little peskies at bay.
- Hike in light-colored clothing to reduce the dive-bombing attacks of Alaska, Minnesota, and Maine's state bird—the mosquito. Studies have shown that mosquitoes are more attracted to dark colors.

---

mad chorus of howler monkeys.

We passed a stratum of dark limestone ledges extending far into the southern bank. The forest grew immense, and the slender isles between trees, darker. Sometimes the gloomy green wall was relieved by orange festoons dangling beneath pao d'orco trees.

Late that afternoon the sky went ablaze between thin rags of clouds, the lime forest cutting across the vivid glare like a ruled line. The river mirrored the sky so precisely that the water shined like liquid gold, from which suddenly rose an Indian paddling downstream, a huge manatee in the floor of his dugout. His chin was smeared red with annatto and on both sides of his face a tattooed streak ran from the corner of his mouth to his temple. He neither ignored nor acknowledged us, standing on the shore. He simply paddled past, stroking slowly and effortlessly with the current, the tail of the huge mammal now and again twitching and flashing in the light. I followed him past, and kept watching till far downstream the Indian fused back into the water.

In this solitary Indian was the greatness Thoreau had discerned in the Concord

(text continues on page 184)

Negotiating a Stream Crossing

What is the safest way to cross a stream? Cautiously! When you must ford a stream, study it first. Crossing where the trail indicates may not be the best place. Slower, wider water may be deeper, but easier to walk through. Water usually moves most swiftly at its narrowest point. Keep the following in mind:

- Always loosen your shoulder straps and unfasten your hip belt before fording a stream, so you can abandon your pack if you get into trouble. Lost gear is preferable to lost life.

- Select a sturdy stick (or two) on the shoreline before crossing and use it as a staff. It'll give you better balance when you are crossing swift water or over slippery rocks. Experienced hikers often pack along several cross-country ski poles without the baskets for just such occasions (plant them upstream or down, whichever feels comfortable). I have tested and really enjoy using Leki's trekking poles.

- To reduce the dragging effect of swift currents, take off excess clothing if the weather is warm. In cold weather, close-fitting long underwear will help keep you warm.

- To prevent slipping and protect your feet, wear boots, or switch to tennis shoes with a good tread. Before venturing into the water, remove your socks; put them back on after you cross.

- Take each step in the stream slowly and deliberately. Plant your forward foot firmly before moving your rear foot. Never hurry.

- Never tie yourself into a rope. If you slip, the rope will only drag you under with the force of the current and could lead to your death. There are specific and appropriate times to use a rope when crossing a stream or river, but only with proper training and additional gear, and at no time should you ever be tied into it. Our advice: If the water is so high and swift that you feel you need a rope to help you cross it, find another point to cross.

Chris Townsend

If the river is flooding, caution is the better part of valor—especially if a safe fording is in doubt. Retreating is always a better option than drowning.

Amphibious Canyoneering

Standing waist-deep in water while contemplating a 1,000-pound log wedged in the narrow canyon walls directly above your head, you may not have the impression of being in a fragile and destructible environment. On the contrary, the rugged and difficult traveling through remote riparian canyons in Utah, Arizona, and other states presents a magnificent, unforgiving, and potentially violent picture. Yet these amphibious canyons demand the highest level of wilderness ethic. Once polluted or vandalized, their resources and beauty are irreplaceable.

- Some of your travel through canyons of this nature will be in the form of raft packing—floating your pack in a streambed and pulling or pushing it. The rest of the time will be spent hiking through wet and lush canyon floors, often wading knee-deep in water. Travel only in small groups. Any group larger than four is too large, and the resulting impacts would be severe.

- Keeping your gear dry can be something of a challenge when canyoneering. If you resort to the old standby—garbage bag–lined packs—your gear is destined to become a tad soggy, guaranteed. The best bet is to use a dry bag with straps, specifically designed for portaging. Basically, it's a daypack that is completely water-

proof, but since it is nothing more than a sack, it will carry like one. Load the dry bag carefully and don't expect complete carrying comfort. Cascade Designs makes a good system that I have been quite happy with. Another alternative, especially if you crave ease of carrying, is a series of small dry bags to protect your gear inside your standard pack. The disadvantage here is that while your gear will remain dry, your pack will become soaked and, after a long swim, fill with water. Don't

A dry bag guarantees that all of your supplies will not get soggy when river wading or swimming.

try to lift your load (unless you plan to rupture yourself) before draining your pack completely.

- Staying warm when wading into and out of cold water can be difficult. One solution is to pack a neoprene wet suit, but this means lugging a bulky item that you may or may not wear. Another alternative, the one I prefer, is to carry a vest and long pants made of Malden Mills' Thermal Stretch by Henderson. Thermal Stretch offers neutral buoyancy and warmth, dries quickly, resists mildew, is abrasion-resistant, and is a heck of a lot more breathable and comfortable to wear than neoprene.

- Do not bring dogs along. Although some people argue that properly controlled dogs have a place in the wilderness, and provide pleasure, canyoneering is not one of those places. The intensity of swimming, jumping, climbing, and rough scrambling will not be a pleasure for your canine friend.

- Always stay in the streambed unless circumstances force you out. Bushwhacking along the lush edges of these canyon-bottom, riparian environments will cause permanent damage to both the delicate soil structure (cryptogamic soil to you naturalists) and the vegetation. Do not pick or even touch the flowers.

- On occasion, traveling through certain sections of a canyon will require you to use climbing ropes, slings, and anchors. It is not a reasonable practice to leave behind an anchor, rope, or sling. If you cannot take your equipment with you, do not use it. Find an alternate method or route.
- It is difficult, but do your best to refrain from sending waste water directly into the stream. Though it is virtually impossible to wash and urinate more than 200 hundred feet from many canyon-bottom streams, at least provide as much opportunity for filtration as possible by dumping waste water in the soil, rocks, and sandy environs away from the stream edge. Periodic flash flooding will flush the canyons clean. Before dumping it, filter all waste water through a bandanna so that all food and particulate matter is removed. Pack out all solid waste.
- Boater's rules apply regarding defecation. Create a miniature river runner's toilet by lining a coffee can with multiple plastic bags. Add small amounts of chlorine bleach as needed to prevent odor and gas production. Do not urinate in the bags. When packing, squeeze out all the air, seal the bags, and then replace the coffee can lid to secure the contents.
- If you stay out overnight, camp only on sand banks, gravel washes, or rocky ledges. Never set up camp in vegetated areas. Campfires are not acceptable, even with significant amounts of driftwood littering the canyon. The resultant blackening of rocks and ash/charcoal production leave behind permanent reminders of your visit. Stoves are the only environmentally sound way of cooking.

Michael Hodgson

Canyoneering is adventure at its best, but the route is often strewn with rocks and filled with water, making travel damp and chilly.

River frontiersman. The Indian paid no mortgage and the frontiersman sought no one's approval. In a fundamental way they were living life on its own terms, clean as rain, and there is greatness in this for anyone who sees and grasps its significance.

But in Kalimantan, Indonesia, when I saw the theme played out all the way, it changed me as much as that first trip down the Grand. We were traveling up a river that didn't have a name, that wasn't even marked on our map, heading for a green alp in the jungled highlands. We rounded a bend and on the lee shore, under a cannonball tree arching over the river, sat a large, oblong hut perched on palm pylons. We pulled over and cautiously made our way into the hut.

The sepulchral hush inside the little dwelling seemed to carry the sighs of forgotten lives, amplified by a wooden basin intricately braided into the reed walls, a carved stool, a coconut grater leaning in the corner, as if carelessly left there an hour before. When we understood that people still lived here, weeks away from the nearest soul on earth, we stole from the hut like thieves. An hour later a young woman, leading a toddler in one hand and dragging a big ripe jackfruit in the other, emerged from the jungle. Near sundown, the woman's husband pulled ashore in a crude, motorized dugout. One of our group spoke fluent Bahasa, and we learned that for five years the man had panned gold from a network of secret creeks nearby, and in fact had tickled out gold enough to move back to Jakarta and do most anything he chose to; but he and his wife had no plans to leave. They would stay there on the riverside, *selama-lamanya* ("forever"), he said. And his wife nodded. I felt a rush of loneliness for these people who would

Little Bastard Flies

Blackflies and no-see-ums are the bane of many a river traveler, especially in the north-woods of Maine. They are so obnoxious that it is uncommon for anyone to live through an attack without resorting to swearing—hence the affectionate label "little bastard flies." Blackflies are perhaps the easier to deal with, even though they leave bleeding and swollen marks where they have penetrated human skin. One solution is to wear a head net—available from most specialty outdoor stores. This will eliminate the annoying buzzing and swarming around your head. Since blackflies seem to enjoy circling the highest point in their fly-zone, you can also "artificially" increase your height, and thereby rearrange their flight plans, by resorting to trickery. Tie a stick to your pack and hang your hat on it so that it rests a foot or so above your head. The blackflies will soon be circling your hat and not your head. Also, try hiking next to a taller partner. He'll soon be swatting and swearing while you are hiking in relative bliss—until he discovers what you are doing, that is.

No-see-ums are a different matter. True to their name, you can't see the little suckers until they are swarming around your head, which they do with alarming frequency. While their bite is not as painful or obvious as that of the blackfly, they are even more annoying because even head netting will not stop them—they simply crawl through the tiny holes and then buzz around, inside the net! The only solutions are either to resort to no-see-um–proof netting (which is so fine that even air does not readily pass through it on a hot day, leaving you feeling stifled and grumpy) or to coat the netting with repellent (which works, but means you live with the lovely odor of DEET all day long—yech).

turn their backs on the world for . . . For what? I wondered, and said nothing for a long time.

The woman fried some rice and we rustled up guavas and alligator pears; then the man said to follow him and for an hour we walked upstream along the river, more feeling our way than seeing it. The sky blazed with stars but there was no moon and the enclosing jungle was dark and the lazy river black as ink. The man stopped and swam out into the river; we followed, and rolling onto our backs, let the current carry us along. For half an hour we floated through the night. Nobody said a word. On both sides the banyans rose in the black decor. Wind moved slowly across the water. On that night in the middle of Kalimantan, I found perfection.

Back in the hut, as we prepared for sleep, the man tapped out his pipe and said that when the day came that he found himself old and tired, he would make amends to God and wait for night to fall. He would have a last meal of durian fruit and rice, and would say good-bye to his family. Then he would wade out into the river and drift with the current. He would not swim to shore. He would just keep on going. *Selama-lamanya.*

When we pushed off the next morning, these three beings waving from the shore felt like memories from another man's life, someone who had

Trail Food: Flavoring the Water

Although water filtration by itself has long been considered safe on many of our nation's backcountry streams and rivers, there is every indication that this belief is changing (see more on this and on filtration in Chapter 3). Bacterial contamination is becoming more common and for that, filtering is not enough. Further, if you are traveling abroad and hiking along Third World waterways, viral contamination must also be considered. For both viral and bacterial pathogens, you need to treat your water with a chemical halogen, most commonly iodine. Of course, most people do not enjoy the taste of iodine, and I count myself among them. There are many solutions. Carbon after-filters, accessories for a number of filters, remove the taste of iodine, but their use may result in too little dwell time (the time required to kill little nasties in your water), leading to water that is inadequately treated. Perhaps the easiest chemical method is to add a small measure of ascorbic acid (vitamin C) to the water after the iodine has completed its recommended dwell time. This effectively neutralizes the iodine and renders the water tasteless. However, if it is flavor you seek, and you want to create a little taste treat for your palate, I recommend the following "bar is open" solutions for trail thirst-quenching:

- For a "fruit smoothie," trail style, add equal parts of powdered whole milk and powdered fruit drink (I prefer dehydrated orange juice) to your water. I have found that the best way to ensure a smooth smoothie is to add no more than ½ cup of each mix to a 1-quart bottle, then add water to fill the bottle one-quarter full. Shake vigorously to blend the ingredients and dissolve the powders. Fill the bottle the rest of the way with water and shake again to mix the contents thoroughly. If you used orange juice, your drink will resemble an Orange Julius—remember those?

- If you prefer something prepackaged, AlpineAire makes a fruit smoothie drink mix that is to die for—on the trail at least. I'm not sure I would opt for this over a blender version using fresh ingredients at home, but then again, it does taste pretty darn good.

died and been forgotten a century before. The simplicity the family shared demolished my notions about what life should be if it were to mean anything. They had no standing in the community, no crowd to verify their "achievements," no television, no phones, nothing to live on but the stars and the river and each other's presence. I'm not sure I ever got over that family, and I'm not sure I ever want to. Sometimes when I buy a new pair of shoes, or "attain" something in this world, I think back to that night in Kalimantan, and wish for a lazy river.

Three weeks later we witnessed the other side of serene waters, a show of natural power that put even the breakers at Waimea in the shade. We were motoring down the Kayan River, heading for the east coast of the island, now less than a hundred miles away. The river broadened with each mile, and presently stretched about one hundred yards across. For several miles the native boatman had hugged the left-hand bank. Up ahead the river pinched to fifty feet across before dropping from sight, as though it had plunged over the edge of the world. As we closed on the breach the air swirled with steam and a low rumbling pulsed through the water and up through the boat. By the time we pulled over, the atmosphere was as steamy as a sauna and we had to yell to hear each other. We made our way through thick verdure and down to the start of a narrow canyon. A large boulder near the rim provided dramatic viewing.

Just below, the river plunged and accelerated into a boiling rage that seemed too savage for rock to contain. Fifty feet farther, the canyon pitched like a ski jump before hooking sharply left. At the elbow,

Ye Olde Swimming Hole

 It's hard to go on a riverside wander and not stare longingly at the water. It's so enticing and often leads the mind to dream longingly of an old swimming hole complete with swinging rope dangling from a branch far above. I'm a big fan of swimming holes—especially if the water is relatively warm and clear, meaning no more than two goose bumps per square inch of skin and no more than a low concentration of algae—but swimming in wild and unknown waters is not without risk. To be safe, you have to be smart. The following tips should keep you from getting into waters that are, metaphorically speaking, way over your head:

- Don't plunge into water that is moving swiftly enough to sweep you downstream. Be sure that the swimming hole doesn't have a current that will suck you into treacherous waters from which escape is difficult.
- Never swim alone. If you get into trouble, a nearby partner decreases the likelihood of becoming another unfortunate river statistic.
- I never swim barefooted unless I know the river has a soft, sandy bottom. All it takes is one sharp rock or a wayward fishing hook to add a bit of trauma to the old swimming hole experience.
- Never dive or jump into waters you do not know. Diving into a swimming hole is appropriate only if you know it to be deep enough (at least 10 feet) and free from obstacles that could cause injury (for example, submerged rocks or logs).
- Children, especially, should be taught never to go near water except where it is shallow and slow-moving. Children should also be instructed never to go into the water without adult supervision.

the entire river heaved fifty feet up the right wall and formed a seething, perpetual wave with a nimbus of vapors swirling above it. A huge log torpedoed past. Stripped bald from its rugged passage, it resembled a huge white bone bobbing atop the whitewater. It suddenly disappeared, then popped back up just before the elbow, arcing forty feet up and sixty feet across the perpetual wave. At the wave's cresting apex, it tumbled down, end over end, and was washed around the corner. The notion of being drawn into this chaos was the scariest thought that's ever crossed my mind.

These stories are mostly extreme

Of Mud, Wet Sand, and Riverbanks

The water's edge attracts humans like ants to a picnic. This is fine as long as safety precautions are followed. Never forget that:

- Mud or wet sand on a riverbank or lake edge is sometimes deep. If you get stuck well away from shore, and the river decides to rise, rescue becomes tenuous at best; the result is an unfortunate drowning at worst.

- Riverbanks are notorious for giving away without giving notice. Be aware of the dangers of sitting or standing on the edge of a riverbank that is undercut by the water flow. Anytime the water is moving swiftly below, undercut banks should be suspect. Should a riverbank give way suddenly, you or your companions could be pitched headlong into rapids or cold, deep water—a potentially dangerous situation.

Chris Townsend, the Grand Canyon

because I am extreme and that's what I remember most vividly. But extremes hinge on excess, which seems foreign or irrelevant to a calmer soul who understands that strength is found in other places besides rapids. Though they understand that still water goes bad, they nevertheless don't feel that way about themselves, are not pulled along by the current, not anxious to see what's around the corner. For us, the disquiet ones, the river is always a spur toward movement. The quieter soul is content to settle in with the subtler moods and deep quiet of a lost lagoon. From this group has come a subgenre of nature writing about fly-fishing and creek mysticism that ranges from plain awful to some of the most elegant prose in the language. To them, the river is about cool depths and opulence, and they get us anxious ones to pause for a moment and see our faces reflected in the water. Or maybe slip into the water, roll onto our backs, and drift with the current. *Selama-lamanya.*

A seashore can run flat and sandy for miles, and often does. Rivers, however, often pass through shoals, between buttresses and mud banks, past islets, and by groves and shrub so thick an earthworm

Quicksand Sucks

What makes quicksand "quick" is water—lots of it. According to the folks at the United States Geologic Survey, quicksand is defined as "A mass or bed of fine sand, such as that found at the mouth of a river or along a seacoast, that consists of smooth rounded grains that will not readily stick together and that is usually thoroughly saturated with water. Quicksand also yields easily to pressure and tends to suck down and readily swallow heavy objects."—Sounds a bit like Hollywood, doesn't it?

What distinguishes quicksand from ordinary beach sand or the spread of sand along a lake shore or at a river's mouth is its tendency to be more liquid than solid. To get a feel for how quicksand works, head for the wet sand at the water's edge and start moving your feet up and down in the same place. Before long, you'll sink in up to your ankles and you'll have a hard time getting your feet out. It's best to try this with a partner who can pull you out if you get sucked in too far. With true quicksand, the grains part so quickly that before you know it, you're up to your waist or beyond.

Should you encounter quicksand, don't panic. Immediately lie down on your back or stomach to spread out your weight; this will enable you to float on the sand, just as you would on water. Gently move your arms and legs in a swimming motion and work your way toward solid footing. Chances are, the area you are floating in is only a few feet wide and terra firma is literally within reach.

Bogs or quagmires in swampy areas can also be treacherous, although they will not suck you in as quickly as quicksand will. Stay especially alert when wandering along tidal flats, marshes, swamps, old bogs, or any place when the ground trembles underfoot. Alaska is notorious for its quagmires. As with quicksand, the best method for self-extraction from a quagmire is to flatten yourself out on either your stomach or back, spreading your arms and legs and swimming or squirming toward safety.

In very extreme cases, your feet may feel irretrievably trapped; in this case, jettisoning your shoes is a good idea. Reach down carefully and untie your laces—not as difficult as it sounds although your face will have to go under sand or mud for a short time—and then pull your feet free.

has to bore its way through. These things mean harsh duty if you're traveling on foot. And unless the river is regulated by a dam and shorn up with cement embankments and so forth, the riverbank can change radically in hours, and minutes in a storm. The option of wading in and swimming around obstacles is often a poor one. By and large a river is a place to go, to hike *to*, rather than hike along. There are many enchanted exceptions, but lengthy riverside travel, which we'll take up shortly, often involves plenty of thrashing, swimming, wading, scrambling, and bog slogging. On a domestic river, brilliant hikes can be had for anyone willing to do a little (or a lot) meandering and boulder hopping. But a river coursing through wilderness rarely affords easy passage along its banks.

Canyons share a distinction with caves: The novelty of entering one often wanes the farther and deeper you go, till you start feeling suffocated and a little panicky and suddenly have to get the hell out and into open spaces. It's a matter of degree, but understand that no known community has ever by choice lived in claustrophobic environs. Even in the middle of the Sumatran jungle, communities are set up in clearings where at least some little sky shows. Paradoxically, it is confronting the strange anxiety of tight confines that makes canyon walking so exciting and original. One of our deepest and oldest natural reflexes is "fight or flight," and if you think you have outgrown this primitive emotion, shimmy into a slot canyon five miles long and five feet wide. A couple of miles into it, when even the swiftest flight cannot immediately deliver you, the error in your thinking will become frightfully obvious. Canyon travel, especially within deep, narrow walls, is not for everyone.

"Canyoneering," however, which has recently become the rage and which commonly tracks rivers with decent elbow room, is one of the greatest outdoor sports going.

The generic goal of all canyoneering is to find a river and follow it to its source. In theory, that means you start at the wide part of the Rio Jarez, say, and follow it, against the current, through Durango, into the Colorado Mountains, up the wide gash in Pico Bravo, and right up to where water drips from a crack in the mountainside. The more common canyoneering practice is to spend a day following a river upstream. As you move higher, most rivers follow a canyon of sorts, hence the name.

Canyons are generally much easier to get into than to get out of. That is, the start of a canyon is typically easy going, but once you've gone some miles, and the surrounding walls have steepened, unless you're heading for a known trail leading to the rim, your only exit might, and often does, require backtracking to your starting point. The few times I've gotten into this position and refused to trudge back out, I scrambled up the canyon walls—and paid dearly for it, once getting poison oak so grievously my whole body was a weeping sore for a month, another time disturbing a yellow jacket nest and getting stung repeatedly till my face looked precisely like Fatty Arbuckle's. Climbing skills help little on steep shrubs and exfoliating chalk and dirt cliffs, which make up the sides of many canyons.

That much said, if you're not dead set on hacking to the very headwaters, don't mind reversing the ground covered, and are willing to tackle most of the things hikers go to extremes to avoid (such as mud and thorns and staying wet for the duration), canyoneering might be for you. All you need is a river and warm

You must step carefully and be sure of your route-finding skills when heading out across steep, rocky terrain.

Chris Townsend

temperatures (count on staying wet, which makes canyoneering a fair-weather sport to be sure).

Provided you don't scramble too far above the ground, use common sense, and always start off heading upstream, there are still a thousand things that can go wrong, though with any luck, getting hurt should not be one of them. The business about starting out pointed upstream is crucial—even for experts—because moving upstream is always more difficult than going downstream. This safeguards you from descending something you will later find irreversible—which I've done. Picture this: You're wading along the edge of a fleet but benign river. A grove of prickly reeds soon runs clear to the shoreline and beyond, so you swim around for twenty yards and are back to casual wading. Returning, however, you find that trying to swim back upstream and past those hateful reeds is impossible, and hand-walking up said reeds will slash your paws to the quick. You can't swim across the river because the river's fifty feet wide and by the time you reached the far shore—if you ever did—you'd have floated a mile downstream. That happened to Bob Gaines and me on the Rio Huerta in Mexico, and we had to make a two-mile detour through catastrophic bogs to reverse that twenty feet we'd swum around.

Play it safe and start on mild rivers; learn what kind of currents are negotiable and what your limits are.

10

Jungle

One always begins to forgive a place
as soon as it's left behind.

—Charles Dickens

John Long

Since it had not rained in nearly two weeks,

which defied every native's memory, the river had waned to a purl and we could hike the normally flooded streambed, skating over river stones submerged for a thousand years, stones that would never feel sunlight until the snarled green ceiling had receded, and by then the stones would be silt, flushed into larger rivers, washed into deltas, into the ocean.

We were five people: a native Iban chief, whose torso was a tattooed cavalcade of deer and snakes and arcane emblems, and whose bare feet crunched over driftwood littering the pebbly route; two young Iban hunters, who carried our provisions in swollen rattan packs and from whose mouthfuls of betel nut came a shocking red spit that stained the river stones like the spore of a wounded boar; a twenty-two-year-old Malaysian soldier assigned to us for reasons only a suspicious government could think of, who, tripping over creepers and slinking through streams, always held his antique single-shot Browning across his chest; and I, who was not going to drag a film crew into the middle of Sarawak until I'd seen the nomadic Punan Dayaks, felt their bark-skin clothes, and drunk their borak.

The soldier was out of his element and the chief fathered him like an heir, showing him just how to swing the machete, pointing out dire insects and critical herbage. Their minds addled by the nut, the young Ibans spat their mouth-

fuls and trudged on. I didn't have much of a pack, and kept pace okay.

We never saw sky through the tangled green roof, but rain was so long overdue we expected it. When it still hadn't come on the morning of the fourth day, we rose early and fell in behind the chief, who seemed to float along the intricate riverbank, the soldier always stumbling an arm's length behind. The leeches were bad.

The weather held, and I noticed everyone (but the soldier) glancing at the surrounding terrain, where black crags soared from stark lime bush. The return of the monsoon worried us, for the river could flood in minutes, forcing us into spiked, squelchy hedgerow that climbed up from the flat river passage.

In late afternoon we camped on a sandbar that hooked with the river's sharp bight. It took the young Ibans and me thirty minutes to clear the scrub and limbs washed there during high water. Mean-while the chief and the soldier, laughing and clowning, collected twigs for a fire in the lee of an ironwood trunk that we couldn't budge.

The young Ibans and I spent an hour damming the river. But no fish ever came.

The next morning it still hadn't rained, so we broke camp at sunrise, eager to cover some dry miles and close the distance between the Punans and us. We could thrash out a roundabout route through the jungle, or follow the riverbed

(text continues on page 197)

Repelling Thoughts

It smells bad, it melts plastic, and don't even think of getting any on your nylon jacket. So why are millions of people liberally applying DEET-based (N, N-diethyl-meta-tolu-amide) insect repellents? Because they work. But is the standard 100 percent DEET formula, once considered essential to combat the attacks of Minnesota's state bird (the mosquito), now considered potentially risky and unnecessary?

The answer is yes, but the Environmental Protection Agency (EPA) has yet to issue an official recommendation and meanwhile maintains that DEET is safe for human use. Still, it is hard to ignore recent revelations that many DEET-based repellents contain a chemical solvent that allows DEET to be more easily absorbed through the skin, leaving one wondering about potential toxicity.

A number of "holistic" repel-lents, made increasingly popular by fear of DEET, rely on citronella (derived from the lemon grass plant; the EPA labels it an essen-tial oil) as well as a host of other herbs to keep the little nasties from alighting. Questions regarding the safety of these so-called "natural" repellents are on the rise, too, because little is known about what concentrations might be toxic or potentially irritating to our skin.

Avon's Skin So Soft, which is not advertised as a repellent (Avon would first have to register it with the EPA), has achieved near cult-like distinction as a repellent among outdoorspeople. Statistics show that Skin So Soft accounts for nearly 20 percent of repellent sales in this country.

But studies also show that Skin So Soft and the holistic remedies can't hold a candle to the effectiveness enjoyed by DEET. DEET masks body odor, creates a smell insects do not like, and creates a surface insects do not like to be on. Even if DEET repellents are bad for you (an assertion that has no definitive support as yet), being "meat on the hoof" for myriad insects is not only unpleasant, in some instances diseases carried by bit-ing insects (Lyme disease, Rocky Mountain spotted fever, malaria, yellow fever, and many more debilitating illnesses) can be more dangerous than the DEET is pur-ported to be.

Nevertheless, products with high concentrations of DEET are losing popularity, especially among people who require frequent appli-cations over prolonged periods—such as hikers on an extended journey—and among parents buy-ing repellents for their kids.

It's not likely that any clear answers will be offered soon, but unless you are inclined to stay home, hide in the tent, or bury yourself in mud, DEET remains the best alternative to the slap-duck-and-run method. My advice: use it as you would a drug or medica-tion—with common sense—and industry experts suggest you stick with products that contain 30 per-cent DEET or less. Use lotion products for the skin (to minimize absorption) and spray products for clothing.

Those inclined to avoid DEET might want to try the following back-woods recipe. I offer it with no guar-antee of success and certainly no claims regarding toxicological safety. Mix ½ ounce citronella, ¼ ounce oil of cedarwood, add 1 ounce Vaseline (heated till soft), and then add ¼ ounce camphor spirits. Allow to cool.

What can you do to fight insects if you don't want to put repellent on your skin?

- Wear a light-colored, long-sleeved shirt and long pants tucked into your boots.
- A good hat and a bandanna around the neck will help.
- Look for a product made from mosquito netting that drapes over your head and seals around the neck. (I find this claustrophobic in the sticky confines of the jungle.)
- Spray repellent on clothing, not on your skin.

If you do get bitten, calamine lotion or a mixture of baking soda and water will help relieve the itch.

John Long

A Papuan tribesman gazes over his measureless hunting ground. Gulf Province, Papua New Guinea.

Cooking from Within

According to a study conducted by physicians at Duke University, physical exertion is considered life-threatening when the mercury reads above 90°F and the humidity level sogs in at 60 percent or above. In this "danger zone," humidity prevents perspiration from evaporating fast enough to keep you cool—no matter how much you drink. Your body begins to cook, and that's not good. Exercising in the danger zone is like turning the burner on high.

Dressing for Success

Even in humid jungle climates, you're usually best off resisting the temptation to completely disrobe. Sweat evaporates nearly as efficiently through loose, lightweight clothing as it does from your birthday suit. And you might need clothing's protection from the sun and biting insects. What's more, many foreign cultures have strict dress codes, especially for women. When it gets really steamy, however, you won't want to hike in anything more than a pair of baggy shorts with a nylon mesh brief. Avoid cotton undershorts; they invite jock rot—a miserable condition anytime but particularly in the jungle.

What do you do when it rains? If the group morals allow it, and you'll know if they do, strip. John reports hiking naked much of the time when rain is sheeting down. After the rain stops, on come the shorts and, if desired, a loose shirt.

Fed by many rivers, mighty Angel Falls (Venezuela) plunges more than 3,000 feet to the rain forest below.

through a steep ravine. The chief chose the riverbed. We'd have to move fast, for the march through the ravine would take six hours, and if it started to rain hard and fast, we'd get flooded. As I made out in my hack Malay, there was little chance of escaping the ravine into the jungle—just too steep. The chief held up a hand vertically and nodded, as if to say, "This steep." My guts turned to water.

The year before I'd filmed an early raft descent of the upper Kapuas. A week into it, we took a wrong tributary and scrambled high onto a bordering crag to try to reckon where the hell we were. A flash flood pinned us down on a crumbling ledge. An hour later and far below, a wall of muddy water and uprooted trees tore past, taking our rafts and a New Zealand boatman along with it. It took us seventeen days to tramp out to Tanjung Sellor. If it rained this time, we wouldn't be walking, we'd be riding the muddy wave, just like the New Zealander.

We entered the ravine after an hour. Overgrown walls rose sheer from the river. The streambed was easily one hun-

dred feet across, so I figured it would take a deluge several hours to fill the canyon, or for the river to rise high enough to add to the many splintered logs teetering atop twenty-foot river boulders.

The first hour passed quickly. On both

Eat for Heat

Foods appropriate for Alaska can be all wrong when the thermometer rises. The body can't process the fats and proteins in hot temperatures that it craves in cold ones. Hot temperatures call for an increase in fruit and vegetable consumption—items packed with water and potassium. Even their natural sugars can be useful for the quick energy they provide. Avoid high-protein foods such as meat unless you have plenty of water; your kidneys use inordinate amounts of water to eliminate the by-products of protein metabolism.

Have you ever wondered why the victuals in warm weather countries are so heavily spiced? Some folks say the spices mask the taste of foods that spoil quickly in the prevailing climate. More likely, fire in the cuisine encourages the body to sweat, thereby cooling itself.

Trail Food: A Sweet Tooth

Aside from an assortment of dried fruits and biscuit crackers, you'll want something sweet to satisfy the inevitable cravings that hit most hikers no matter where they are. Of course, in the jungle you'll not do too well with chocolate (unless you opt for Tropical chocolate, sold in some stores—it doesn't melt, but it doesn't taste too great either) or anything else that is inclined to get soggy or soft. That's why I love peanut brittle. It's practically indestructible, even if it does get a little tacky. You can buy it at any candy store, but it's a lot more fun to make your own, and making it is quite easy.

Take 4 tablespoons of butter, 2 cups of sugar, a pinch or two of salt, and cook over low heat in a nonstick pan until the mixture is smooth. (To be sure you've cooked it long enough, drop a small amount into a bowl of ice-cold water; it's done when the mixture forms a hard ball.) Now you can get creative. Tradition calls for 2 cups of peanuts, but I prefer to add 2 cups of mixed nuts—including chopped walnuts, pecans, and cashews. Pour the mixture onto a greased cookie sheet and place it in the refrigerator. Once the mixture is cool, break the brittle into chunks and transfer it to plastic bags.

sides, the vertical walls were spangled with dripping red orchids. Furry corkscrew vines spiraled from the cliffsides, looping and crossing the shallow river, then sweeping back up the opposite bank. Dawn vapors crept slowly up the wild cliffs to form a steamy nimbus, broken in spots to expose the green twine of the canopy, two hundred feet overhead. The air below was gummy and still, and the river was so low it barely made a sound. We stopped.

The chief gave a short speech, his outstretched arm waving to one, then the other, canyon wall. He emphasized words I could not understand. The soldier nodded quickly, sweat pouring down his bronzed face like a triton's in a fountain. He twice checked the safety on his rifle, making sure it was off. The chief resumed his march, his dark eyes traveling between the canyon walls, the soldier's eyes burning holes through his back.

The chief barked and the soldier closed the distance between them to a rifle's length. I followed the soldier nearly as closely as he shadowed the chief. On both sides, the young Ibans flanked out.

Suddenly the chief stopped and raised his hand. The young Ibans froze, but the soldier jumped and for the first time moved the rifle away from his chest. His knees flexed. His face was twisted with fear. Since violence is essentially wordless, it finds play only when communication breaks down. The soldier hadn't said a word for several hours. He looked ready to shoulder his rifle and blast the chief into the next world. I had long given up trying to understand why the soldier shadowed the chief with his gun, and in my terror of getting flushed out of the ravine, I almost wanted the soldier to shoot, to do something to shatter my anxiety. The chief simply dropped his gaze from high on the right-hand wall and marched on. The soldier brought the rifle back across his chest and fell into file.

The heat and humidity hung on us like a curse. I tramped on, drunk with adrenaline, staring at the soldier. A thin drizzle

Unlatching Leeches

 You've been slogging through dense undergrowth and along muddy tracks for an hour when, as you lean over to catch your breath, you notice your legs do not appear as you remember them. In fact, they are dotted with . . . whooyah, leeches! Before your skin begins to crawl and fold up right over your head, seize control and wrest your emotions. Although leeches do drain small amounts of your body's fluids, they're fairly innocuous. Did you know, for example, that hospitals in the United States still occasionally use leeches after surgery to keep blood away from a wound, to keep the wound clean, and to prevent infection?

Leeches are small, dark, bloodsucking, wormlike creatures. They reside happily in stagnant waters and in the dank understory of vegetation along the jungle floor, and they readily attach themselves to exposed skin. Although I know a few sadistic lads who revel in pulling and stretching leeches with forceps or pliers until they snap off with a twang, more subtle methods for leech removal exist. Though it sounds archaic, touching a hot match to a leech will encourage it to let go. Sprinkling the leech with salt will encourage it to detach and ultimately kill it. Once you've removed the leech, treat the bite area as an open wound; wash it with soap and water and then disinfect it with a good antiseptic. Open wounds, no matter how small, can quickly turn septic in the jungle.

began bleeding through the canopy. Our hours, I thought, were numbered.

The chief started hiking fast. In another hour, the vapors had burned off and through holes in the canopy gleamed shafts of blistering sunlight intermittent with sheets of scalding rain.

The chief's attention returned to the cliffsides, which slowly eased in angle. I tore my eyes away from the soldier and panned up the left wall; it looked like the same verdant brawl from waterline to sky. Meanwhile the chief weaved silently from shadow to shadow. Off to each side, the young Ibans did the same. The soldier's face was a study in awe. When he stumbled, the chief shot him a glance I thought would cost the chief, but the soldier only nodded bashfully. His rifle shook in his hands and I didn't care. I felt like shouting. A copper taste hung on my tongue. The river had risen a foot and in spots covered most of the riverbed.

We moved through a cut of sunlight. The chief treaded lightly along a spit of gravel, three creeping shadows playing across the still water to our left. For several minutes the chief's gaze had lingered high upon the right-hand wall. With a last step so slow it took some balance to perform, the chief's hand came up; with his eyes still riveted up and right, he froze. The soldier froze. Spread out on both sides, the young Ibans froze. I froze, and could feel my heartbeat in my hands and could hear it in my ears.

The chief wheeled around. The soldier extended the rifle at arm's length, one hand clasping the middle of the barrel, the other, the butt of the stock. In one motion the chief snatched the rifle, shouldered it, turned, and no sooner had the barrel settled on a spot high on the right-hand wall than a flash leaped from the muzzle as the report banged off the canyon walls, volleyed up and out through holes in the thinning canopy. A dark object rolled down the wall, tumbling with greater and greater speed till it plunged over a last, vegetated ceiling and splashed

John Long

A nameless river wends through unexplored jungle. Irian Jaya, Indonesia.

into a pool one hundred feet away.

The young Ibans were instantly on it, machetes drawn. But when I raced over I saw my concern was over nothing because the chief was a dead eye: a gaping hole right through the deer's head. A brain shot.

I spun to face the chief but he had already wandered downstream, his eyes probing high on the left wall. The young soldier fumbled to thumb a new shell into the chamber, fumbled because he kept looking up to see how far ahead the chief had gone. Gun loaded, safety off, the soldier scampered after and took up his position, walking quietly and in step behind the chief.

In ten minutes the storm shot through the canopy like a blast from a fire hose, and I broke into a jog with the other four men. When the ravine opened up an hour later, we'd been bodysurfing a waist-deep torrent for half an hour and were barked and bashed all over. The young Ibans had lost the deer and the soldier had lost his old Browning. We were sad about that. And we never did find the Punans. But the experience instilled in me a conviction I stick to: of all the world's varied terrain, the jungle is the most magnificent.

The musk of stewing peat waters your eyes. The green fastness extends forever. Mighty trees stretch for light, two hundred feet overhead. A hornbill shrieks in the dead of night.

The spider fern arises from an infinite, indivisible emptiness felt only through the contour of the fern itself. The jungle's immutable energy is a display of this emptiness, as is every ant and every drop of water dripping from a black rock wall. Change is supreme, the cycle of existence endless and audible in the nervous buzzing of the ancient peat, in boulders grinding in a river bottom during high monsoon. The fallen banyan seems lonely, but the green shoots rising from its moldering trunk show that even death cannot lie still in the jungle. Our presence there is high drama.

Fancy Footcare

Call it swamp foot, call it trench foot, but whatever you call it don't expect it to be fun. Particularly virulent forms of foot fungus are brought to life in the hot, wet, and steamy jungle environment. Dry feet? Forget it! Foot comfort is possible, however, even if your feet are wet most of the time. You can start by tearing a page out of the native way of wandering, and that's walking barefoot. While you can't beat the technique for breathability (and I don't recall ever seeing a native with foot problems), going barefoot is probably too far out there for most "civilized" shoe wearers. Opt, instead, for comfortable footwear (John is partial to Nike Air Madas or Five Tennies) that offers just enough support without being stifling. Thin, synthetic socks will dry quickly and resist becoming fungus gardens. Most of us have some form of athlete's foot, so be sure to take care of it aggressively before heading into the jungle. A week or so before your jungle jaunt (if you wait until your feet are cooked, it will be too late), and throughout the trek, use a strong prescription antifungal as a prophylactic. Nizoral 2% Cream is expensive, but this is the only one that works on John's feet. And if it works there, it will work anywhere—trust me. Use foot powder liberally; whenever possible, take off your shoes and let your feet breath. Why not wear Teva sandals, you may wonder? Well, try slogging through knee-deep mud in sandals just once. Sandals become more trouble than they're worth when faced with the sucking power of soupy mud.

We itch, sweat, swear, and do a hundred other things—some bliss, some hell; but forgetting is not one of them.

Like my first time in Canaima, Venezuela, a small jungle resort in the middle of tropical jungle. My future wife, then a Canaima schoolteacher, invited me to go to the *piedra*, the rock. We hit the little trail leading out of the village. Monkeys screeched high above as orange birds shot through the thick air between columns of hardwood trees. Rain drummed the snug vine ceiling, but by the time it seeped through, the hot rain fell in a misty curtain through the shade. Twice we forded steaming tongues of red mud that flowed over the small trail.

The piedra was a river boulder set in a big lagoon. On every side the sky bled through the canopy, streaking the green fastness topaz, emerald, gold. Beside the rock, under an awning of palms, Indians fished for giant eels prowling in the pool. As twilight dappled the sky, the Indians spooled in their droplines and faced the night with stony enchantment. I sat there for hours. Never had I felt so knitted into the restless surge of life.

Three years after my first visit I returned to Canaima to film some pickup shots for *King Kong Two*. The film was a bust, but my experience in the Venezuela jungle was another miracle. I had gone there to get a few high vista shots of the vast jungle, and had the helicopter pilot chopper me to the top of a towering apui, a limestone plug rising from the jungle like a massive green fist. The top of the apui was more than two thousand feet above the jungle and the terrain was from another world. Owing to intermittent fog, I couldn't get the shots I needed, so we bivouacked on top, with plans to grab the shots at dawn, weather permitting. We'd brought a local jungle expert along with

us, a veritable Pablo Bunyan who went by the name of Plutarcho; a few hours after nightfall, he invited me on a hike. Following the dim penumbra of Plutarcho's flashlight, we plodded through ankle-deep ropes to a wafer of rock extending out off the lip of the apui. The wet rock angled slightly and horribly toward the lip, and I thought Plutarcho mad to walk right to the edge of it.

"Eeeejole!" Plutarcho cried, peering over the edge. "You could drop a stone off here and it would fall a kilometer before it touched anything." He continued gazing into the void for a long while. "Tomorrow the sky will clear and the sun will pour down on us." Plutarcho looked down over the edge and pointed. "Look, Juancho. Look at the river."

Crisscrossing shafts of moonlight beamed through holes in the clouds to glint off the mighty river, far below them.

"That river, this view—we don't have to share them with anybody. They are all ours tonight."

We stood out on the wafer of rock, looking down at the river, over the silvered sweep that stretched beyond my last thought. Plutarcho found a fresh pool of rainwater in a hollow in the rock, and we drank the water, which was crystal and cool and tasted like the earth.

Serenity and wholeness abide under the green canopy. Much of my fascination is owing to the jungle's knack of soothing my past and conditioning, both of which led me to a mistaken sense of terminal otherness. You cannot be an individual in the jungle. The only role is as a participant in something far more inclusive than our private lives. Yes, the jungle has bugs, and pounding rain, and hip-deep mud and funky miasma; but there is magic in the ancient shade, and I hope every one of you gets the chance to someday feel it.

11

Weekend Warrior

For reasons ranging from mortgage

obligations to weeds in the backyard, even the outdoor fanatic is lucky to spring free for a long trip more than once every couple of years. But weekend—or extended weekend—trips are usually possible no matter how busy your docket. Oftentimes a few days in the wilds is the very medicine to relieve an overwhelming schedule, allowing you to take a few deep breaths and recover some gusto for the Big Grind. Weekend trips also serve as training for short trips into other areas as well as for extended treks.

The weekend-warrior adventure can be divided into a lot of different categories, but let's look at two main types: the "goal trek," where you have a specific peak to bag, say, or a divide to cross, and the "rejuvenation junket," where you might schlep to a certain swimming hole and spend a couple of days doing exactly as you please, including a lot of dreaming and dozing in the sunlight.

THE GOAL TREK

The goal trek—the standard outing—is a backpacker's mainstay and is carried out by clubs and outdoor programs every week of every year, much as regional playhouses can be counted on to stage productions of *Faust* and *Othello*. Time and tradition have fashioned classic outings

that almost everyone with a pack yearns to undertake.

In Southern California, for example, the classics include treks up San Gorgonio, San Jacinto, Mount Baldy, and Mount Whitney (all are nontechnical climbs). Hiking clubs often award badges and such for peaks bagged and treks completed. These ventures add a sense of direction and accomplishment not achieved by simply wandering in the wilds.

By and large, peak baggers and weekend warriors of the past were working stiffs, so they figured out ways to bag most classics over a weekend. For many years the routes were inside information. No more. Popular demand has triggered a boom in regional hiking guidebooks, which break such trips down to the last shrub on the trail.

Take San Gorgonio. The standard itinerary starts with the point of departure, determined by the nearest roadhead. That immediately gives you two fixed points of reference: the roadhead, and the summit of San Gorgonio. Since a classic almost always follows well-established trails, the trek simply involves connecting the trails between the two fixed points.

Mileage is normally posted on well-traveled paths. Twenty years ago, such postings could be highly inaccurate. A distance marked on a sign as ten miles could just as likely turn out to be six or sixteen.

With modern technology the Forest Service now accurately reckons trail distances to close tolerances.

In addition to mileages, regional guidebooks detail elevation gains and terrain, provide a general take on the time required for various legs of the trek, and point out favored campsites. Guides also list lush vistas, famous landmarks, and obstacles such as log crossings. Indeed, the new guides are so thorough they do everything but roll out your sleeping bag for you.

Weather can radically alter the timetable and the list of gear required to bag a classic. Slogging to the top of San Gorgonio in the dead of winter when the snowdrifts are high as a ship's prow and nighttime temps plunge is a very different venture than jogging to the summit in July. The need for snowshoes or skis and other cold-weather gear is discussed in the guidebooks, as well as time adjustments for completing the trek in winter conditions.

Tradition has determined—through thousands of outings over the years—an average time frame, drawn from the average hiker's experience. Viable programs and worthy guidebooks take seasonal con-

Foiling the Criminals

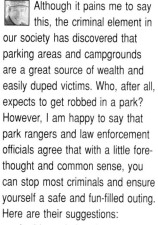 Although it pains me to say this, the criminal element in our society has discovered that parking areas and campgrounds are a great source of wealth and easily duped victims. Who, after all, expects to get robbed in a park? However, I am happy to say that park rangers and law enforcement officials agree that with a little forethought and common sense, you can stop most criminals and ensure yourself a safe and fun-filled outing. Here are their suggestions:

- Avoid wandering alone on a campground trail, no matter how short it may be. This is especially important for children and young teens.
- Travel in pairs around a campground. No one should go to the bathroom alone.
- Report all suspicious activity to rangers.

- Never stay in an urban park after dark.
- Sign in at all trailheads.
- Never leave a wallet or anything of value locked in your car. Take it with you or leave it at home. I tuck my driver's license, credit card, and money into a waterproof nylon pouch that I take with me; I leave my urban wallet at home.
- Check in with rangers to determine if your trailhead has a high incidence of break-ins. If so, try to choose another parking place. I have often found a garage owner in a nearby town willing to allow me to leave my car and drive me to and from the trailhead for a small fee.
- Use your older vehicle and not the brand new SUV for the outing. Nothing announces valuables for stealing louder than a new and expensive vehicle. If your new car or truck is all you

have, be sure your insurance will cover vandalism.
- Try to leave your car at a parking area where lots of people are coming and going throughout the day.
- Never hide your car keys on the vehicle. There are few options for hiding a key, and the crooks know them all.
- Park with your trunk or hatch facing the main parking lot and not the woods. No sense in giving thieves any more privacy than necessary.
- Refrain from leaving a note on your dashboard that tells where you're going and when you're returning. Why? Because although the note will help searchers in the event you are reported missing, it unfortunately also serves as a written time frame for crooks, telling them how long they have to thrash and trash your car.

ditions into account in making time esti-mates. Also, outings conducted by local clubs and shops—offering a sound baptism into the society of weekend trekkers—set a pace geared for the slowest participant. A classic is a classic owing to popularity, meaning most everyone can do it.

Most classics follow the easiest and most popular route. But often there are longer or more direct or technical routes up the same peak or across the same divide. Such variations on a classic theme provide ambitious hikers with variety and chal-lenge not found by sticking to the old chart.

Goal treks share some aspects of mountaineering. Take a major peak like Everest or K2. There are various ways—or routes—up these mountains. Each route varies in length and difficulty. The shortest route is the most direct one. It is likely to be the most difficult as well, because instead of following lines of natural weakness—which usually describe a wandering, not a direct, line—the direct route blazes straight over all obstacles.

The classic hiking route up a moun-tain does not make a beeline for the

Lost and Found

By paying attention to your surroundings, you can avoid losing the way while hiking. But if you get lost, there also are ways to survive until you can find your way out or searchers reach you.

- Keep your eyes moving in 360-degree sweeps as you hike. Yes, that means looking behind you frequently. Remember important and easy-to-recognize landmarks for reference in finding your way later. Use your eyes, ears, and nose in helping determine where you are relative to your car or camp.
- Carry a whistle around your neck and know how to use it. The sequence of three sharp and distinct blasts from a whistle followed by a long pause, repeated several times, is a uni-versal sign that trouble is brew-ing and help is needed.

- Sit and think quietly if you become disoriented. Panicking will only get you more lost. If you are able to remember clearly the way back to camp or the trail-head—and chances are that after sitting for a few minutes, you will—then by all means pro-ceed as long as everything con-tinues to look familiar. Otherwise, stay put.
- If you decide to stay put because you're obviously lost, follow these four steps for survival: First, find or build a shelter. A shelter made of sticks and debris that you essentially burrow into is effective and quite warm, even in severe weather. Second, find a source of water. Third, make a fire for warmth and for signal-ing. As the fourth and final prior-ity, find food. Do not eat plants unless you are certain they are not poisonous. With shelter and water—even if no food is avail-

able—a person can survive for many days.

Tips and Tricks for a Successful Trip

The following are a few suggestions, many already covered in detail in this book, to help you keep your weekend escape memorable for the right reasons.

- Don't leave home without the essentials: duct tape, flashlight, map, compass, extra food and clothing, sunglasses, first-aid supplies, pocket knife, water-proof matches, fire starter, and baby wipes (to wash your hands).
- Set up your tent at least once before you leave home. Ever try to set up a tent in the dark and forget how? Or discover that a mouse had set up house over the winter, leaving the tent looking like Swiss cheese? Hold a prac-tice assembly in your backyard to get the routine down. Another tip:

summit. Instead it follows gullies and ramparts in wandering its way to the top, essentially bypassing difficult and technical terrain. Variations of the classic "easy" path range from slightly steeper and more strenuous routes to forging cross-country straight for the top, hacking through bushes and clawing up cliffs.

Most goal treks can be approached many different ways, allowing you to choose a route that matches your abilities and desires. And most every way is probably described in a regional guidebook.

THE REJUVENATION JUNKET

The drawback with the goal trek is that the more prestigious the outing, the more it's apt to take on the aspect of hard work. If you are grinding things down to a nub all week long, sometimes the motivation is not there to drive two hours, throw on a forty-pound pack, and hike your pins off to get another feather in your cap. Sometimes you don't feel like earning your wilderness experience.

---

try color-coding tent poles by size with colored tape to make assembly quicker and easier.

- Don't snack where you sleep. In bear country, never bring food into a tent, don't sleep in clothing that smells of freshly caught fish, hang your food away from camp, and always yield the right of way to a bear.
- Cool your jets. Unless you're trying to launch the space shuttle (or your dinner), running the camp stove on full power all the time is a waste of fuel.
- Watch your pee for cues. If your body is producing relatively clear urine five times a day, your fluid intake is fine. Cloudy or dark urine means you need to drink more—at least two quarts per day. No, Hawaiian Punch does not count. Neither does beer.
- Lose the scent. The only thing you'll attract with perfume is bees. If you want to see wildlife,

remember that Bambi doesn't like cosmetics, neon clothes (you're not in Vegas), or perfume. And, shhhh! Be quiet.

- Keep it light. Mosquitoes are naturally attracted to darker colors. When hiking, keep covered and wear light colors.
- Don't dry wet boots in front of a fire unless you plan to eat them. Can you say "barbecued boots"?
- Skip the death march. A weekend outing is no time to try to cram in a year's worth of activity. Your family and friends will soon learn to avoid your camping trips if all you do is schedule grueling hikes, early rising, and constant activity. Learn to relax and enjoy the quiet moments.

Food Planning

Major considerations in putting together a menu for your trip include taste, nutrition, and energy content. Both adults and

children need high-energy carbohydrate foods when adventuring outdoors. This is not to say your diet should become one of sugar and fat during an extended trip. Planning meals and snacks that include pasta, milk, cheese, rice, seeds, nuts, dried fruit, and vegetables will adequately meet nutritional needs for everyone. Weight, ease of packaging and handling, and variety are other necessary considerations.

Water is a critically important part of menu planning. It's vital that each person drink two to four quarts of water per day. Just as important is maintenance of the body's balance of water and salt. The normal diet typically includes an adequate provision of salt. But if the trip is extremely difficult or the weather unusually hot, an electrolyte additive to the water is appropriate. Avoid overdoing the salt intake, as too much salt is more harmful than too little.

The rejuvenation junket is the ticket when you want to get out of Dodge, but don't want to crawl back to the OK Corral more exhausted than when you started. Sometimes we need to venture into the wilds to recover—emotionally, spiritually, and physically. Here, the idea is to slip into nature and wander around—or simply hang out—till we find the healing mojo.

This kind of trip can take many forms, but a favorite method is to hike to a certain bend in the river or a shady arroyo, make camp, and kick back. The usual aim is to get away from everything and everybody, so beware if your destination is a popular one; you'll likely be hiking right into the teeth of a mob. Most any landmark (especially lakes and waterfalls) within an hour's walk from the roadhead is likely to be busy as an anthill on the weekend. To find solitude, you might have to walk a little farther afield or head for a lesser-known area. Few people ever leave the trail, so a little cross-country work can usually carry you away from the masses. Just make sure you know how to get back.

Proper hydration will help prevent hypothermia, frostbite, heat stroke, heat cramps, and altitude sickness. If water is not going to be available at the campsite or as you travel, be sure to pack it with you.

KEEPING IT LIGHT

You can keep the weight of your food to a minimum by using dried, dehydrated, and freeze-dried foods, in addition to any fresh selections on your menu. Further lighten the load by repackaging all dry foods into resealable plastic bags (such as the Ziploc brand). Choose sturdy freezer-quality bags, not flimsy ones designed to hold sandwiches. Stay away from canned goods.

It's most convenient and efficient to prepackage each meal into a large resealable plastic bag. Whenever possible I premeasure and premix all the dry ingredients for a meal together in the same bag.

Don't forget to label the bag with its contents, and drop in briefly written preparation instructions for each meal.

You can package bulk foods in doubled resealable bags or in plastic bottles with a wide mouth. For beverages, sugar, and such items as dehydrated milk or instant coffee, I prefer wide-mouth Nalgene bottles. They are easy to open and close and won't tear or break. Food items like pancake mix, flour, pasta, and dried fruits pack and carry nicely in a double-bag system. I recommend the double bagging to prevent accidental bursting or puncturing.

Set up a mini assembly line to package your food before the trip. A get-together with everyone measuring the food and writing labels is both fun and efficient. The kids will enjoy sealing the bags (be sure to squeeze out all the air first) and sticking on the labels.

Fresh produce for the trip is best carried in a breathable mesh bag near the top or to the outside of a pack. The produce will tend to spoil in plastic.

Because of the danger of spoilage, stay away from real butter, cooked meats, eggs, and non-canned bacon. Real cheese is fine outdoors, but avoid processed cheeses and spreads. The softer the cheese or the higher the oil content, the more the cheese will turn gooey and oily—and unappetizing. Just try to get a child to eat oily-looking cheese and you'll soon see what I mean about avoiding the softer cheeses. I prefer hard cheeses like Jarlsberg or Gouda.

Meals: What to Eat

Try to plan your meals and snacks so they will be easy and fun to prepare, visually appealing, and tasty. The following list can

UPPING THE ANTE

The evolution of one's outdoor education is usually determined by where a person lives, transportation options, and the amount of time available. If you live in downtown Trenton, have no car, and can't leave town, it's doubtful you'll become the next John Muir. But if you can break free for weekends and can find a ride, you can probably get to the nearest wilderness and have at it.

If the nearest wilderness features a big expanse, you will in time crisscross it every which way. If it features a prominent peak, you'll work it from various angles. This is the normal approach: squeeze the local resources dry. Work the classics to stay in shape and to have fun. When the urge strikes you, try more ambitious routes to expand your curriculum.

People follow this same strategy with mountain biking, tackling the easier runs to hone the basic moves and plunging down the grim single-track courses as skill and experience increase. Over time they know the whole area intimately and in the process acquire a medley of skills

aid in your menu planning. Don't forget to solicit the input of everyone—including the children—who will be eating the meals.

BREAKFAST SUGGESTIONS

Drinks. Cocoa, orange juice crystals, Tang, tea, coffee, low-fat dried milk.

Cereal. Oatmeal, granola, muesli, Cream of Wheat, Cream of Rice, Malto Meal.

Main dishes. Pancakes (Bisquick works great), freeze-dried western omelet, dried eggs.

Dried fruit. Apricots, prunes, raisins, apples, pineapple, plums, cherries, pears, peaches.

TRAIL LUNCH SUGGESTIONS

Drinks. Juice crystals, individual serving-size boxes of juice, Kool-Aid, Wylers, Tang, Gatorade instant mix, hot cocoa (nothing better for a cold day).

Meat. Bacon bits or bar, jerky (beef or turkey), salami, pemmican, beef stick.

Cheese. Any nonpasteurized, non-processed cheese that does not require refrigeration.

Nuts. Peanuts, pecans, cashews, pine nuts, walnuts, hazelnuts, almonds.

Seeds. Pumpkin, sunflower, soya, sesame.

Fresh vegetables. Carrots, radishes, cauliflower, jicama, celery, turnips, broccoli.

Fresh fruits. Apples, oranges, tangerines.

Dried or freeze-dried fruits. Dates, apples, pineapple, bananas, peaches, prunes, apricots, raisins.

Breads, crackers, pastries. Lebanese flat bread, sourdough, rye, pilot biscuits, Ritz crackers, Waverly crackers, Triscuits, Rye-Crisps, Japanese rice crackers, Cheese Nips, Melba toast, trail

biscuits, Pop-Tarts, Danish Go-Rounds.

Sweets. Licorice, lemon drops, candy orange slices, tropical chocolate, malted milk tablets, Tootsie Rolls, Life Savers, fruit bars or rollups, sesame seed bars, pudding, cookies.

DINNER SUGGESTIONS

Drinks. Tea, coffee, hot cocoa, Kool-Aid, Wylers, Tang.

Soups. Lipton Instant, Knorr Instant, Top Ramen.

Prepared dinners (freeze-dried). Favorite brands include Richmoor, Natural High, Back-packer Pantry, AlpineAire, and Mountain House. If you've never tried freeze-dried dinners, buy several, take them home, and prepare them. I admit a personal preference for Backpacker Pantry desserts and side dishes and AlpineAire and Natural High main

that will help when they venture to other areas.

Once one has followed this progression, the hankering to move on to other — and possibly bigger—pastures is automatic. A common delusion, however, is that by mastering a local area, you're set for anything under the sun. Flash back to the various chapters on desert, alpine, jungle, and other environments and recall the special demands particular to each area.

The key word here is "special." A person used to hiking over varied terrain and in different conditions, setting up camp, cooking with a portable stove, and so forth, already knows the basic composition. But each different ecosphere will impose its own arrangement on the song. Desert travel can be learned only in the desert. But the experienced backpacker is not starting from scratch when he or she first ventures to Death Valley or the sands of Arabia. This person is simply gaining familiarity with a new arena and with the gear and special skills necessary to navigate the land in safety. Every outdoor person I know learned the fundamentals by exhausting an area close to home, only later applying their skills the world over.

courses, but everyone's tastes are different.

Rice. Uncle Ben's quick brown rice for curries, casseroles, and stir-fry.

Flour mix. Bisquick, for dumplings, breads, and biscuits.

Pastas. All kinds, including macaroni and cheese.

Lentils, pinto beans, lima beans. All make great dinners or can be added to soups and stews.

Instant potatoes. For thickening soups or making potato pancakes.

Bases: Tomato base, chicken base, beef base, miso, instant gravy, sauce packets, bouillon cubes or powder. Flavoring and bases for soups, stir-fry, casseroles, curries.

Textured vegetable protein. Made of soybeans; add to soups or casseroles.

Freeze-dried chicken, beef, fish. Add to soups or casseroles.

Freeze-dried vegetables. Add to soups, casseroles, or stir-fry.

SPICES AND OTHER FOOD ITEMS

Margarine. Squeeze Parkay, Country Crock, or other.

Cooking/frying product. Crisco, carried in a small container. Better than oils and butter for cooking and frying, and it doesn't burn or break down as easily on a hot flame. After each use, pour back into container and reuse.

Honey. Healthier than white sugar for sweetening. Package in a squeeze tube or eight-ounce plastic bottle.

Brown sugar. Alternative to honey and not as messy.

Cinnamon sugar. Sprinkle on cereal, hot biscuits, pancakes, and so forth.

Peanut butter and honey mix. Premix two parts peanut butter to one part honey, and package in a squeeze tube; add more honey to soften consistency.

Dry milk. Low-fat Milkman powder for flavoring and mixes. To help prevent lumping, use just enough water to turn the powder into a paste before adding all the water required.

Spices. Cinnamon, nutmeg, curry, oregano, chili powder, garlic, black pepper, salt, dry mustard. Package each in a one-ounce plastic bottle and label.

Spicy sauces. Soy sauce, the backpacker's ketchup. And Worcestershire Sauce and Tabasco Sauce, packaged in flip-top bottles, for spicing-up freeze-dried meals.

FAVORITE MEAL SUGGESTIONS

Breakfast

Pancakes and wild berry syrup; hot cocoa or orange juice crystals; dried fruit.

Lunch

Gorp; peanut butter and honey mix on Ritz crackers or party rye bread;

beef jerky; Wylers lemonade mix or water; candy bar.

Dinner
Freeze-dried spaghetti mix; Knorrs instant vegetable soup; instant chocolate pudding using instant milk; Tang, Wylers, or water.

Cookware

 The choices in cookware for backpacking are relatively simple. We'll take a look here at the various materials used for cookware and how to care for your pots and pans. (See chapter 12 for a rundown on your choices in stoves and stove fuels.) In selecting cookware, essentially there are four basic materials to consider.

Enamel. This is nothing more than thin steel coated with a kiln-baked enamel finish that looks good, is easy to clean, and is hard to scratch. The downside is that this stuff will chip and dent over time and rust will appear wherever a chip occurs.

Aluminum. It's very light and conducts heat very well, making cooking quite efficient. On the downside, burned-on foods stick tenaciously to aluminum, which is why nonstick coatings are so popular and such a good idea. There was some fear in

the past of possible health hazards from eating foods cooked in aluminum, but my research has turned up no evidence of such risks.

Stainless steel. This material is extremely durable, cleans quickly and efficiently, and won't scratch easily. The downside is its inability to conduct heat evenly, leading to scorched food in the pattern of a stove's intense flame.

Titanium. This will be your choice if saving weight is your primary concern. It is durable and extremely lightweight. On the downside, it is very expensive and it does not conduct heat evenly, making boiling anything more than water a creative affair.

I use a titanium cup and aluminum pots most often. This selection combines the best of weight and cooking performance.

PROTECTING YOUR POTS

What are the best ways to keep your pots and pans looking clean and new? If the pots you own are coated, then it is a simple matter of wiping them clean with a soft, soapy sponge and rinsing them with warm water. If the pots are made of uncoated aluminum, stainless steel, or titanium, a bit more elbow grease

will be required. Prolong the finish on any cookware by using only nonabrasive scouring pads—not steel wool, scouring powders, or other abrasives.

A few other do's and don'ts to help prolong the life and looks of your cookware:

- Never cut with a knife inside nonstick cookware.
- Don't let cookware boil dry.
- Use only nylon or wood utensils, which won't mar the pots.
- Adjust the stove's flame to a medium heat for all frying and cooking, being sure the flame does not extend up the sides of the pot at any time.
- When storing or packing pots, keep in mind that exposed metal surfaces and Teflon coatings don't mix. So place a paper towel, a soft cleaning towel, or other soft and thin fabric or paper between pot surfaces to prevent scratching.
- Avoid packing a stove inside cookware, a practice that can lead to fuel residues and tastes that are less than appetizing. A far better alternative is to pack foodstuffs inside cookware.
- Pack cookware midway in your backpack and as close to your back as possible to minimize denting or crushing.

Choosing a Backpack

Following are some key features to look for when shopping for a backpack. Also check back to chapter 2 for other useful information and advice on packs.

- Durability. Is the pack built strong enough to withstand beating through willow, dense brush, and alder and being scuffed and dragged over rocky surfaces? Look for reinforced stitching at pocket corners, materials such as packcloth and Cordura, and double layers of fabric on the pack's bottom—this is especially important for internal frame packs.
- Ease of use. Some packs have just too many "damn straps" for adjusting fit and function. Some adjustments are necessary; too many simply become confusing and frustrating.
- Good fit. Your pack needs sufficient adjustment to fit your body, with a waist belt and shoulder straps that take into account the width of your hips, the curves of your body, the width of your shoulders, and so forth.
- Comfort! Comfort! Comfort! No pack will make a load disappear, but there's a tremendous difference in comfort between a poorly designed pack and one

that is built to carry the load close to your body, with minimum pack movement and maximum weight on your hips rather than on your shoulders. Look for contoured and well-padded shoulder straps, a hipbelt that is cupped or angled to sit comfortably on your hips with minimal gaps, and a frame system that transfers the weight effectively to the hipbelt.

- Floating top pocket. The pack's top pocket should adjust up or down—that is, it should "float"— to accommodate your load as it grows or shrinks.
- Accessory pockets. By purchasing accessory pockets that can be strapped to the main pack, you can customize the pack in terms of function and volume.
- Hydration accessories. You need to keep up your fluid intake as you hike, so look for a pack with at least one pocket that can accept a hydration bladder with its attached drinking hose. You also will probably want to get a water bottle holster for carrying a wide-mouth, one-quart bottle.

Choosing Your Boots

 (See chapter 2 for other information on boots.)

Choosing A Tent

Buying a tent is something like buying a home: you decide what you must have for comfort and safety and then do your best to find the dwelling that meets your needs within your budget. Following is a list of basic features any tent should have. After that, I've listed additional features specific to tents designed for various climatic variations: summer tents; three-season tents; and all-season tents. (See chapter 12 for supplementary information on tents used in mountaineering and winter camping. Also see chapter 12 for guidance on choosing a sleeping bag.)

Along with the tent, add a ground cloth. With nothing more than the clear polyethylene sheeting available at most hardware stores by the roll, you can make a trim-to-fit ground cloth that is slightly smaller than the footprint of your tent's floor. The ground cloth, not your precious tent floor, will then take the wear and tear of earth and grit abrasion.

Also, a word to the wise before we begin: Just because a manufacturer says a tent will sleep three doesn't make it so. How much space you require inside a tent is a personal thing that needs to take into account how tall you are, how wide you are, how much "toss and turn" room you need, and how much extra sitting-up room you desire. I've seen so-called two-person tents that won't even accommodate two full-size sleeping pads side-by-side without overlapping.

ESSENTIAL FEATURES OF ANY TENT

Look for the following features in whatever tent you buy.

- Collapsible tent poles of aluminum, high-strength aluminum, carbon fiber, or tubular fiberglass.
- Tent poles that are all the same length so that they can be used interchangeably, making it easier to set up the tent in less than ideal conditions. As an alternative, the poles may be color-coded, with each color corresponding to a specific pole sleeve on the tent.
- A free-standing tent design. Free-standing tents set up easily on sand, rocks, snow, or anywhere else, with no need for pounding in a bunch of stakes. However, even a free-standing tent needs to be tethered to a stake, a tree, or a rock unless you want to risk turning it into a very expensive and disposable kite.
- Nylon or polyester fabric, for

durability and lightest weight.
- A one-piece floor, which promotes waterproofness.
- Steep walls, which increase usable interior room, shed precipitation well, and help vent out humidity.
- Mesh windows and doors with zippered closures for battening down the hatches when things get blustery and damp.
- Tent body of yellow, white, or beige, to let the most light in.
- Storage pockets inside the tent, for organizing small items.
- Gear loops inside the tent, to use for hanging flashlights and other equipment.
- Waterproof rain fly that clips to poles and requires only minimal staking.
- Beefy nylon webbing stake loops at each pole end on the tent body.

ESSENTIAL FEATURES OF A SUMMER TENT

Summer tents are designed for use during summers and in hot climates. Look for:

- Two-pole construction for weight savings.
- Generous amounts of mesh in the tent body. The breezier the tent, the better it will ventilate.
- A rain fly that stops several

inches above the ground, allowing for a high level of protection combined with a good deal of ventilation.

ESSENTIAL FEATURES OF A THREE-SEASON TENT

Three-season tents are built to handle light snow and the harsher conditions of autumn, in addition to being suitable for warm climates. Features should include:

- Three poles of high-strength aluminum, to stand up to strong winds and heavy rains.
- An inside gear loft. The loft attaches to the ceiling for additional gear storage.
- A large vestibule. This covered protrusion at one end adds room for wet boots and damp dogs.
- Two entries, or one extra-large entry, in tents designed for two or more people. This allows for easier entrance and egress without stepping on your partner's face.
- A full-coverage rain fly that extends to the ground.
- Sturdy guy-out points sewn to the rain fly for helping to tie down the tent when things get blustery.
- A skylight window in the rain fly for additional light.
- A rain fly that can be set up by itself, independent of the tent, for

the ultimate in weight savings and go-light travel.

ESSENTIAL FEATURES OF AN ALL-SEASON TENT

All-season tents, also known as convertible tents, can serve for all seasons. However, they are still not fully intended for hard-core mountaineering or serious winter camping (see chapter 12). In an all-season tent, look for:

- Four high-grade aluminum poles as part of the tent's free-standing construction, with the option to use only three poles in the interests of saving weight.

- Removable vestibule. For trips where light weight is a must, the vestibule can be left behind.
- Generous mesh in the tent body, with zip-out panels for added ventilation when needed or full closure when maximum protection is required.
- The all-season tent should also include the special rain-fly features of the three-season tent: sturdy guy-out points sewn to the rain fly for tying down the tent in high winds; a skylight window in the rain fly; and the option to set up the rain fly by itself, independent of the tent.

FEATURES TO AVOID IN A TENT

Now that you know what to look for in buying a tent, here are a few things to reject:

- Solid fiberglass poles. These are the poles that discount stores and cheap tents rely on, and they are the poles that shatter with alarming frequency.
- Metal zippers of any kind.
- A tent design that requires full staking in order to remain standing.
- Any tent so small that you feel like the filling in a nylon burrito.

12

Long-distance Hiking

Countless scenic turnouts on countless

byways throughout the world can snatch your breath away with the drop into a velvet arroyo, the fan of trees that stretch to the horizon, the stark desert emptiness that runs off the edge of your mind. Such views whisper things to us. But if you want to hear the words you must leave the car and trek out into the arena. And if you really want to grasp the language, you've got to stay out there and live with it for a while. The farther you penetrate the view, the more it creeps into your bones. And that means covering some ground—probably a lot of ground, spread over a lot of days.

The topics we've covered put us in reasonable shape to examine the particulars of heading into the wilds for the Long March. However, you face a handful of special demands when a trek puts you afield for a week, a month, or longer. The first thing is that the "long" in Long March is a very fluid term.

I remember topping out on Mount Watkins in Yosemite Valley after a five-day ascent of the South Face. Starving and exhausted, humping a haul bag (full of climbing gear) the size of a beer truck, the four-mile trudge from the summit back to the valley floor—all downhill—seemed to take a month and nearly killed us. Several years later, Dwight Brooks and I set off from Wamena (in Irian Jaya) and lit out across jungle trails hoping to traverse Indonesian New Guinea on foot. Our loads belonged on mules. Better yet, elephants. But we were fit, the trails were generally flat and, most off all, we were fresh and eager. We put in more than a hundred miles the first week and could easily have done more. Twenty days later, when the muddy path wound over 10,000-foot cols and the cold drizzle never let up, every step seemed a mile.

With shifts in terrain and altitude, distance becomes a relative term. Sure, there are legendary treks that would sap an Army Ranger. We humans have limits, and nature has a way of making us meet them. Hiking above 12,000 feet, say, is real work for anyone. And when the trail describes a staircase, or works up a scree field, it's rugged duty for us all. These things considered, it's often the time spent afield, rather than the mileage covered, that defines the Long March.

Nevertheless, you will cover some ground, and no matter the terrain or the obstacles encountered, when big mileage is involved, the key elements usually are fitness, gear, weight, attitude, pace, and rhythm.

FITNESS

The age-old adage says that anything worth having requires hard work. In other words, if you crave nature's grandeur, you'll be hiking your ass off or you'll never get past the edge of the magic. Another adage says that the best things in life are free. You can pull your jalopy over on the Pacific Coast Highway, walk thirty yards to the shoreline, and watch the fireball fall into the sea—and who's to say this isn't Nature at her finest hour? What's at issue here is the quality and depth of experience.

Any adult can attest that it takes years to really know one's spouse—if you ever do. You've got to see her from many angles, witness all her moods. You've got to travel into his uncharted territories braving tornadoes, earthquakes, mudslides, and a thousand mirages. The same holds for Mother Nature. You cannot know her at a glance. You must cover some ground—together. Here, it's best you be in shape or you won't be communicating with the natural world so much as hating life for all the screaming muscles. It's hard to appreciate, let alone understand, anything when you're exhausted.

The media love to idealize long-distance hiking. Given articles might touch upon the effort required to slog the length of the Dolomites or to traverse the Bob Marshall Wilderness. But note how the photos are usually of shimmering sunsets and dewy meadows. Articles, posters, brochures and so forth typically promote the aesthetic glories of the long trek. I would invite you to look a little closer.

Say I'm going to Sequoia National Park and plan to make a sixty-mile loop up to a group of alpine crags and high lakes. I block out a week to complete the expedition. Aside from seven days' food, I'm lugging cooking and sleeping gear, camera, notebooks, first-aid kit, and probably another couple pounds of widgets and doo-dads that I don't need and will never use. But I paid green money for these things and damned if I'm going to leave them collecting dust in the garage. I stuff all this gear into a pack, heave it up onto my back, and amble down the trail. No one can question that I'm moving through God's country. But I'm not floating along the path like an angel on the wing, harp in hand. First and foremost, I'm a beast of burden. If I'm in shape and used to the load, those dewy meadows and shimmering sunsets seem heavenly. But if I'm so overburdened I can barely look up, everything around me will seem hateful because all my attention is glued to the physical torment of humping a load I'm unfit to handle.

Consider it this way: you've got tickets to the J. Paul Getty museum, home to a billion dollars worth of frescoes and marble nudes. At the museum entrance, you're given a ten-pound pack. Over the past six months you haven't done anything more physical than walk the mutt, but a ten-pound pack is no big deal and you slip into the wing featuring Grecian statues and admire them. You move on. Each time you leave an exhibit, a man drops another ten pounds into your pack. By the time you get to the European masters, your pack weighs seventy pounds, your legs are buckling, and your spine is crooked like a horseshoe. Rembrandt can go to hell, or rather, join you there. All you want is to get that load off your back. You notice a woman beside you. She also hefts a seventy-pound pack. The effort of schlepping her load is written on her face, but she seems to enjoy the superb canvasses before her just the same. How is this possible? Simple. She is mentally and physically prepared to handle the load. In short, she's in shape.

For a trek of any distance, fitness is prerequisite, the foundation upon which rests most everything else. It is very hard and always painful to acquire endurance on the trail unless you are an athlete rounding back into shape and the trek is long enough for you to work through a breakdown and recovery cycle—something usually requiring several weeks. If you bring some fitness and endurance to the venture, and if your rations are good, your tackle is squared away, and you understand how to pace yourself, you will likely get stronger as you go. But if you jump straight from a hot tub onto the John Muir Trail, your effort probably will not be one of enjoyment, but rather one of survival.

Not surprisingly, many poorly conditioned folks decide to get back into shape by embarking on a Long March. This strategy breeds a survival ordeal. The mind-set of surviving a long hike carries with it the idea of victory and accomplishment—once you battle through it. The hike, and nature, are reduced to a mere utility in the service of a personal agenda.

Of course, nature is—thank God— totally indifferent to our personal agendas, and here lies the rub. When we walk into the outdoors with too rigid a plan, we stop embracing the unknown and start judging it on the basis of how well, or how poorly, it accommodates our intention. If we're trying to get in shape and the switchbacks seem to climb to Venus, we curse the trail and the rascal who made it. That much said, no person who has ever hiked a grueling trail—regardless of that person's fitness—has not cursed the loose footing, the blazing calves, and the shoulder straps cutting through the bone. It's just that if you're in shape, you don't hold the trail responsible for being what it is. As a rule of thumb, your fitness level must be equal to the task or any long-distance hike will literally turn into a pain in the ass. And quickly.

Comfort Ratings

Temperature ratings are no guarantee of warmth. It's not uncommon for people to judge the minimum comfort limit of an identical sleeping bag up to 20 degrees apart. Even without the variables of environmental factors, clothing worn, food eaten, pads used, body size, fitness, and so forth, perceptions of comfort vary wildly.

GEAR

I've always worked off the notion that the best gear is that which most increases my enjoyment. It's also worth recalling the old mechanics' saying that good work depends on having the right tool for the job. Keeping track of these two ideas helps clarify the confusing task of selecting the "best" gear for a long-distance trek.

If you're in shape, preparation is a determining factor on whether a long trek is a dream or a nightmare. Preparation is largely a matter of learning what you really need. A great and essential mantra among experienced outdoors people is, "The more you know, the less you need," or simply, "Less is more." If you want to be a pack mule, you certainly can. Many do. But it is a much better business—on both your body and the land—to travel lightly, touching down as a breeze stirs the leaves, rather than plowing across the tundra on mule hooves. Of course, to travel lightly you must have knowledge—navigation and survival skills, a rucksack full of common sense, and ease with being in the backcountry even if naked and alone. Again, such skills naturally issue from experience. The quickest way to achieve the "less is more" philosophy is to make that motto your goal.

A second essential factor in preparation is to learn about the climate and terrain of the place you're going. Most any long-distance trek will engage different terrain and conditions—perhaps all the way

Choosing A Sleeping Bag

Sleeping comfy in the outdoors can take on all the adventure of Goldilocks attempting to find a comfortable bed—some too soft, some too hard, some too warm, some too cold. It doesn't have to be that way if you take into account a few basic concepts.

ESSENTIAL FEATURES

Look for these features in the bag you buy:

- Lining of taffeta or other softer, non-cotton material: comfy, warms quickly, breathes supremely.
- Dark-colored lining. This absorbs heat better and uses the sun's rays most efficiently should you need to dry out your bag.
- Semirectangular shape for sleepers who toss and turn; narrower mummy-style bag for sleepers who manage to stay put.
- Differential cut, with the inner lining sewn smaller than the outer shell, allowing insulation to loft up to its maximum. More loft, more warmth.
- A filling (insulation) of either synthetic fibers or down. Down is lighter and more durable. Synthetic fills fare better than down when bags get wet.
- Insulated draft collar to seal in the warmth and keep out the cold around neck and shoulders.
- Hook-and-loop (Velcro) tab to cover the zipper toggle by the hood, preventing unplanned unzipperings while you slumber.
- Multisectioned or shaped hood to cup the head naturally.
- Two-way zipper for more ventilation and flexibility. If you desire companionship, be sure your bag has a right- or a left-side zipper that is compatible with another bag.
- Ample full-length flap of insulated material (known as a draft tube) that hangs over the zipper to seal out cold air. A windproof and water-resistant outer shell is a plus; DryLoft is my favorite.
- Highly desirable option: a fleece-lined stuff sack. Turn it inside out

from desert to mountaintop. For example, my first climbing trip was a six-week affair into the Wind River Range in Wyoming. The fringes of the area were fairly temperate but rainy. However, we wanted to go deep into the range and bag a few famous peaks, and this required crossing glaciers and stomping up snowy cols. The range was renowned for high winds, frequent summer rains, and wild temperature swings. That was enough information to roughly know the basic gear I'd need. Lightweight mountaineering boots would get me across the glaciers. Rain gear was certainly required; same with warm clothing, a sleeping bag good to 20 degrees, plus a lightweight tent to sit out any storm.

This was a sort of first-level gear checklist, including the basic stuff I'd need to simply survive. Twenty years ago, one could fill out this list rather easily since the market offered a limited product line. For instance, there were perhaps half a dozen good lightweight mountaineering boots to pick from. Now there are probably five hundred. The same goes for all the other gear. Exactly what boot and tent and pack to buy is largely a matter of what you can afford, combined with personal preference. Personal preference is a sticking point for those who haven't the experience to yet know what they like and don't like.

Most people I know who venture out on long treks have amassed a collection of gear that works best for them. Over the years they have used various products and narrowed the huge field to what they like (which often depends on style and fit), can afford, or managed to get for free. This trial-and-error process is only possible if

and stuff it with a parka or extra clothes for a comfy pillow.

Your bag will only be as warm and your night only as comfortable as your sleeping pad is good. Closed-cell foam pads such as ensolite are fine, but spartan. I prefer Therm-a-rest brand self-inflating pads.

WHEN COMPARING BAGS

Here are a couple of factors to think about as you rate one bag against another:

- Look at the foot section, the hood area, and the draft tube that is meant to cover the zipper. How are they designed? Are there any obvious cold spots? Does the hood cup the head or look flat? Is the foot section roomy or does it appear as if it will constrict your toes?
- How much insulation is in the bag? Bigger bags require more insulation to provide equal insulating qualities as smaller or more narrowly cut bags.
- On down bags, do the compartments feel firm (a good sign that the down will not shift and permit cold spots), or are they soft and fluid (a poor sign, indicating that the down is free to move around and create cold spots)? An exception is the type of bag designed to permit the user to shift the down from top to bottom to adjust for temperature fluctuations.

Choosing a Mountaineering and Winter Tent

A tent that can withstand the rigors of mountaineering and winter camping is much like the three-season and all-season tents discussed in chapter 11—but even tougher and more adaptable. (Chapter 11 also covers the main things to look for in any tent.)

ESSENTIAL FEATURES FOR MOUNTAINEERING AND WINTER

The mountaineering tent is the bomb shelter of the portable domicile world, designed for harsh conditions and winter use. Features to look for:

you are filthy rich or work in the outdoor-recreation field and have access to a lot of gear. Either way, there is little consensus so far as brand names go. Herman's favorite tent might not be my favorite. Tastes vary extravagantly. And a few prominent outdoors people use (or have used) gear you wouldn't believe.

Take Norman Clyde, mountaineer and father of Sierra Nevada exploration. Clyde, a distinguished eccentric and hard-head, used to foray into the Sierras for months at a time. The weight of his pack was legendary, and included—among other things—cast-iron crockery and a smattering of bulky tomes in Greek and Latin. Only a lunatic would recommend such a load. Conversely, woodsman Jedadiah Smith cast off on monthlong wilderness junkets with only a bedroll, a rifle, and a satchel of pemmican. John Muir did the same—without the rifle.

Long-distance treks require so much gear that I avoid anything unnecessary and make certain the gear I do bring is good quality, fits well, and is as light as possible. Extra gear adds up to needless pounds on my back. When something doesn't fit, it can be worse than worthless. Shoddy gear falls apart, which can be disastrous when your survival might depend on having a functional tent or weatherproof boots. A prototype backpack once self-destructed on me in Borneo, and I had to lash it back together with climbing webbing. My boots delaminated during a trek in Mexico, and I had to hoof it out barefoot.

Don't be seduced by all the new electronic gizmos that dazzle us from the pages of magazines. Electronic aids—most

- Four to five high-grade aluminum poles as part of the tent's free-standing construction.
- Steep sidewalls to shed wind and snow.
- Two doors, on opposite ends or sides of the tent, each with a vestibule for maximum gear storage and ease of entering and leaving in the face of anything Mother Nature tosses your way.
- Vestibules with their own poles for support.
- A versatile rain fly, with full tent coverage, sturdy guy-out points for tying down in high winds, and the option to put it up independent of the tent—making it possible to pitch the fly as a roof over a partial snow cave (essentially a snowpit with a fabric roof) and to save the weight of packing the full tent.

ESSENTIAL FEATURES OF A SINGLE-WALL TENT

This is a category unto itself, for trekkers who desire minimalist features and ultralight shelter—and who don't mind doing the meticulous seam-sealing that is required to keep the rain out. (Most other tents come partially factory seam sealed on the floors, leaving you to simply finish seam sealing the rain fly.) As the name implies, the single-wall tent is designed to be used without a rain fly. Important features:
- High/low ventilation ports for maximum flow-through of air even when the hatches are battened down.
- Vertical sidewalls for maximum interior space and shedding precipitation.
- Free-standing design.
- Sturdy guy-out points sewn to the tent body for tying down the tent when things get blustery.

Choosing a Stove

It's a burning question: What stove should I buy? And the decision brings up a question that's just as important: Which fuel should I use? You've got your single fuels, dual fuels, multifuels, solid fuels, liquid fuels, gas fuels. There are stoves you have to prime, stoves you don't; fuels that burn clean, fuels

notably the global positioning system (GPS) units that use satellites to pinpoint your location—are advanced tools that presuppose a thorough understanding of basic navigation. They supplement—they do not replace—map and compass and the skill to use them.

If you're exploring the middle of Borneo or racing in the Eco Challenge adventure race, electronic devices are invaluable. But if you're humping along a trail in the High Sierras, a GPS unit is needless weight. If you get to depend on electronic devices to find your way, and never learn basic map and compass skills, what happens when the batteries go dead or a bear steals the contraption? You're cooked. Electronic devices are handy tools for the experienced explorer. They are not crutches for the inexperienced.

As you complete a few long marches, you will get a feel for what best works for you and be able to develop a personal inventory of favorite gear. As you read articles and run into others on and off the trail, you'll be introduced to new developments and can update your gear as money allows. Any experienced outdoors person can tell you what basic gear you will need on a given trip, but no one can tell you specifically what make and model to buy. That's part of the discovery process that makes the whole business interesting.

WEIGHT

Up till perhaps a dozen years ago, hikers usually faced a tradeoff between weight and durability. Modern fabrics have largely—but not entirely—

that don't. So what are you to do when you suddenly realize, I need a stove.

Relax. It's not all that difficult.

The fact that you're going backpacking, rather than car camping, essentially determines one important decision: how big a stove to carry. A backpacker will usually choose a one-burner model, rather than a bulky stove with two or more burners.

As you begin to look at stoves, you will also need to decide on the fuel to use. They all have advantages and drawbacks. Usually your principal decision will come down to choosing one of the liquid-fuel stoves or one of the pressurized gas-canister stoves.

LIQUID-FUEL STOVES

Liquid-fuel stoves have two obvious advantages over pressurized gas-canister stoves. Their cost of operation per hour is less, and they are far more versatile because they can be designed to burn more than one type of fuel. With all the redesign features of liquid-fuel stoves in recent years, the old argument that they are too hard to keep clean and maintain is no longer valid. The fuels:

White gas. Burns hot and clean and can be used as its own priming agent. Has limited availability outside the United States and Canada.

Kerosene. Can be quite finicky to prime and light, and burns with a

dirty flame. But once properly preheated and burning efficiently (say your fuel mantras), kerosene has a heat output as good as that of white gas. Widely available internationally.

Denatured alcohol. A fuel that is making a comeback of sorts since it burns so cleanly and quietly and is virtually explosion-proof. However, it generates much less heat than other fuels.

Multifuel stoves. If you are traveling where white gas or pressurized canisters are not readily available, it's a great advantage to use a multifuel stove—one capable of burning white gas, unleaded gas, kerosene and, in a pinch, aircraft fuel.

eliminated this dilemma. Capaline, Gore-Tex, and various other synthetic materials have come to replace the wool, goose down, and bulletproof (and heavy) nylon of years past. As these materials have gone through stages of refinement, they've become lighter and more durable. However, there is always that point where a piece of gear becomes flimsy, regardless of the quality of construction or the textiles employed.

Since every ounce counts on a long trek, you avoid taking gear you don't need ("less is more"). This means that if the gear you do bring falls apart, you're probably looking at trouble. For that reason, I tend to avoid super-featherweight gear. I don't want my stuff giving out while far afield. I also understand that the caving and climbing I enjoy stresses gear more than if I was simply hiking the trail. Therefore I put a premium on durability, and go with heftier models. The other advantage of this strategy is that you beat the ultrapremium prices of the very lightest stuff. If you think a silk suit touches you for serious money, try buying a three-ounce parka good to absolute zero. Your grandkids will still be paying it off fifty years hence.

Every crowd has its share of maniacs—the folks who'll head across the Gobi Desert with a tube tent and two cans of Spam. Most people, however, err on the side of too much stuff and too much weight. The goal is to learn what you don't need or can live comfortably without. Equipment makers pitch everything from seventy-dollar sun hats to portable showers as essential tackle. Most hikers find otherwise once they have to hump these "essen-

PRESSURIZED GAS-CANISTER STOVES

If convenience is your primary concern, you can utilize any of the pressurized gas-canister stoves. With them, you get out of the chores of pouring liquid fuels, pressurizing, or priming. The choice of fuels in these stoves includes:

Butane. Loses some performance capability in cold temperatures. Available internationally.

Isobutane and butane/propane blends. Higher octane performance than butane alone, getting the stove somewhat out of the cold-temperature doldrums.

Propane. Uses larger, heavier cartridges than the butane or isobutane cartridges in order to accommodate higher pressures. Offers the best performance of any of the pressurized canister fuels. Limited international availability.

Coleman Max fuel. Designed to counter the problem faced by all pressurized gas cartridges: how to operate and burn consistently at temperatures down to and below zero degrees Fahrenheit. Using a standard propane/butane blend, Coleman gets around the drop-off in performance by utilizing a version of fuel injection. A hose inside the cartridge pulls liquid fuel into the stove, where it vaporizes—a switch from the standard approach of pulling only a gaseous form of the fuel into a stove.

SOLID FUEL STOVES

These stoves, burning twigs and pine cones, are a good alternative for the trekker out for a long time where store-bought fuel is unavailable or not practical to carry in the quantities needed. You must be prepared to tinker and fidget with the flame, with can be made very hot. For use only where dry wood is legally available.

OTHER CONSIDERATIONS

As you choose a stove and fuel, you will also want to determine the weight and carrying size of the stove and check out some of its other fea-

tials" on their backs. The trail has a way of thinning out one's gear. The tricky part is finding a cozy line between what you need to simply survive and what you need to enjoy yourself. Once you assemble the bare essentials, everything else is a luxury.

The importance of keeping the weight down on a long trek cannot be overstated. Conversely, the longer you spend "out there," the more you might want to pamper yourself, which usually entails added gear. There is no set list that applies across the divide. It takes several trips to figure out what you need, which will vary from what Bathsheba needs.

Ultimately you end up with two lists: what you need and what you want. You can't whittle down the "need" list. And the "want" list should include only what you can physically bear to carry without

breaking your back. Chances are you won't know how many extras you can carry till experience shows you. "Less is more" translates to less weight. The trick is discovering just how much "less" you can get away with and still squeeze maximum bang from your experience.

ATTITUDE

The attitude we haul into the wilderness profoundly shapes our experience during an extended trek. No matter our fitness, our gear, or our experience, there will be problems simply because we're in an environment that cannot be controlled and that is not beholden to our needs. "Freak" storms wash out trails; varmints burgle our vittles; ankles twist; people's moods—quite possibly our own—

tures. Boiling times for water, often listed by manufacturers as a means of comparison, should be utilized with a bit of skepticism—like those infamous sleeping-bag temperature ratings. Many variables affect a stove's operating efficiency, including operator familiarity, fuel quality, the type of pot, stove cleanliness, wind conditions, air temperature, beginning water temperature, altitude, and more.

You will be most likely to match the "laboratory" conditions that allowed the boiling time to be so fast if you utilize a full-coverage windscreen for the stove and if you use a pot that is blackened for better heat absorption, with a tightly fitting lid. Remember that it takes longer to

cook meals at higher altitudes because the air pressure is lower and water boils at a cooler temperature than at sea level.

Stove Repair and Maintenance

Take care of your stove and it'll take care of you. You simply need to get to know your stove a bit so you can keep it in good repair.

TIPS ON FIXING COMMON STOVE PROBLEMS

Let's take a look at a couple of the common problems of liquid-fuel stoves that can be cured in the field—or better yet, at home before you have an impatient group waiting for dinner at the campsite.

Clogged jets. Here's the problem you'll run into most often. Liquid-fuel backpacking stoves usually come with a cleaning needle and a jet-removal tool. If a jet is really clogged, you'll need to remove it from the stove with the tool. Then soak the jet in white gas, a solvent that will eat away most carbon buildup or other residues. MSR backpacking stoves have a built-in pin that self-cleans the jet when you simply shake the stove or turn it upside down.

No pressure. If a stove does not seem to be generating pressure, even with continued pumping, chances are the leather pump cup needs lubricating. Apply mineral oil to both sides of the cup, and mold it

take on demonic aspects. The ace trekker is not he who avoids problems, but rather she who uses them as learning experiences and makes course corrections en route.

This is especially true when traveling in a group, which is typically the case on multiday trips. A long trek presents countless daily decisions. Should we push on, or rest. Should we cross the swollen creek, or walk around. Should we take a day trip into the volcano, or to the rock that looks like a dinosaur. Everyone has an opinion and rarely are they all the same. This can lead to conflict, especially if one continually gives in to the person with the loudest mouth and the strongest energy.

Avoiding the conflict of contrasting opinions means that no conflict gets resolved, resulting in the party living in conflict. Eventually the pressure gets so great that a trip-ending blowout occurs. I've seen it happen to the best of them. The key is to always voice your opinion and feelings in a contained way and take things from there. If one person demands things always be done his or her way, the pot will eventually boil over.

Another trap is to haul a load of rigid expectations onto the trail. Whenever I trek afar and expect things to conform to what I think I want, I fight myself and nature most of the time. When I go on a long trek with a spirit of openness, hoping to learn something new, obstacles are seen as opportunities, not things God has set in my path to thwart my will and frustrate my plan.

Whatever experiences I have along the way are important because they are mine, not because they confirm something I already know or validate my sense of

back into a slightly conical shape if it has gone flat. If the stove still does not pressurize, the fuel bottle O-ring might be cracked (look for fuel leaks).

Getting to know your stove. Each manufacturer has a specific set of remedies for its particular stove design. It's not enough just to read the instructions. Spend some time taking your stove apart and putting it back together—never right before a trip, mind you. Become familiar with your stove and how to keep it healthy.

STOVE REPAIR KITS

For most trips, all you really need to carry for repair of liquid-fuel stoves is the cleaning needle and jet-removal tool that comes with the unit. You might also take along an extra jet.

An advanced repair kit for international travelers or for those heading out on expeditions should also contain:

- extra jets to be used with fuels other than white gas, such as kerosene.
- Spare O-rings for the fuel bottle, the fuel tube, and the control valve on the pump if the stove has one.
- Spare bushing for the fuel tube.
- Small bottle of mineral oil to lubricate O-rings, bushings, and the leather pump cup.

PREVENTIVE CARE

Simple maintenance and storage precautions will prolong the life of your liquid-fuel stove.

- It's most important to take apart your stove and lubricate any O-rings and leather pump cup (if your stove has a pump) at least once a year—more often if you use the stove frequently.
- Never store a fuel bottle with the pump still in it. Instead, remove the pump and store the bottle in an upright position.
- Never store opened fuel for more than one year. The older the fuel, the more likely it is to contaminate a stove with soot and other lacquer-type residue.
- Burn only the highest-quality fuel. Most liquid-fuel stoves are designed to burn white gas. In

mastery. Whenever we venture afield with too fixed a plan, we ride the tide of willpower and often miss opportunities to follow our gut and act spontaneously. Because nature is fluid and ever-changing, if we are not at least somewhat flexible we'll not be able to flow with the shifting sands and at some time we'll likely sink. No matter how strong you are, when you venture deep into the wilds, you are up against far greater forces than your own.

On the other hand, you carry a limited amount of food and probably have a finite amount of time. So without some structure, without sticking to some kind of timetable, you'll likely find yourself stumbling toward the nearest roadhead on last legs. The greatest experience I ever had in the wilds was when Dwight Brooks and I went to Papua New Guinea with no immediate plans but to seek out adventure. We had a month to get into trouble. We bumbled our way into the Gulf Province—one of the most remote and unexplored regions on earth—and discovered the world's largest river cave. We also overshot our rations by a week, and our starved march out from the cavern reduced us to staggering scarecrows.

The trick is to find a balance between sticking to a general plan and allowing yourself the freedom to explore novelty as it presents itself. Without a plan of some kind, you're hiking yourself into chaos. But if you set out on a week-long, seventy-mile trek and insist on staying on the trail every second and hiking exactly ten miles a day, you've reduced your wilderness journey to a quasi-military operation.

Again, our attitude is greatly influ-

such stoves, use only the highest grade of white gas, and use another fuel only if absolutely necessary.

COMMERCIAL TRAVEL WITH YOUR STOVE

What are the regulations for taking stove fuels with you as you travel aboard a plane, bus, train, or boat? The answer is simple: you can't do it. Commercial carriers prohibit the transport of any type of fuel, be it liquid or pressurized.

You can carry the stove without fuel as long as the fuel lines are completely clear of any residue. A friend of mine received the third degree from baggage inspectors who wanted to know what his Coleman Xpedition stove was, and then he had to prove the fuel lines were clean.

If your stove has a permanently attached fuel tank, as is the case with some of the Optimus and older Coleman stoves, you may be prohibited from taking even the stove on board a plane, even if the tank is clearly empty—depending on how strict the officials are feeling. We contacted major airlines at least twice and received enough variation in their answers to convince us the policy is arbitrary.

My recommendation? If you plan to travel by commercial carrier, check with that carrier ahead of time. Of course, what is said on the phone and what happens at the check-in counter are often two different things. If you attempt to travel with your old fuel bottles, they must be so clean they're practically odorless, with absolutely no evidence of fuel residue. To be sure of no hassles, I suggest you purchase new bottles that have never seen a drop of fuel inside. Of course, for the return trip, you may have to part with your new purchase.

The U.S. Postal Service also has strict rules on handling fuels. It currently accepts only one specific fuel for shipment: the three-pack of 170-gram Coleman Max fuel, which can be mailed to any address in the fifty states and Puerto Rico.

enced by the expectations we place on the trek. Perhaps the most limiting expectation we can have is—figuratively speaking—to continually chase after the rainbow. Life in the wilds is a mosaic of countless parts, few of which can be controlled. The natural world moves in phases and cycles, so the mosaic is ever changing. When the pieces constellate into a beautiful sunset or heavenly view, the experience is only a moment in time because, urged on by restless forces, the mosaic cannot hold one form for long. Storm clouds fill the horizon and the fog moves in.

When we become overly attached to the mosaic as it used to be, we resist the natural change and measure the current experience against a more pacific past. This fosters feelings of resentment, rather than an openness to the new. It also flattens out the dynamics of experience in an attempt to keep things at a single sustained pitch. But nature won't have it, and you'll inevitably end up feeling disappointed.

No matter what experiences you have had in the wilds, you never really know what you'll find in the environment or inside your soul. Much depends on your adaptability to change. Having the discipline and moxie to forge on when you need to, and the flexibility to explore or do nothing when you want to, allows you to get maximum value from any extended trek. Flexibility is also a survival skill. Every person I know who has made a habit of taking long treks has faced a per-

sonal epic in the wilds. They need not be life-threatening to be epic. Friends have tried fording rivers only to have their packs ripped off and whisked away, leaving them to hike out fifty miles with virtually no gear. Fuel bottles have come open, meaning there is no gas for the stove—a problem when you're above tree line. Parkas get blown away, snow falls by the yard, hornets come from nowhere, folks get separated. Such events leave you to ad lib, a difficult procedure when one is locked into a rigid mind-set. When the plan goes south and you start raging and blaming, you waste the very energy needed to find a solution.

A good attitude is also a realistic one. Even with the best team and the best-laid plans, some trips simply can't get off on the right foot. The trek seems jinxed from the start. Everything goes wrong. Then it's often wise to postpone the junket and to return when the stars are realigned. No need to force the thing.

PACE

Every aspect of a long trek needs to be monitored in terms of pace. You need to pace your food consumption, not plowing through all your stores at once, yet making sure to eat often enough during strenuous stretches. You need to keep hydrated by drinking at steady intervals. You need to keep covering ground lest you make no progress. You need to pace your energy output, taking rest days when your body screams for a break. And you need to spend as much time enjoying the fun as harping on the hardships.

A key to pacing yourself is learning to vary things according to the way you feel, while keeping in mind the essential aspects that consistently need attention, such as sanitation, your physical condition, and the weather. The ability to respond to a situation with a degree of flexibility is, for most of us, an acquired skill. You can learn a lot from someone who has mastered this art. A brief apprenticeship (even if it's just one trip) with a veteran long-distance trekker is an invaluable experience. When you see the principles of pacing put into practice, the lessons are not easily forgotten.

RHYTHM

Everything has rhythm. In the wilds we are taken by the cadence of sun and moon streaking across the sky, beneath which towers the granite butte whose countenance hasn't changed in ten thousand years. But the butte was not always a butte. It too has a rhythm and is subject to natural forces of weathering so slow that to feel the rock's pulse is to appreciate the power of time.

Everything is in movement, changing, becoming something different. To surrender to the rhythms around you is to open up to novelty. To resist nature's varied pulse is to fight for a frozen future, a battle we cannot win, especially in the wilds. At some level everyone and everything is afraid of change. But if we can ride the edge of change, still keeping our feet

beneath us, our life will expand beyond what we ever imagined possible. Only then might we glimpse into the very womb of Mother Nature, the void which gives birth to all things and all rhythms, where change and permanence live in perfect balance. Because we are all part of both the rhythm and the void, neither can be captured. We don't find it, we surrender to it and experience the Great Knowing. Happy trails!

HUT TO HUT

A Long March with minimal loads? No food, cooking gear, or tent to hump on your back? The idea makes as much sense as a marriage sans guff. But believe it, the Europeans have worked out a system, based on long tradition, of hut-to-hut marches that can start in the Alps and take you all the way to the ocean.

Many different routes exist, allowing you to carry little more than rain gear and camera and perhaps a sleeping bag—and still traverse hundreds of miles through postcard vistas and over high mountain ridges. You can stop and start where you like, linking favorite or classic routes over a period of years, as whim and schedule allow.

If there's a drawback to these trips, it's that hut fees (for a bunk and meals) are sometimes pricey and the fixed distance between huts is often substantial. But if your legs and lungs are up to it, and you have a free month and enough dollars, some of the hut-to-hut routes are to die for.

The "Secret" Dilemma

OF AN

Outdoor Writer

Though this is not a guidebook, it will,

hopefully, encourage you to go walking and, thus, will probably lead you to a guidebook or two—perhaps even a guidebook or magazine article that I have written. And so I share the following with you.

Many years ago, *Motorland* magazine published an article about the clamming in Bolinas, California, north of San Francisco. Much to the dismay of Bolinas residents, and ultimately the magazine, some of the magazine's two million readers descended on the area with shovels, depleting the clam population and tearing up the beaches to such a degree that locals are still talking about it. More recently, in 1993, *Outside* magazine listed Lavender Canyon, a remote corner of Canyonlands National Park, as one of 15 "perfect spring campsites." According to park officials, the fragile desert landscape was subsequently overrun by so many people that local property owners closed the access road to the canyon, and the park has been forced to create a strict permit quota for others who wish to visit.

Such instances tempt me to keep to myself the sanctity of the special places I am fortunate enough to visit. After all, it can be argued that sharing a "secret" by regaling readers with the merits of a secluded spot serves only to destroy its charms and turn its beauty into a sacrifice sold for the sake of book profits or editorial whims.

It is not uncommon for writers and editors to receive pointed letters from readers taking them to task for selling out the land, for pillaging a place by making it public. Land managers frequently ask writers to remove public trails and recreation sites from guidebooks and articles because they are afraid the areas will be overused (and in some cases, used at all). On the other side of the coin, rangers, land managers, park officials, and visitors are often grateful for the "secret spot" revelations because it is through a writer's carefully chosen words that travelers are made aware of recreational alternatives and destinations they otherwise might not have known about, or perhaps cared about—choices that offer alternatives to relieve the congestion of other, often overcrowded recreational locations.

It's hard to walk a middle road here. I do question the wisdom and ethics of giving up the few quiet places of our world to a public that may or may not appreciate the land. More and more I hear from friends, "I'll take you into this great spot, but you have to swear to me that you won't write about it." It's a promise I won't make because I know I can't keep it. So sometimes I miss out on a great hike and my friends end up feeling hurt. While it's true that I do selectively withhold information regarding the exact location of pristine areas I believe would suffer by my writing about them, the question remains: Should writers and editors be bound by an oath of secrecy to protect public lands because they fear the public might destroy what it is they supposedly love?

Every action has a consequence. If those who would write and publish an article keep quiet about a site, that site remains subject to the whims of the select few who know about it already or happen to stumble upon it. That is not necessarily a good thing. Recent history is filled with pages detailing land abuses and misuses at the hands of a "knowing few." Glen Canyon used to be one of the secret places, until it was dammed, its beauty drowned under hundreds of feet of water. It could be argued that had writers such as Ed Abbey written about Glen Canyon and shared its secrets with the public, the dam might never have been built and Glen Canyon might still exist. Idealistic? Perhaps. But remember that without John Muir, a writer and consummate walker, there may not have been a Yosemite.

The land has no voice to tell those who might care how wonderful and special it is. The call of loons echoing across a fog-enshrouded bay or the beauty of desert canyon walls carved by wind and rain—these are things the public can care about only if it knows their meaning. Protectionism is a dangerous game and often ends up hiding things from those who might love them most. You can be sure that most of the "secret" and out-of-the-way places you read about in magazines, newspapers, and books are already well known to mining, logging, and business concerns who utilize satel-lites and aerial photography to scour regions for their own gain.

By publicizing an area, we run the risk of thrashing that sacred secret under the wheels, hooves, or feet of unthinking visitors who come only to say that they came. There are people who believe that we don't really own the land and are but stewards charged with keeping it safe. That view could mean that all of us should have access to all of the land, or that none of us should be able to enjoy what a few of us are keeping "safe." It depends on our perspective.

What's the answer? There isn't one, pat solution. For now, I will continue to share with those who choose to read about the places I have visited. Does that invite destruction of the lands I love, the lands I care enough to write about? No matter how honorable the writer's inten-tions, warnings to "tread lightly" are mere words on a sheet of paper. There is nothing earned by reading about a site— no sweat equity, no thrill of risk or dis-covery. I have always believed that you care most about what you have worked for, or have been given as a treasured, per-sonal gift. That said, the best answer to the question of possible destruction rests with you and how you choose to visit those sites you find revealed within pub-lished pages. Awareness of those sites is a writer's gift to you. Treat the gift with respect and hold the wild places of this country sacred. Wherever you choose to travel, do so as a breeze upon the earth, and we'll all be better off.

Appendix 1

The Hiking Adventurer's Checklist

In addition to the items listed in "The Essentials" (pages 15–17), the following checklist will help you plan your next adventure. Not all items will be needed on every trip; pack only what you need and leave the rest at home. Remember, you've got to carry what you pack.

Dayhiking

PACKS

Daypack or fanny pack
Child carrier (if camping with a child under four who has difficulty walking long distances)

FIRST AID

Antibiotics
Antiseptics
Acetaminophen (such as Tylenol)
Antihistamine (such as Benadryl)
Tincture of benzoin
Sterile gauze pads
Gauze roll
Nonadherent dressing
1-inch-wide adhesive tape
Steri-Strips
Ace wrap
Large compress
Moleskin
2nd Skin
Tweezers
Bandage scissors

Irrigation syringe
Low-reading thermometer
SAM splint
Space blanket
Sawyer Extractor snakebite kit
Emergency report form
Pencil
Emergency phone numbers and money for a phone call

CLOTHING

Base Layer
Underwear
Long underwear (tops and bottoms)
Liner socks
Wool outer socks
Sport-specific socks (such as those made by Thorlo)
T-shirt (cotton/synthetic blend such as those made by Sierra Designs or Patagonia)

Insulating/Thermal Layer
Wool shirt
Synchilla, Polartec, or wool sweater

Shorts
Long pants

Protective Layer
Wool, A16 Bomber, or Synchilla hatSun hat
Bunting, Polartec, or Synchilla jacket
Parka (synthetic fill or down)
Wool mittens
Rain suit (jacket and pants)
Gaiters
Windbreaker
Hiking boots

MISCELLANEOUS GEAR

Fishing gear and license
Thermometer
Bandanna
Note pad and pencil
Camera, film, lenses
Binoculars

Overnight Treks

Consider including the following, in addition to the items you would carry for a dayhike.

PACKS

Backpack (external or internal frame)
Waterproof pack cover

HOUSING

Tent (appropriate to the trip and season)
Mosquito netting (for around head when sleeping under the stars)
Nylon tarp with grommets (9 x 12 feet)

BEDROOM

Sleeping bag (down or synthetic)
Sleeping pad
Pillow
Ground cloth

KITCHEN

Stove
Fuel/fuel bottle
Primer paste
Lighter or matches
Windscreen
Cook set
Frying pan
Water bag (collapsible)
Storage containers for food
Zip-top bags (freezer variety)
Large spoon
Pocketknife

Spatula
Can opener (GI folding variety)
Small whisk
Small grater
Pot grips
Knife, fork, spoon
Plate, cup, bowl
Cutting board (small nylon variety)
Ice chest
Scrub pads
Biodegradable soap
Paper towels
Aluminum foil
Spice kit

BATHROOM

Comb/brush
Toothbrush/toothpaste
Dental floss
Deodorant
Small towel
Shaving kit
Biodegradable skin and hair soap
Moisturizing lotion
Towelettes
Sunscreen (15 SPF or better)
Lip balm
Tampons
Toilet paper

CLOTHING

Camp shoes or sneakers

MISCELLANEOUS GEAR

Butane or candle lantern
Trowel
Plastic trash bags

FUN AND GAMES

Frisbee
Nerf ball
Hacky Sack
Miniature games (backgammon, checkers, chess, etc.)
Harmonica
Kazoo
Paperback books
Coloring books
Star guide
Mini microscope
Magnifying glass
Small plastic collection containers
Aquarium net
Sketch pad
Pencils
Crayons
Colored felt-tip pens
Gold pan and mineral book

SPECIAL CONSIDERATIONS FOR INFANTS

Bottles and extra nipples
Rubber or plastic pants
Diapers
Plastic bag for dirty diapers
Sleep suits
Extra clothing
Warm snuggle suit
Rain suit
Baby food
Baby wipes
Baby powder or cornstarch

Appendix 2

Gear Manufacturers

All of the gear listed here is available through specialty mail-order companies or at your specialty outdoor store. Call the numbers provided to find a retail outlet near you that carries the gear you desire. To view products from the following manufacturers, including web links to their sites, visit www.geartrends.com.

Packs

BACKPACKS

- Arc'Teryx Equipment: 800-985-6681
- JanSport: 800-558-3600
- Kelty: 800-423-2320
- Gregory: 800-477-3420
- Osprey: 970-882-2221
- Dana Design: 800-972-4066

DAYPACKS/FANNY PACKS

- Dana Design: 800-972-4066
- Overland: 800-487-8851
- JanSport: 800-558-3600
- Lowe Alpine: 303-465-3706
  Ultimate Direction: 800-426-7229

CHILDREN'S DAYPACKS

- Osprey: 970-882-2221

CHILD CARRIERS

You'll need one of these if you're walking with a child under four who has difficulty walking long distances.

- Tough Traveler: 800-468-6844
- Kelty: 800-423-2320

Tents

- Eureka: 800-661-9086
- Mountain Hardwear: 510-559-6700
- Sierra Designs: 510-450-9555

Clothing

BASE LAYER

Long Underwear

- Hind Drylete: 800-952-4463
- Patagonia Capilene: 800-638-6464
- Lowe Alpine Powerstretch: 303-465-3706
- Moonstone Mountaineering Bipolar: 800-390-3312
- Helly-Hansen Lifa (polypropylene): 800-435-5901

T-shirts (cotton/synthetic blend)

- Sierra Designs: 800-736-8592
- Patagonia: 800-638-6464

Long-Sleeved Shirts

- Ex Officio's Baja Plus: 800-644-7303

Shorts

- Ex Officio's Amphi Short: 800-644-7303
- Kavu's Chillawack: 206-285-9124

Long Pants

- Ex Officio's Amphi Pant: 800-644-7303
- RailRiders' Weather Pant: 800-437-3794

Wool Socks

- Wigwam: 800-558-7760
- SmartWool: 800-550-9665

Sport-Specific Socks

- Thorlo: 800-457-2256

INSULATING/THERMAL LAYER

The following companies make products manufactured with Malden Mills' Polartec 100 or 200, Power-stretch, or Bipolar—all good materials for this layer.

- Lowe Alpine: 303-465-3706
- Marmot: 707-544-4590
- Moonstone: 800-822-2985
- The North Face: 800-719-6678

Kid's Fleece

- Molehill Mountaineering: 303-271-1106

Bunting, Polartec, or Synchilla Jacket

- Lowe Alpine: 303-465-3706
- Sierra Designs: 800-736-8551
- The North Face: 800-719-6678
- Mountain Hardwear: 800-579-9093
- Patagonia: 800-638-6464

PROTECTIVE LAYER

Waterproof/Breathable Jackets

For Men:

- Columbia: 800-547-8066
- Nike: 800-344-6453
- Lowe Alpine: 303-465-3706
- Marmot: 707-544-4590
- Mountain Hardwear: 800-579-9093

For Women:

Granted, I don't wear women's jackets, but I depend on some very reliable testers who regularly beat the life out of any jackets I send their way, and these hard-hiking, hard-working women can't stop raving about the following companies:

- Lowe Alpine: 303-465-3706
- Sierra Designs: 800-736-8551

- Marmot: 707-544-4590
- The North Face: 800-719-6678
- Mountain Hardwear: 800-579-9093
- Moonstone: 800-822-2985
- Juno: 802-862-3351

Water-Resistant Windbreakers

- Pearl Izumi: 800-877-7080
- Sierra Designs: 800-736-8551
- Patagonia: 800-638-6464
- Hind: 800-952-4463

Hats

Sun Hats

Sequel makes my favorite sun hat, the Desert Rhat, that resembles something a Foreign Legion soldier might wear. Their loose-fitting clothing line is also excellent hot-weather wear: 970-385-4660.

Baseball-Style Caps

- Kavu: 206-285-9124

INSULATED HATS

While I am very partial to my British military wool beret, there are times when I wouldn't think of heading outdoors without donning a fleece-lined bomber hat (I look like Elmer Fudd but who cares), such as the Adventure 16 Bomber (619-283-6314). If it's really nasty, you'll want a balaclava too, and my favorite is one made of Drylete from Hind (800-426-4463). They call it a face mask.

Footwear

Any of the companies listed below offers a good shoe that'll hold up in most conditions:

APPROACH SHOES

These low-top shoes with sticky rubber soles are great for rock scrambling.

- Five Ten's Five Tennie: 909-798-4222
- La Sportiva: 303-443-8710

HIKING BOOTS

- Merrell: 888-637-7001
- Tecnica: 800-258-3897
- Asolo: 800-892-2668
- Vasque: 800-224-4453
- Adidas: 800-448-1796
- Nike: 800-344-6453
- Montrail (makes an excellent women's shoe): 206-621-9303
- Salomon: 800-225-6850

MUKLUKS

- Steger Mukluks: 800-543-0773
- Sorel, manufactured by Kaufman Footwear: 800-265-2760
- Northern Outfitters: 800-944-9276
- Timberland: 800-445-5545

Walking Staffs/Hiking Poles

- Leki-Sport U.S.A.'s Super Makalu: 800-255-9982

Stoves

- MSR: 800-877-9677
- Optimus-Suunto USA: 800-543-9124
- Peak 1, Coleman Company: 800-835-3278
- Primus: 800-435-4525

Maps

- U.S. Geological Survey: 800-USA-MAPS

- Map Link (includes USGS maps): 805-965-4402
- Trails Illustrated: 800-962-1643
- DeLorme Mapping: 800-452-5931
- Earthwalk Press: 800-828-MAPS
- Tom Harrison Cartography: 800-265-9090
- Maptech: 800-627-7236
- Wildflower: 800-265-9090

Compasses

- Brunton: 800-443-4871
- Silva: 888-245-4986
- Suunto: 800-543-9124

Water Filters

- PUR: 800-845-7873
- SweetWater: 800-531-9531
- MSR: 800-877-9677

First Aid

- Adventure Medical Kits: 800-324-3517
- Atwater Carey: 800-359-1646
- Outdoor Research: 800-421-2421
- Sawyer Products (both first aid and Extractor snakebite kits): 800-940-4464
- Chinook Medical Gear (excellent first aid and emergency medical gear at reasonable prices): 800-766-1365

Sun Protection

- AloeUp Sunscreens at 25 SPF or better are my favorite: 800-537-2563
- Sun Precautions makes a featherweight, cottony soft fabric called Solumbra that is reported to block 97 percent of the sun's harmful rays. (The shirts and pants are light and loose and quite comfortable.): 206-441-6688.

Appendix 3

Cyberhiking

The Internet is exploding with more and more companies and organizations offering services and opportunities on the World Wide Web. Here are some of the best sites I can recommend for cyberhiking. Enjoy, but don't get too lost in the electronic world: there's a real world waiting right outside your door.

- **Adventure Network**
  www.adventurenetwork.com
- **Total Fitness Network**
  www.totalfitnessnetwork.com
- **GearTrends**
  www.geartrends.com
- **Fogdog.com outdoor products**
  www.fogdog.com
- **Planet Outdoors**
  www.planetoutdoors.com
- **REI**
  www.rei.com
- **Yahoo Hiking Reference Page**
  dir.yahoo.com/recreation/outdoors
- **Yahoo Outdoor Magazines Reference Page**
  dir.yahoo.com/recreation/outdoors/news_and_media/magazines
- **Hiking and Walking**
  www.teleport.com/~walking/hiking.html
- **GORP—Great Outdoor Recreation Page**
  www.gorp.com
- **AMI Recreation and Snow News**
  www.aminews.com
- **Leave No Trace**
  www.lnt.org
- **Orienteering and Rogaining**
  www2.aos.princeton.edu/rdslater/orienteering
- **Volksmarch and Walking Event Index**
  www.winternet.com/~stachour/vm/index.html
- **Hosteling Information**
  www.hostels.com/hostels
- *Outside* **Magazine**
  www.outsidemag.com
- **American Hiking Society**
  www.americanhiking.org.

- **Sierra Club**
  www.sierraclub.org
- **Appalachian Mountain Club**
  www.outdoors.org
- **DeLorme Mapping**
  www.delorme.com
- **Topo Interactive Maps by Wildflower**
  www.topo.com
- **Trails Illustrated Maps**
  www.trailsillustrated.com
- **Maptech**
  www.maptech.com
- **U.S. Geological Survey Topographic Maps**
  info.er.usgs.gov
- **Bureau of Land Management**
  www.blm.gov
- **National Park Service**
  www.nps.gov
- **Fish and Wildlife Service**
  www.fws.gov
- **Forest Service**
  www.fs.fed.us
- **American Discovery Trail**
  www.discoverytrail.org
- **Canadian Parks**
  www.worldweb.com/parkscanada-banff
- **New Zealand Hiking Information**
  www.gorp.com/gorp/location/newzeal/newzeala
- **Australia Bushwalker's Page**
  www.anatomy.usyd.edu.au/danny/bushwalking/index.html
- **General Outdoor and Hiking Information News Group**
  news:rec.backcountry

Index

A
Abbey, Ed, 230
acetazolamide, 125
Aconcagua, 24
Adidas Adventure Sandal, 173
Adrenalin, 32, 95, 96
alcohol, as a diuretic, 111, 125
alpine walking, 126–32
    boots for, 131–32
AlpineAire, 185
altimeter, 86, 167
altitude, acclimatizing to,
    124–25
altitude sickness, 121, 124, 125
    preventing, 125
American Hiking Society, 8
American Volkssport Association,
    8
Amphi Pant and Short, 132
Angel Falls (Venezuela), 18–19,
    32
animals, wild, 7, 130, 140,
    142–43
    See also wildlife
Annapurna Circuit (Nepal), 43
antihistamines, effect on sweat-
    ing, 111
Appalachian Mountain Club, 8
Appalachian Trail, 21, 53, 131
Appleseed, Johnny, 18
approach shoe, 54, 55, 62
Aquaduct Vest, 65
archaeological sites, guidelines for
    visiting, 40–41
Arches National Park (Utah),
    109–10, 119
Arizona Outdoor Institute, 113
Arkansas Stone, 138
arms, swinging, 12
ascorbic acid, 185
athlete's foot, 200
Auerbach, Dr. Paul, 125
Avon Skin So Soft, 194

B
Baby Ruth, 24
backpack, choosing a, 211
Backpacker magazine, 71, 128
backwoods skills, 18
Baja Plus Shirt, 132
Baker, Dave, 127
balaclava, 152, 154
balance, 12
balloons, 71
Banzai Pipeline, The, 175–77
barometric pressure, 86
*Basic Essentials of Desert
    Survival, The*, 113
bathing, 40
beaches
    camping on, 40
    shoes for, 172
    walking on, 170
    See also coastal hiking
bearings, field, 81–82
bears, 130, 140, 142–43
    food storage and, 206
beef jerky, 130
beer, alcohol-free, 24
    See also alcohol, as a diuretic
Big Bend National Park (Texas),
    34
Big Mac, 24
binoculars, 41, 117
    care of, 141
    choosing, 140–41
Biwell leather conditioner, 57
blackflies, 184
blanket, emergency, 17, 20
blisters, 95, 96
blood, drinking, 114
Boer, Stan, 45
Bolinas (Calif.), 229
Bollé, 159
Boone, Daniel, 82
boots, 52–57
    alpine walking, 131–32

care of, 57
choosing, 211
dryers for, 162
drying, 57, 206
high-top vs. low-cut, 57
lug-soled, 154
mukluk, 164–65
pac, 164–65
snowshoeing, 161
warming devices for, 162
Borneo, 45, 179
bottles. *See* water: bottled
breakfast, 24, 25
Bridwell, Jim, 18–19, 45, 66,
    142–43
British Mountaineering Council,
    123
Brooks, Dwight, 24, 25, 215
Brunton compasses, 76
budget, 47
bushwhacking, speed of, 22

C
cactus, 109
caffeine, as a diuretic, 111, 125
calamine lotion, 194
cameras, 41, 146, 153
Campbell, Joseph, 7
campfires, and safety, 38, 40
camping
    canyon, 183
    winter, 155
Camping and Woodcraft, 69
*Camping Healthy: Hygiene for
    the Outdoors*, 102
campsites, finding, 38
Canaima (Venezuela), 18, 32, 201
canyoneering, amphibious,
    182–83, 189
Canyonlands National Park
    (Utah), 229
canyons, 182–83, 189–90
carbohydrates, 26

Carstensz Pyramid (New Guinea), 1
Cascade Designs, 182
Casey, Tim, 126
cattle, in weather forecasting, 87
Cébé, 156
cellular phone, 126–27
Center for Disease Control, 43
Chapman, John, 18
checklists, 46, 231-32
child carriers, 28–29
children
    age considerations, 28
    games for, 33
    hiking with, 28–33
    infants' checklist, 232
    medical and safety considera-
        tions, 96–97
Chilkoot Trail (Canada), 123
citronella, 194
climbing, speed of, 22
clinometer, 166
clothing, 7, 16, 58–69
    children's, 29
    cold-weather, 64–65, 160–67
    color of, 153, 206
    desert, 113, 114
    jungle, 195
    manufacturers of, 233-35
    rafting, 182
    snow, 151–54
    warm-weather, 61–63
    washing, 39
    water-resistant, 64–65, 66–69
    windy-weather, 63–64
    zippered, 61
    See also fabrics and fibers
clouds, in weather forecasting, 87
Clyde, Norman, 220
Coachella Valley (Calif.), 107, 112
coastal hiking, 168–77
    clothing for, 170
    dangers of, 170, 177
    See also beaches
coffee
    as a diuretic, 111, 125
    in weather forecasting, 87
Cole, Charles, 24
Colorado Plateau, 119
compass, 16, 76, 77
    manufacturers, 235
    sighting mirror on, 76, 77
    taking bearings with, 81–82
Con-Tact paper, 84
Concord River, 179

conduction, 110
convection, 110
cooking utensils, 232
cookware, 210
crampons, 57, 155, 156
criminals, foiling, 204
Cryptosporidium, 90
Cutters repellent, 31
Cutters snakebite kit, 99

D
Dani, 25, 58
Dayak tribe (Malaysia), 7, 45, 193
declination, 77
deer, in weather forecasting, 87
deerflies, 7, 117
DEET, 29, 31, 101, 115, 184, 194
    alternatives, 194
defecation, 38–39, 183
dehydration, 92–93, 114–15, 125
DeLorme maps, 79
Dennis, John, 121
descent, techniques, 13–14
Desert Rhat hat, 62
desert travel, 107–19
    flash-flooding in, 108, 115
    night-hiking, 109–11, 114
    tips, 115
deserts, 46
dew, in weather forecasting, 87
Dharma Bums, 44
Diamox, 125
diapers, 28
diary, keeping a, 34–35
Dickens, Charles, 192
Diet Coke, 24
diseases, travel-related, 42–43
dogs, walking with, 36–37, 39, 182
Donner, Dr. Howard, 95
Douglas, William O., 18
Dry Comfort Footwear Dryer, 162
duct tape, 54, 70, 84, 145
Duke University, 195
Dumba tribe (New Guinea), 93
dunes, 170
durable water-resistant finish (DWR), 64, 66
dysentery, 73

E
Earthwalk maps, 79
El Tigre (Venezuela), 20

Elderhostel, 9
Ellesmere Island (Canada), 151
emergency plan, 103
    for children, 29, 31
emergency supplies, 16–17, 19–20, 32, 102–03
Emerson, Ralph Waldo, 136
energy bars, 24
environmental impact of hikers, 38–41
Environmental Protection Agency, 194
Epi Pen, 32, 95, 96, 99
Ex Officio, 132
excrement, dealing with, 38–39, 183
exotic locales, 42

F
fabrics and fibers
    bicomponent knits, 60
    canvas, 58
    Capilene, 59, 64
    ClimaGuard, 65
    cotton, 60, 152, 195
    Driclime, 64
    Dry-Fit, 60, 65
    Drylete, 60, 65
    Gore-Tex, 66
    Lifa, 64
    Lycra, 60, 62
    microdenier pile, 60, 63, 65
    nylon, 58
    Polartec, 64
    polypropylene, 59
    spandex, 58
    stretch fleece, 60
    Therma Fleece, 60, 65
    Thermal Stretch, 182
    Thermax, 64
    Thinsulate, 59
    Ultrasensor, 60, 65
fanny pack, 49, 51
fastpacking, 20, 128–29
Fawcett, Ron, 91
Felany, Henry, 179
field bearing, 81–82
field guides, 41
Finley, John, 18
fire pan, 40
fire starter, 16, 20
fires, 38, 40
first aid kit, 6, 16, 20, 32, 94–95, 231
    manufacturers of, 235
fishing kit, 103

fitness, 9–10, 104–05, 216-17
flashlight, 16, 17, 20
   batteries, bulb, 70
food, 6, 16, 20, 24–27,
   206-10
   dessert, 116–17, 118, 208
   dried fruit, 26, 29, 118, 149,
    208
   fruit chew, 149
   fruit drinks, 185, 208
   fruit leather, 118, 208
   in hot temperatures, 197
   jerky, 130, 208-09
   planning, 206-07
   sweets, 197, 208
   trail mix, 171
   utensils, 232
   when to eat it, 26–27
   winter trail, 158
foot powder, 6, 54
foot warmers, 162
footwear, 6, 12–13, 45, 62
   approach, 54, 55
   beach, 172
   care of, 57
   children's, 29
   conditioners for, 57
   crossing streams, 181
   desert, 113, 114
   drying, 57
   fit, 52
   jungle, 200
   lacing, 54–56
   manufacturers, 234
   mukluks, 164–65
   multisport, 172–73
   sandal shoes, 173
   "waterproof," 54
   winter, 162, 164–65
   See also boots
foraging, in desert, 113
fording (snow), 158–60
forest walking. See woodland
   walking
Forgey, Dr. William, 98, 111
French Alps, 121
Freud, Sigmund, 120
frost, in weather forecasting,
   87
frostbite, 154
frozen lung, 154
fructose, 26
fruit, dried, 118, 149, 208
   packing, 26, 29
fruit chew, 149,
fruit leather, 118, 208

G
Gaines, Bob, 166, 191
gaiters, 52, 132
games, hiking with children, 33,
   232
Ganci, Dave, 113
garbage, handling of, 38
Gatco sharpeners, 139
Gatewood, Emma, 53
gear, lists of manufacturers of,
   233-35
   selecting, 46, 218-25
   long-distance hiking and, 218-
   21
Gerald, Clive, 24
getting started, 6
Giardia, 90, 113, 148
Gissing, George, 73
Glen Canyon, 230
global positioning system (GPS),
   126–27, 167
gloves, 65, 95, 152, 153
glycogen, 26
goal treks, 203-06
Goddard, John, 5
goggles (winter), 156–57
   fogging on, 157, 159
   lens color, 159
Goldfarb, Steve, 24
Gore clothing, 64
gorp, 27, 29
Grabber Toe Heaters, 162
Grand Canyon, 179
Grand Tetons, 8
Granite Mountain (Calif.), 117
Green River, The, vi
gullies, 74–75

H
hair, in weather forecasting, 87
Haley, Jim, 108
Half Dome, Yosemite National
   Park, 9, 126
halo, around moon or sun, 87
hand lens, 117
Harrison, Richard, 153
Harrison maps (Tom Harrison
   Cartography), 79
hats, 62, 97, 113, 152, 184
   for children, 31
   manufacturers of, 234
head net, 184
health, good, 90–93
heat, paths of, 110
heat cramps, 97
heat exhaustion, 97–98

Heat Factory Insole Boot
   Warming System, 162
heat prostration, 93, 114–15,
   195
heat stroke, 98
Henderson, 182
Hensley, Robie, 131
Hi-Tec boots, 29
High magazine, 123
hikers, famous, 18
hikes, essentials to bring on,
   15–17
   length of, 7
hiking
   alone, 18–22
   environmental considerations,
    38–41
   for mileage, 20–21
   long-distance, 214-27
   preparing for, 82–83
   safety during, 83–84
   speed of, 22
   straight-shot, 74–75
   timing, 22–23
hiking associations, 8–9
hiking poles, 234
Hillary, Edmund, 125
Hind clothing, 64
hips, 12
Hix, Kim, 159
hoods, jacket, 67–69
Horgan, Paul, vi
horseback riders, 39
hose clamps, 71
Hotronics Foot Furnace, 162
Hudson, George, 24, 25
Hurt, Leroy, 161
hut-to-hut hiking, 227
hydration systems, 115
hygiene, backcountry, 102–03
hyperthermia, 97–98
hypothermia, 98, 123, 155

I
Iban, 193
ice, hiking on, 155–56
Idyllwild (Calif.), 123
illnesses, travel-related, 42–43
immersion foot, 154
Indonesian New Guinea, 215
In Southern Light: Trekking
   through Brazil and Africa,
   106
Inca Trail (Peru), 42
insect bites/stings, 73, 95, 115,
   117, 184

prevention (repellents), 29, 31, 99, 101, 115, 180, 184, 194
treatment, 99, 194
Internet sources, 233, 236-37
intertidal zone, 170
Inuit, 151
Irian Jaya, 25, 58
irrigation syringe, 94–95

J
jackets
down, 68–69
fitting, 68–69
hoods on, 61, 67–69
manufacturers, 234
ventilation in, 67
waterproof/breathable (WB), 66–69
wind-resistant, 61, 62–65
Jakarta (Indonesia), 42
Jaya highlands (Irian), 25, 215
Jefferson, Thomas, 18
Jenkins, Mark, 71
John Muir Trail (United States), 43, 128
Joshua Tree National Monument, 8, 46, 107–08
journal, keeping a, 34–35
Journal of Wilderness Medicine, 95
jungle hiking, 192–201

K
Kalimantan (Indonesia), 90–91, 151, 184–86
Kanyan River (Indonesia), 186
Katz, Mike, 24, 25
Keds, 53
Keller, Helen, 72
Kelty child carriers, 29
Kennedy, Dr. Barbara, 96
Kephart, Horace, 69
Kerouac, Jack, 44
knees, saving, 13–14
knife, 16, 70
sharpening, 138–39
Koukoulus, Andrew, 99

L
laces, flat vs. round, 55
lacing shoes, 54–56
land use guidelines, 38–41
Lansky sharpeners, 139
lay of the land, 20
layering, 59, 60–65, 152
by season, 61–65

learning to walk, 12–17
Leatherman Tool, 16, 70, 115
Leave No Trace, 38
Lectra Socks, 162
leeches, 198
legs, 12
Leki trekking poles, 181
lightning, dealing with, 88
Livingstone, David, 18–19
Loma Linda University (Calif.), 8
long-distance hiking, 214-227
attitude and, 223
fitness and, 216
gear for, 218
hut-to-hut, 227
pace, 226
rhythm, 227
weight of gear for, 221
Longs Peak, 119
lost, what to do if, 83–84, 166–67, 205
Lowe Alpine pullovers, 64
Lyme disease, 101–02

M
Macunaima mine (Brazil), 180
Malden Mills, 182
Malibu Creek (Calif.), 32
manufacturers of hiking products, 233-35
maps
Bureau of Land Management, 167
contour lines on, 80, 167
declination on, 77
folding, 84
need for, 7, 16
orienting, 79
publishers, 234-35
topographic, 78–79
US Geological Survey, 77, 79
using GPS with, 167
waterproofing, 84
Marker pullovers, 64
Martin, Greg, 23
matches, waterproof, 16, 20
McHugh, Pat, 71, 103
meals, for weekend trips, 207-10
meats, 26
Medical Guide to Traveling with Children, A, 96
medications, first aid, 94–95, 231
personal, 17
See also first aid kit
Melville, Herman, 168
Merrell boots, 29

metabolism, as a heat source, 110
Milford Track (New Zealand), 42–43
Miller, Dana, 128
mirror, signaling, 16, 17, 20, 31–32
mittens, 152, 153
Moab (Utah), 73, 109–10
Moby Dick, 168
Moffat, Gwen, 150
molefoam, 54
moleskin, 6, 53, 54, 94, 96
mosquito netting, 71, 194
mosquitoes, 180, 194
Motorland magazine, 229
Mount Baldy (Calif.), 74–75, 203
Mount Gorgonio (Calif.), 10, 203
Mount Thor (Canada), 128–30
Mount Watkins (Calif.), 66, 215
Mount Whitney (Calif.), 9, 128, 203
mountain climbing, 74–75, 133
Mountain Hardware, 65
mountain missiles, 131
mountain travel, 2
mountain walking, 121–35
alpine, 126–32
altitude's effects on, 124
clothing, 132
pace, 123
timing, 123
mountainous trekking, 132–35
dangers of, 134–35
MPI Outdoor Safety Products, 71, 103
mud, hazards of, 187
Muir, John, 19, 43, 145, 220, 230
multitool, 16, 70, 115
myths, outdoor, 148

N
Nalgene bottles, 115, 145
Nardone, Joe, 116
National Outdoor Leadership School, 95
National Park Foundation, 9
National Weather Service, 86
navigation, 74–85
desert, 116, 119
forest, 138
GPS, 126–27, 167
natural, 84
needles, for repairs, 70
nettles, stinging, 7, 144
New Guinea, 1
Nike shoes, 172, 200
Nikwax shoe conditioner, 57

Nizoral, 200
no-see-ums, 184
noise, 39
NPD Group Inc., 128

O
Ohlone Wilderness Trail, 128
Outside magazine, 229

P
packs, 48–51
  backpack, 211
  donning, 50
  fanny, 49, 51
  fitting, 50–51
  manufacturers of, 233
  rain cover for, 50
  size of, 48–49, 50
  straps on, 48
  weight of, 6, 17, 29–30
  zipper pulls on, 51
pain, 12
Pamons, 33
pants, 58–59, 62
Papua New Guinea, 25, 93, 144, 195
Patagonia Go-T, 63
  Pneumatic, 64
  Velocity, 64
peak bagging, 9–10
Permanone repellent, 31, 101
permethrin, 101
photography, 146
plastic bags, for rain, 50–51, 66
pocketknife, 16
poison ivy, oak, and sumac, 99–100
Polo, Marco, 18
poncho, 68
Pony Express Trail, 116
postholing, 158
powerwalking, 20–21
Private Papers of Henry Ryecroft, The, 73
pullovers, 64
Punan Dayaks, 193
  See also Dayak tribe

Q
Quest fanny pack, 49
quicksand, 187, 188

R
radiation (heat), 110
radio, two-way, 126–27
raft packing, 182

rafting, 179–80
Rails to Trails Conservancy, 9
rain, clothing for, 66–69, 132
Red Rocks (Nev.), 153
rehydration, 95
rejuvenation junket, 206-07
repair kits, 70–71
resting, how often, 26
Ridgeway, Rick, 90
Rio Huerta (Mexico), 191
river wandering, 40
rivers, 179–91
  See also streams
Rob Roy, 69
Rochester Shoe Tree Company, 162
Rocky Mountain National Park (Colo.), 119
Rocky Mountain spotted fever, 101–02
Ross Allen Reptile Institute, 99
rubber bands, 71
running, 22
  See also fastpacking

S
safety, 73–105, 186, 194
Salmon River (Idaho), 179
salt tablets, 95
Samburu tribe, 12
San Juan de los Callos (Venezuela), 169, 177
sandals, 52
sandpaper, 70
sandwiches, 25, 26
Sarawak (Malaysia), 7, 24, 193
Sassan, Kathy, 24
sastrugi, 84
Sawyer Extractor, 96, 98, 99
Sawyer repellent, 31
Schimelpfenig, Todd, 95
Scott goggles, 157
scree, 57
Seam Grip, 70
2nd Skin (Spenco), 54, 94, 96
Sequoia National Park (Calif.), 130, 216
Service, Robert, 33
shelter, emergency, 84
shoes. *See* footwear
shorts, 58–59, 62
Shoumatoff, Alex, 106
sidestepping, 13
Sierra Club, 128
Sierra Club Outings, 9
Sierra Designs' Ray-T-ator, 62, 63

signaling devices, 16, 31–32
Silva compass, 76
Skeedadle repellent, 31
skiing, cross-country, 160
  repair parts for, 70
Skin Cancer Foundation, 97
sky colors, in weather forecasting, 87
Slade, Jim, 45, 179
sleeping bag, 155
  choosing a, 218-19
slogging, 158
slots, 119
Smith, Jedadiah, 220
Smith goggles, 157
smoke, in weather forecasting, 87
snacks, 6, 155
  for children, 29
  See also food
snakebite kits, 96
snakebites, 98–99, 117
sneakers, 53
snow, varieties of, 151
snow blindness, 154, 156
snow hiking, 151–67
  avalanches, 163–65
  clothing for, 151–54
snowmobiling, 45–46
snowshoeing, 22, 159, 160–61
  boots for, 161
  techniques, 161
Snyder, Gary, 44
soap, 39, 40
  germicidal, 102
socks, 52, 59, 62
  changing, 54, 59
  electric, 162
  neoprene, 173
  sizes of, 59
  synthetic, 200
  wool, 154, 162
Sog tool, 16, 70, 115
"Song of the Open Road," 4
Space Below My Feet, 150
speed, estimating, 21
splints, SAM, 95
sports drinks, 92–93
sprains, 95
Springer Mountain (Ga.), 131
staying in shape, 9–10
Steger mukluks, 164
sternum strap, 48
Stormproof, 84
Story of My Life, The, 72
stove-repair parts, 70

stoves, 38, 220-25
   choosing, 220-23
   manufacturers of, 234
   repair and maintenance, 223-25
strap, spare, 70
streams
   crossing, 135, 181
   walking along, 179–80
Street, John, 102
stretching exercises, 7, 15–16, 28, 30
stride, 22
Stuffitts scented shoe inserts, 162
Suicide Rock, 161
Sullivan, Roy C., 88
Summit Hut (Ariz.), 127
sun protection, 97–98, 235
sunburn, 95, 97–98
sunglasses, 17, 114
   for snow, 154, 156–57
sunscreen, 6, 17, 29, 31, 97, 153
surfing, 172–77
survival kit, 102–03
Suunto compasses, 76, 156
sweating, 111, 195
sweatpants, 58–59
swimming safety, 186

T
Tahquitz Mountain (Calif.), 123
talus slopes, 124
Teague, Richard, 119
Tecnu, 100
"10 Essentials," 15–17
tennis shoes, 52
   for children, 29
tent-pole sleeve, spare, 70
tents
   choosing a, 211-13, 219-20
   manufacturers of, 233
   mountaineering and winter, 219
   single wall, 220
terrain, understanding of, 20
Thompson's Water Seal, 84
Thoreau, Henry David, viii, 18, 179
Thorlo socks, 59
ticks, 100–01
tide pooling, 175
tides, 170
Tilton, Buck, 26, 102
timing a trip, 22–23
toilet, chemical, 40
toilet paper, 38, 39
Tough Traveler child carriers, 29
Tour du Mont Blanc (Europe), 42

Townsend, Chris, vii
trail food. See food
trail running, 22
   See also fastpacking
trails
   caring for, 147
   marked, 7, 74
   outstanding, 42–43
   weather's effect on, 74
Trails Illustrated maps, 79
trash, handling of, 38–39
trekking poles, 13, 123, 160, 181
   manufacturers of, 234
trench foot, 154, 200
turkey jerky, 130

U
Ultimate Direction clothing, 128
umbrella, for deserts, 115
underwear, 58, 60, 63, 64–65
urine, color of, 92, 111, 206
   to keep away animals, 148

V
Vasque Kids Klimber boot, 29
Velcro strips, 71
vests, 65
vitamin C, 185

W
Waimea Bay (Hawaii), 172–77
walkers, famous, 18
walking
   balance, 12
   health value of, 8
   technique, 11–12
"Walking" (Thoreau), viii
walking sticks, 160, 234
   See also trekking poles
Walking the Yukon, vii
waste, 40, 183
   human, 38, 40
water
   bottled, 43, 153
   containers, 6, 16, 26–27, 92–93, 115, 145, 153
   creating, 111
   diseases in, 90–91
   finding, 112
   flavoring, 185
   need for, 17, 27, 84, 92–94, 111, 114–15
water purification systems (filters), 16–17, 43, 90–92, 113, 185
   manufacturers of, 235
waterways, 135, 178–91

waves, 172–77
weather, 86–89
   forecasting with altimeter, 86–88
   lightning, 88
   signs in nature, 87
   wind, 86–88
weekend trips, 203-13
Weiss, Dr. Eric, 96
Weston, Edward Payson, 20–21
whistle, signaling, 16, 20
White River Expeditions, 179
Whitman, Walt, 4
wicking, 59, 60, 62
Wilderness Education Association, 98
Wilderness Medicine Institute, 26
Wilderness Medical Society, 95, 96, 98
Wilderness Medicine, 111
wilderness travel, 2
   safety, 73–105
wildflowers
   desert, 109
   mountain, 128
wildlife
   bears, 142–43
   desert, 110, 117
   stalking, 144
   watching, 41, 117
Williamson, Peter, 32
wind, in forecasting weather, 86–88
wind pants, 58–59
Windstopper, 64–65
Wingo, Plennie, 21
winter camping, 155
winter hiking. See snow hiking
woodland walking, 136–49
Woods Walker, Inc., 102
Wordsworth, William, 18, 121
World Health Organization, 95
World Wide Web, 236-37
wound management, 95–96
writing, journal, 34–35

Y
Yeats, W. B., 178
Yeti boots, 164
Yosemite National Park (Calif.), 8, 9, 128, 166, 230
Yosemite Valley, 66, 91, 215

Z
Zion National Park (Utah), 8, 119
zippers, 61, 69